TRANSOCEANIC STUDIES
Ileana Rodriguez, Series Editor

Writing AIDS

(Re)Conceptualizing the
Individual and Social Body
in Spanish American Literature

Jodie Parys

THE OHIO STATE UNIVERSITY PRESS
COLUMBUS

Copyright © 2012 by The Ohio State University.
All rights reserved.

Library of Congress Cataloging-in-Publication Data

Parys, Jodie, 1975–
　Writing AIDS : (re)conceptualizing the individual and social body in Spanish American literature / Jodie Parys.
　　p. cm.—(Transoceanic studies)
　Includes bibliographical references and index.
　ISBN 978-0-8142-1204-2 (cloth : alk. paper) — ISBN 978-0-8142-9306-5 (cd)
　1. Spanish American literature. 2. AIDS (Disease) in literature. I. Title. II. Series: Transoceanic studies.
　PQ7082.N7P364 2012
　860.9'3561—dc23
　　　　　　　　　　　　2012024209

Paper (ISBN: 978-0-8142-5676-3)
Cover design by Juliet Williams
Text design by Juliet Williams
Type set in Adobe Fairfield and Ellington MT

CONTENTS

Acknowledgments   vii

Introduction   1

Chapter One
    The Body as Weapon: HIV as Revenge   17

Chapter Two
    Eroticism and AIDS: The Confluence of Desire, Death, and Writing   57

Chapter Three
    Isolation and Exile: AIDS and the Solitary Body   94

Chapter Four
    Forging (Comm)unity through Hybridity:
    Pedro Lemebel's *Loco afán: crónicas de sidario*   138

Concluding Thoughts
    Future Markers of Identity: An Ever-Shifting Landscape   172

Works Cited   180

Index   185

ACKNOWLEDGMENTS

THIS BOOK would not have been possible without the support, direction, and encouragement of so many people. A tremendous thank you to Ksenija Bilbija, Rubén Medina, and Juan Egea for the insightful feedback they provided when this project was in the dissertation stage. Our conversations challenged me to think in new directions and taught me how to find my critical voice. Many of their suggestions and feedback have been integrated into this final manuscript.

I am also grateful to the peer reviewers and copyeditors of the initial draft of this manuscript, all of whom provided detailed and thoughtful feedback that allowed me to examine and strengthen several areas of the manuscript.

I am indebted to Pilar Melero for her careful editing of my translations of textual quotations. Her nuanced knowledge of languages and her skill as a writer and editor added depth and richness to the final version. Any errors or omissions are my sole responsibility.

I am also tremendously grateful to the faculty and administrators at the University of Wisconsin-Whitewater for their ongoing encouragement and support of my research. It is a pleasure to work in an environment where I am surrounded by colleagues who readily collaborate and administrators who creatively work to enable faculty success.

And, most importantly, I extend my most heartfelt appreciation and love to my family: to my parents, for their unwavering love and belief in my abilities, and especially to Ryan and Alexander, who provide me with constant inspiration, love, and encouragement and help me see and enjoy the beauty, joy, and poignancy of life. My love for you both grows and deepens every day.

AN EXCERPT of chapter 1 was previously published under the title "The Violent Seductress: Using the Female Body as Retribution for HIV in Ana Solari's *Luna negra de noviembre*," *Journal of the Midwest Modern Language Association* 44.2 (Fall 2011), and has been reprinted with permission from the editors. Also, a small section of this chapter appeared as "The Body as Weapon: HIV as Revenge," in *Ciberletras* 14 (2005), and has been reprinted with permission from the editors.

An excerpt of chapter 2 was previously published under the title "Eroticism and AIDS: The Confluence of Death, Desire and Writing in Manuel Ramos Otero's 'Invitación al polvo,'" *Cincinnati Romance Review* 26 (2007): 142–61. Another section appeared as "Confronting HIV/AIDS through an Erotic Rewriting of the Classic Fairy Tale 'Rapunzel' in Andrea Blanqué's 'Adiós, Ten Ying,'" *The International Journal of the Humanities* 7.5 (2009): 105–16. Both are reprinted with permission from the editors.

An excerpt of chapter 3 was previously published under the title "Confronting the Reality of HIV/AIDS: Self-Imposed Exile as a Journey of Self Discovery in Nelson Mallach's 'Elefante,'" *Journal of the Midwest Modern Language Association* 42.1 (Spring 2009): 117–32. It has been reprinted with permission from the editors.

Portions of chapter 4 have appeared in two previous publications: "Forging (Comm)Unity through Hybridity, HIV, and Marginalization: Pedro Lemebel's *Loco afán: crónicas de sidario*," *Dissidences* 4/5 (2008); and "La creación de (com)unidad mediante la hibridez: *Loco afán: crónicas de sidario* por Pedro Lemebel," *Memoria histórica, género e interdisciplinariedad. Los estudios culturales hispánicos en el siglo XXI*, edited by Santiago Juan-Navarro y Joan Torres-Pou. Madrid: Biblioteca Nueva, 2008, 113–21. Permission has been granted to reprint from both.

This publication was supported by an award from the University of Wisconsin-Whitewater. All views expressed in this publication are those of the author.

INTRODUCTION

SINCE 1981, the world has been profoundly impacted by the human immunodeficiency virus (HIV) and acquired immunodeficiency syndrome (AIDS). On an individual level, HIV and AIDS possess the potential to cause the body's immune function to become compromised and, as a consequence, may undermine an individual's control over his or her own body, thus forcing a rethinking of the conceptualization of self, both individually and in interaction with others. In my examination of this reconceptualization of self in the face of AIDS, I argue that the body is a fundamental element of self-identity and, consequently, that the drastic changes wrought by AIDS impact the way the individual sees his or her self. Part of this new self-perception is also expressed in relation to others. The social meanings of the disease as well as the historical tendency to marginalize those who are HIV-positive have resulted in a rethinking of the relation of the individual to society.

This exploration of self and society often takes place in the pages of literary texts, infiltrating narratives with an altered conceptualization of the individual and his or her relation to those around him or her in light of the AIDS epidemic. I illustrate the way AIDS has pervaded the personal and social imaginings of the body by focusing specifically on textual representations found in Spanish American literature in which AIDS has a significant role.[1] The thematic emergence of AIDS as a literary topic in

---

1. By "significant," I mean works in which one of the main themes is AIDS, whether ex-

Spanish American literature was rather slow at the outset of the epidemic (1981), but as the virus has become more widespread and impacted more individuals, the topic has slowly begun to appear in more works. Nonetheless, one notes a dearth of literary works from the 1980s, the decade in which AIDS became a reality for most Latin American countries, with many recording their first cases in the middle of the decade. Ironically, the earliest work I uncovered, included in this study, Ricardo Prieto's drama *Pecados mínimos*, hails from a nation (Uruguay) that did not record its first case until 1993.[2] In the 1990s through the present, the epidemic has begun to appear in increasing numbers of fictional works from Spanish America, but it still has not received widespread literary or critical attention. For example, in the context of U.S. literature, critics refer to "AIDS literature"[3] and "AIDS narratives"[4] to denote the vast quantity of fictional narratives depicting AIDS. In the Spanish American context, however, no such category exists. My study addresses that void by drawing together a representative corpus of literary texts from various Spanish American countries and diverse literary genres, including novels, short stories, poems, theater, and testimonials, to illuminate not only the ways in which these Spanish American writers have chosen to depict this disease, but also the ways in which the literature will be archived for future generations.

For the protagonists who inhabit the works that I study, the prospect of being a carrier of a potentially fatal virus gives way to fundamental existential questions and necessitates a renegotiation of one's position in the world given the drastic changes caused by the disease. As a result, various questions inform my examination of AIDS narratives in the Spanish American context: How can the subject negotiate the contradictory reality of *living* while being inhabited by a deadly virus? How are the protagonists' actions influenced by the recognition that they carry a potentially deadly weapon within their cells? Consequently, how is the interplay of life, death, and desire played out in interpersonal relationships? Finally, what strategies are employed by the subjects to help them face, and even overcome, the fear of death?

Widening the scope to encompass the collective as well as the personal plane, this work additionally examines the individual's relation to the world around her- or himself, examining the opposite poles of iso-

---

plicitly or implicitly referenced. Works that make only a simple mention of AIDS without any further exploration of how the disease affects the characters are not considered in this study.
  2. http://www.country-studies.com/uruguay/health-and-welfare.html.
  3. See Treichler.
  4. See Krueger; and Morris.

lated exile versus the creation of community. On the one end, protagonists struggling with myriad personal, familial, and societal taboos must decide how to negotiate their position in the collective space. In some texts, they opt to relinquish community in favor of a cloistered existence. Conversely, others see in AIDS a common ground, one capable of uniting diverse individuals in a collective struggle against the virus that they all share.

Parallel to these central thematic thrusts, this work also examines the role of writing itself—how the disease has impacted the narrative structure and expression, as well as how narrative is altered by the appearance of AIDS itself as a protagonist. One area where this impact is apparent is the vast use of metaphorical language when referring to the virus. In her seminal works on the metaphorical language connected to illnesses such as cancer, tuberculosis, and AIDS, *Illness as Metaphor and AIDS and Its Metaphors*, cultural critic Susan Sontag affirms that in every era, certain illnesses have special significance and often become mechanisms for the projection of particular values and social dynamics. In the same way that tuberculosis and cancer carried mythological connotations in the nineteenth and twentieth centuries, respectively, so also do HIV and AIDS in current society. Sontag's work highlights the particularly important role a disease may hold in society and illustrates the potential impact of a disease on a society's values, morals, and interpersonal interactions. These "mythological connotations" imbue many of the texts of this study with an additional level of meaning, reflecting pervasive stereotypes and (mis)conceptions that have been intentionally, and often unintentionally, embedded in many works about AIDS, including a large number of those examined here.

In fact, the treatment of AIDS exemplified in these texts often follows a well-documented and unfortunate trend throughout history to stigmatize diseases viewed as mysterious, while morally condemning the individuals who contract them. Sontag's work, in particular, helps to draw this parallel between the current stigmas surrounding HIV/AIDS and those seen in relation to tuberculosis in the nineteenth century and cancer more recently. She explains that "any disease that is treated as a mystery and acutely enough feared will be felt to be morally, if not literally, contagious" (6). Consequently, this perception impacts the treatment of those affected and perpetuates stereotypes and stigmas, particularly in the absence of solid information about the disease involved. For example, according to Sontag, "having TB was imagined to be an aphrodisiac, and to confer extraordinary powers of seduction. Cancer is considered to be de-sexualizing" (13). Diego Armus, in an article published in his self-edited collection *Disease in the History of Modern Latin America: From Malaria to AIDS*, has also analyzed this depiction of TB as a disease of passion by explaining how "nineteenth-century writers depicted tuberculosis as a romantic disease mainly affecting individuals with rarified sensibility, spiritual refinement, or some tragic character flaw" (101–2). Consequently, this perception bred a new metaphorical language that referenced a "white plague" and obfuscated the realities of the disease (101–2). This sexualization of diseases that are not even transmitted sexually conflates their meaning and consequently produces damaging stigmas, ultimately affecting the concept of selfhood and conceptualizations of identity in those afflicted.

When the disease in question *is* indeed a sexually transmitted one, such as syphilis or HIV, many additional layers of stigma and bias often come into play because of the cultural meanings attached to sexuality, gender identity, and eroticism. As a consequence, cultural beliefs affect the language used to describe, represent, and archive these illnesses and reflect the stereotypes circulating about each disease. For example, "syphilis was often assumed to 'confess' the patient's otherwise private sexual involvement with someone who had had at least one other sexual partner" (Bliss 186). Bliss further explains that the "confession" often manifested itself through physical symptoms, such as chancres, sores, lesions, or other outward manifestations of the illness (186). In this way, the physical manifestations of the disease are interpreted as a revelation of an individual's private (sexual) interactions, regardless of whether that socially based assumption is indeed true. In the process, assumptions project upon the victims additional layers of societal shame by connecting the contraction of the illness with behaviors deemed socially unacceptable, or even deviant, such as infidelity, promiscuity, or, in the case of HIV/AIDS, homosexuality, IV drug use, or other proscribed behaviors. In fact, in the early media accounts of the HIV epidemic in Brazil, the reports often implied that "information on the new syndrome was relevant to the public more for the scandalous 'confessions' it exacted from celebrities so diagnosed than because HIV presented a real threat to 'average' Brazilians" (Larvie 297). This inaccurate, divisive, and stigma-laden representation of the AIDS epidemic is not uncommon, as I will illustrate throughout my analysis.

Like many diseases that predominated before it, AIDS is the most recent example of an illness that is rife with misconceptions, often discussed using taboo-laden and metaphorical language, and consistently conflated with social, moral, and cultural meaning. As Armus posits in *Disease in the History of Modern Latin America*, "diseases are not only sites where society, culture, and politics interact in a certain period of time, but also analytical tools to understand the always elusive complexity of the historical experience" (16). AIDS follows that same trajectory and, as such, literary representations of the AIDS epidemic across Spanish America provide us with an archive of the multiplicity of meaning that AIDS has acquired throughout its history in this region. Additionally, the very act of writing as a means of facing mortality and a truncated and often isolated existence reappears frequently throughout these works. Perhaps most intriguing is that this interplay of literary production and bodily destruction can be seen in texts from divergent genres, including poetry, short story, diary, and chronicle. These divergent texts illustrate how writing and literature can, and often do, address cultural and societal issues, with the textual space serving as the arena in which the seemingly divergent realms of fiction and disease converge.

A further preoccupation of this project is the notion of silence and how it figures prominently in the narratives and works analyzed. One notes an overriding trend to refuse to name AIDS, even when it serves as a central concern. Even when silence is broken, it is often only with the equivalent of a whisper, rarely thrusting the disease into the forefront for scrutiny. Instead, AIDS is a plague, "el mal," "la peste," or is simply described through its symptoms. This cult of silence is intriguing and will be examined throughout this study in relation to its various manifestations and in regard to the influence it has on the overall message of the works in which it appears. Part of the examination of silence surrounding AIDS involves asking several questions, including why does AIDS appear in these works and what role does it play in the larger narrative and artistic projects at hand? How is the silence (of AIDS) trying to speak? Additionally, is this textual lacuna representative of the pervasive taboos surrounding AIDS in many societies? If so, how do these texts dialogue with and challenge those taboos?

In fact, "void" and "lack" are terms that come to mind when summarizing the critical corpus that exists at present with regard to the representation of AIDS in Spanish American literature. This apparent void is perhaps best summarized by a correspondence I received from Ricardo Chávez-Castaneda, a contemporary writer who has also served as a panelist on several juries for competitions in the field of contemporary literature in Mexico: "Como verás, es una muestra de lo poco que ha invadido este asunto nuestros imaginarios latinoamericanos. Es increíble. . . . El tema, dicho de la manera más simple, brilla por su ausencia" [As you will see, it is an indication of how little this topic has invaded our Latin American imaginary. It's incredible . . . the topic, said in the simplest way, stands out for its absence].⁵ The very idea that a disease that is so omnipresent on a global scale could be considered *absent* from the literary production of the writers from Central America, South America, and the Caribbean seems an amazing paradox, and one that has provided stimulus for this project.

Extensive research into the bibliography regarding AIDS in Spanish America reveals that two writers dominate the attention of critics in this area: Reinaldo Arenas and Severo Sarduy. Their stature is not surprising given their importance to the literary canon and perhaps also because it is widely known that both died from AIDS. In this sense, they have legitimacy as messengers on the topic of AIDS. The primary focus of the critical corpus at this point is on Arenas's last work, his autobiographical *Antes que anochezca* [*Before Night Falls*].⁶ As an autobiography written in the twilight of Arenas's life while facing a death sentence imposed by AIDS, *Antes que anochezca* has provided quite a bit of fodder for critics examining the treatment of exile, political dissidence, homosexuality, and AIDS. Most often, one finds some or all of these topics intertwined in critical analyses, particularly since they all were integral parts of defining Arenas himself and his focal work. Literary critic Ricardo L. Ortiz recognizes this point and affirms that this autobiography also has a very poignant political critique and that it is "against the murderous boredom of repressive, totalizing systems that Arenas laughs and screams" (106). Ortiz further points out how Arenas's depiction of AIDS as an unnatural disease that began as an "orchestrated political conspiracy against marginalized communities" is one facet of that critique (101).

Taken in a different light, Arenas's autobiography can also be seen as an end-of-life exploration of his own love–hate relationship with Cuba, intensified by the knowledge that his moments on Earth were limited by the disease.⁷ Another critic, David Vilaseca, deviates from the political and social interpretation in favor of a more individualistic evaluation of how AIDS can be envisioned as literal and metaphorical elements of the Lacanian symptom, or *sinthome*, and how, when seen through this lens, AIDS functions both as a threat to the subject's well-being and also as a source of "an oblique, forbidden *jouissance*" (271). Vilaseca bases his interpretation not only on the more explicit allusions to AIDS in the prologue, but also on the displaced expression in the body of the text of the experiences of the disease on the narrator. This silence in regard to the

---

5. Personal correspondence, December 2003. This and all other translations are the author's. A special thank you to Pilar Melero for her careful editing of all translations.

6. This text received even more attention because of the popularity of the movie that was made of it.

7. See Schulz-Cruz.

disease in the textual body raises an interesting set of questions that will be addressed in my own analyses. Is this silenced text representative of the fact that the disease itself, although a silent visitor to the body, "speaks" in other ways? Does the silence bespeak the marginalization and repression that accompany the label "AIDS"? Although Arenas's text will not be a focus of my current project because it has received ample critical attention, the idea of silence presented in it will inform my reading of many other works in which the disease is felt, sensed, intuited, but is never heard or displayed in an explicit manner.

The process of deciphering a text that refuses to name or that circumvents the idea of naming has been addressed in critical articles focusing on the other main literary figure whose work constitutes part of the current (limited) AIDS canon: Severo Sarduy. Leonor Álvarez de Ulloa and Justo C. Ulloa have played the role of literary detectives in their readings of *Colibrí, El cristo de la Rue Jacob,* and *Pájaros de la playa,* examining the various linguistic fragments and plague metaphors that, when taken together, show a progressively increasing reference to the disease that ultimately stole Sarduy's life in 1993.

Other than the aforementioned Arenas and Sarduy, only a few other figures have been detected on the critical radar at this point. A few disparate articles on the topic have been published, but to date, still no critical corpus to speak of exists. One article provides a hemispheric overview on the topic and is perhaps one of broader perspectives I've seen, albeit limited to the scope of an article.[8] Another provides an examination of some of the literary and visual representations of AIDS from the Caribbean but does not limit the scope to Spanish-language works, as I examine here.[9] Still another makes a brief mention of Luis Zapata's masterpiece *El vampiro de la colonia Roma* in relation to AIDS, but the reference depicts how the view of sexuality presented in that novel has changed since the arrival of AIDS on the global scene.[10] Other critics have chosen to direct their attention to the works of Latinos in the U.S. instead of looking south of the border.[11]

The tendency to divert attention from Spanish America is further exemplified in critical anthologies about the writing of AIDS and the use of literature as a vehicle for expressing the effects of the epidemic on a society. The primary focus is on the prolific literary response to the epi-

   8. See Ingenschay.
   9. See Romero-Cesareo.
   10. See José Joaquín Blanco.
   11. References to Chicano and Latino representations of AIDS are seen in *Ollantay Theater Magazine,* which has dedicated an entire issue to the topic, as well as segments of Taylor and Villegas's *Negotiating Performance* (article by Sandoval), Foster's *Chicano/Latino Homoerotic Identities,* and other texts dealing with gay and lesbian perspectives (see Navarro).

demic in the U.S., a response that does not have even a passing mention of Latin America, even though other articles focus explicitly on France and Germany, for example.[12] Even in criticism autochthonous to Spanish America, there still exists an overriding tendency to look outside, elsewhere, for literature in order to understand AIDS, such as was seen in an article in a Cuban journal about cinema and AIDS, in which, besides three brief mentions (and no analysis) of Latin American movies (*Solo con tu pareja, Bienvenido—Welcome,* and *Fotos del alma*), the central focus was on U.S. cinema.[13] Similar patterns are seen in articles from Argentina, Mexico, and Puerto Rico.[14] This tendency to divert attention from one's own issues may be part of the reason that this disease has yet to receive significant critical attention despite the fact that writers, artists, and filmmakers (other than Arenas and Sarduy) are indeed producing works that reflect, combat, and at times celebrate the disease. One of the goals of my study is to help bring some of those works to light and to generate more critical discourse about the perceived lack of response thus far to the pandemic.[15]

When examining and selecting texts to include in this study, I considered works from many countries across Spanish America, ultimately selecting those that not only have HIV/AIDS as a primary preoccupation, but that also represent trends seen in literature and criticism across the region, paying special attention to genre and its relation to the overall messages conveyed. Although the specific texts that I analyze do not necessarily represent each country or region of Spanish America, the overall analysis does maintain such broad scope and hopefully will help initiate further critical dialogue on this topic through which an even broader range of works can be examined. Because of a dearth of theory about AIDS produced by Spanish American intellectuals or Spanish American texts, I

---

12. See, for example, anthologies edited by Nelson; and Murphy and Poirer.

13. See Nodarse.

14. Both Liguori and Cranwell respond to Sontag's work. Interestingly enough, they make no attempt to apply Sontag's theories to Latin America's situation. Latin America is still treated as "other," foreign. Garasa's article is provocatively entitled "SIDA y literatura," and given the fact that it is from an Argentine newspaper, one would anticipate finding an enlightened discussion of Argentine literature; the focus, instead, is on U.S. literature. Along these same lines, the entire volume of *Ollantay Theatre Magazine* (1994), which has articles titled "SIDA y teatro," for example, is devoted to AIDS and the Puerto Rican (primarily Nuyorican) community.

15. Even when the scope is widened to examine responses to AIDS across the humanities, there still is a remarkable lack of critical attention. In fact, in a recent article, Gregory Tomso noted a "decline in scholarly attention to HIV/AIDS in the humanities" something he attributed in part to the decrease in AIDS-related activism and the fact that "nearly a generation has passed since the pandemic first appeared" (443).

recur to a multidisciplinary approach to these works while paying particular attention to the social and historical contexts underlying the primary texts, thus modifying the critical approaches to take into account the specific Spanish American contexts in which these narratives were produced. In addition to specific AIDS-related theories, I draw upon cultural studies, sociological and medical discourses, psychology, postcolonial theory, feminist theory, and queer theory, among others, as I approach each text.

Despite the divergent backgrounds of the primary texts, as well as the critical theory used to analyze them, all of these works are united under the broad topic of the body, conceived of as an individual composed of a physical, emotional, and spiritual entity both in isolation and in communion with others. Because HIV and AIDS are physical viruses that attack real bodies, the individual body is the initial portal of entry into the exploration of the notion of identity and the way in which it is impacted and altered by the arrival of AIDS. However, each individual is also a part of a larger community, and the virus itself impacts society as well as individuals. These separate but related concepts—the individual and social bodies—are the uniting themes of the first two chapters and the last two chapters of this study, respectively.

The first two chapters of this work are concerned precisely with the individual body and reactions to the virus that appear, at least on the surface, to be polar opposites: the vengeful utilization of the diseased body as a weapon to exact revenge on a sexual partner and the erotic exaltation of the self as a way to celebrate life rather than mourn death.

Chapter 1
THE BODY AS WEAPON: HIV AS REVENGE

Chapter 1 explores the drastically altered body that results from HIV infection and examines the more sinister side of sexual relations in the AIDS era: the fatal potentials of the disease and the silent manner of transmitting this hidden disease as a means of exacting revenge. Three texts, which I will refer to collectively as "revenge narratives" owing to the centrality of the theme of retribution to the overall plot, will serve as the backbone of this chapter. The first two texts, "Luna negra de noviembre" by Ana Solari and "El secreto de Berlín" by Ramón Griffero, are short stories from Uruguay and Chile, respectively, while the third, *El vuelo de la reina* by Tomás Eloy Martínez, is a novel from Argentina. These narratives recognize the fact that HIV, as a virus that often leads to the fatal AIDS, is in essence a biological weapon whose transmission is possible through one of the most intimate interactions human beings have: sexual intercourse. In the course of that transmission, the virus is silently passed from one person to another. These texts depict the deliberate exchange of the virus by one of the two parties in an act of revenge on the recipient as well as the reconceived notion of self that results from being infected by a virus that grants power and agency at the same time that it systematically weakens and destroys. Theories by Arthur W. Frank, sociologist and author of *The Wounded Storyteller,* on the diverse types of "wounded bodies" illuminate various ways in which individuals compromised by a disease choose to interact with others. Specifically, we see how the avengers function as both "dominating bodies" and "mirroring bodies," allowing them to seduce and eventually infect their unwitting victims.

What is notable about the works discussed in this chapter is the way that the identity of an AIDS-altered individual is constructed. Each of the protagonists fails to examine the entire scope of his or her altered identity, eschewing the more reflective journeys of identity conceptualization that the protagonists in the texts I examine in later chapters undertake. Instead, the protagonists focus on one aspect of their new corporal reality: the potential to harm another through the deliberate transmission of the virus. In essence, these authors have chosen to depict the sadistic potential of those affected by AIDS, showing how the AIDS-infected body can effectively function as a weapon. The dynamic that is established in these works, then, is a victim–victimizer relationship, with the protagonists opting to exert their own distorted form of agency through the violent overtaking of another individual's body. Elaine Scarry's theories from *The Body in Pain* on "unmaking" and the use of torture as a means of exerting power over one's victim will shed light on many of the interactions depicted in these narratives. We see this tendency most clearly in Eloy Martínez's work *El vuelo de la reina,* which describes the sadistic, destructive steps that the protagonist takes to destroy his ex-girlfriend, although attempts to destroy also surface in the ritualistic acts undertaken by Griffero's protagonist as he selects and systematically destroys his victim. Cognizant of the fact that these texts are all postdictatorial texts from the Southern Cone, I also analyze the echoes of the authoritarian discourses and rhetoric that have resurfaced in these works' depiction of the victim–victimizer relationship and the interchange of power.

While the notions of a reconceptualized identity and the utilization of the body as a weapon thematically unite these works, they also share stylistic commonalities as well, namely, the recurrence of metaphors that, according to Sontag, continue to perpetuate stereotypes about AIDS. These authors recur to militaristic, apocalyptic, and plague-ridden metaphors that follow tendencies seen in other works, but they fail to question or reinvent the representation of AIDS through their own works. Furthermore, these three texts all refuse to name the disease "AIDS," choosing instead to shroud references in metaphor, euphemism, and textual clues. I will show how these stylistic traits, combined with the overtly dark themes that pervade the works, contribute to, rather than deconstruct, many of the negative stereotypes that continue to pervade public perception about HIV and AIDS. In effect, through the depiction of individuals who knowingly construct their nascent post-HIV-infection identities on the deliberate infection and destruction of others, these works further contribute to the demonization of HIV-positive individuals and perpetuate rather than erode stereotypes surrounding HIV transmission.

Chapter 2
EROTICISM AND AIDS: THE CONFLUENCE OF DESIRE, DEATH, AND WRITING

In this chapter, I focus on how two authors attempt to defuse the power that AIDS has over their protagonists' sexual expression and eventual deaths. The first is the Puerto Rican poet Manuel Ramos Otero and his collection of poetry, *Invitación al polvo*, published in 1991 after his death from AIDS-related complications. Ramos Otero's work is overtly erotic, exalting both homosexuality and unabashed sexuality despite the impending demise brought on by AIDS. I compare this collection to Andrea Blanqué's (Uruguay) short story "Adiós, Ten-Ying," in which she narrates the exploits of a young girl who chooses to leave her cloistered existence in Montevideo, opting to prostitute herself to sailors in exchange for worldly travels. Contracting AIDS as a result of her adventures, the protagonist reflects fondly on her sexual exploration and what she views as both personal and sexual freedom, thus opting to celebrate her life and sexuality rather than fear her rapidly approaching death.

Both Ramos Otero and Blanqué choose to assert the sexualities of their protagonists in a way that defies current notions about protection and caution in this AIDS-affected epoch. Because of the enhanced risk associated with sexual activity, bodies have increasingly been policed and disciplined by the political hegemony that has determined which sex acts are "safe," and by extension acceptable, and which are considered "unsafe" and therefore reprehensible (Singer). This increased projection of the sexual being into the political and social discourse has appropriated some of the individual power over one's own body and sexuality and has created a marginalized view of any practitioners of "unsafe" sex, such as the protagonists of these narratives. In response to this marginalization, the authors use divergent strategies to transgress the boundaries of sexuality imposed by society and, in the process, are able to deflate some of the symbolic currency attached to AIDS.

In Ramos Otero's case, I explore the connection between disease, desire, and death, utilizing Georges Bataille's theories regarding eroticism as well as the connections that Jonathan Dollimore has made between sexuality, desire, and death in his work *Death, Desire, and Loss in Western Culture*. The confluence of these seemingly discordant forces surfaces as the central tenet of the majority of Ramos Otero's collection. I analyze three key moments that appear throughout the work: the celebration of life, love, and eroticism that occupies the majority of the initial poems; the devastating void resulting from the loss of his lover and the solitude that haunts the poetic voice as he faces his dismal future because of AIDS; and, finally, how sexuality and eroticism, combined with the powerfully indelible force of writing, allow the poetic voice to accept death on his own terms without erasing or negating the pleasurable experiences that led to his final moments of life.

The confluence of eroticism, death, and narrative can also be seen in Blanqué's treatment of AIDS. I explore these three concepts against the backdrop of the fairy tale trope, which underscores this story. Ten-Ying becomes a modern-day Rapunzel, choosing to flee her sequestered existence despite the risks that await her. I utilize theories from Christina Bacchilega's work *Postmodern Fairy Tales* to analyze this reworking of a traditional story against a nontraditional backdrop consisting of prostitution, eroticism, AIDS, and untimely death.

In contrast to the first two chapters of this study in which my primary concerns are the different manifestations of the individual body through both destructive, vengeful sexuality and celebratory, defiant eroticism, in the last two chapters I shift focus away from the individual body and her interaction with *one* other being onto the notion of the solitary being *in relation with* the community or social body. I examine both the rejection of interpersonal bonds through self-imposed isolation as well as the formation of unity through the shared bond of AIDS and a peripheral existence.

Chapter 3
ISOLATION AND EXILE: AIDS AND THE SOLITARY BODY

This chapter centers on the individual AIDS-infected body as it purposively separates itself from the social body, whether physically or emotionally. Here the focus is on the new markers of identity from the position of isolation and the altered perception of the body and AIDS itself, as viewed from the protagonists' positions on the physical and psychological margins of society. The works I use to illustrate this point are Ricardo Prieto's play *Pecados mínimos* (Uruguay), Nelson Mallach's (Argentina) short story "Elefante," and Pablo Pérez's (Argentina) diary *Un año sin amor*. In essence, the protagonists in these narratives attempt to erase themselves from the social body by fleeing the society or social group they are part of, thereby self-destructing. Particularly in the first two works I study, there is an internalization of the early messages by many societies toward AIDS patients: they were treated and seen as a type of leper who should be isolated from the general population. These narratives perpetuate that urgency to cleanse the social body by showing the protagonists willingly removing their diseased bodies from the collective realm. In contrast, Pérez's work focuses more on the destruction that AIDS wreaks on the individual rather than playing into the paranoid notion of the risks posed by the HIV-positive individual to society.

I recur to various theories on both internal and external exile, particularly those offered by Amy K. Kaminsky and Sophia A. McClennen, to scrutinize the types of isolation and exile depicted in these works. While not the overt variety experienced by individuals forced to leave their homes and countries because of war, repression, or other reasons, these three works depict varying degrees of both physical and psychological exile consistently imposed by the protagonists rather than by the society around them. I have termed the depicted social separation "radical isolation" in Prieto's and Mallach's works because the protagonists take extreme measures to depart from their previously known existences. In Pérez's work, I use the term "solitary separation" to refer to the increasing separation between the protagonist and the life and world he knows, despite the fact that he never physically leaves that space.

The most drastic of the three works is Ricardo Prieto's play *Pecados mínimos*, in which Marcos, the protagonist, sadistically isolates both himself and his mother, Julia, from the outside world in an attempt to separate both of them from the malicious "Sr. Sida" [Mr. AIDS] that exists beyond the threshold of the family home. While the protagonist ostensibly claims to be protecting his mother from the evils of the world and the disease that he himself carries, his methodical psychological and physical destruction of her reveal the apocalyptic tones of the work, which were particularly common at the inception of the epidemic when this play was written (1981). I examine this notion of AIDS = death = end of the world, showing how it not only motivates the extreme isolation of the protagonist, but also further informs his fatalistic views of his own state of being. Last, I explore the deplorable treatment of the mother, connecting it to the hatred Marcos feels toward his own loss of agency as well as his conviction that the destruction of society as he knows it is impending.

The second example of "radical isolation" is Mallach's story of a young, HIV-positive man, Rodrigo, who flees home, family, and, for the majority of the work, self, in order to avoid the realities of his condition. During his two-year journey away from home, I examine his attempts to redefine himself in relation to his new condition. Central to this process is the notion of the "other" as theorized by Jacques Lacan, who, through the gaze, reflects back to the individual the idealized version of the self. Rodrigo passes the majority of his time avoiding contact with others, thus avoiding the alterations in self that their gazes could reflect back to him. Slowly he begins to face his new version of self through a series of interpersonal interactions and solitary experiences. All of these moments ultimately comprise the modified "mirror stage" that Rodrigo undergoes as he comes to terms with his changed identity as a result of AIDS.

In contrast with the representation of individuals who flee from society as they grapple with their experiences with AIDS, the last text discussed in chapter 3, Pablo Pérez's *Un año sin amor*, illustrates an individual who becomes trapped because of the overly signified body that has been taken over, both physically and symbolically, by AIDS. I refer to Pérez's work as a reflection of "solitary separation" because it chronicles one year in the life of the author, who is certain that death will visit him before the end of the year. As a result, he sinks into an increasingly deeper state of psychological depression and physical solitude, even though he lives in the same apartment, works at the same job, and studies at the same school as he did before AIDS took over his life. It is as if a barrier exists between Pablo and the world, and in this chapter, I explore his life on both sides of that barrier and the ways in which the cumulative experiences influence the portrait of self that he creates.

Chapter 4
FORGING (COMM)UNITY THROUGH HYBRIDITY:
PEDRO LEMEBEL'S *LOCO AFÁN: CRÓNICAS DE SIDARIO*

In contrast with using exile as a solution and thereby further allowing society to isolate and marginalize those suffering from AIDS, others have asserted their agency to build a community of support and create a unified front within the existing political and social body with which to combat hegemonic subjugation. Providing an illuminating example of this confluence of community and social identity is Pedro Lemebel's stunning collection of chronicles about the effects of AIDS on the (homosexual) transvestite community in Santiago de Chile, entitled *Loco afán: crónicas de sidario*. The collection details the fate of the transvestite community ("las locas") from the fall of Allende, through the Pinochet dictatorship, and into the transitory period of democracy that followed in its wake. In this chapter, I utilize the theories of Homi Bhabha, particularly those expounded in *Locations of Culture*, to show how Lemebel's text takes advantage of the liminal space between what Bhabha identifies as the pedagogical and the performative aspects of national identity in order to create an alternative cultural identity based on the experience of multiply marginalized protagonists: AIDS-infected, homosexual, transvestites.

By utilizing this liminal space, Lemebel continually employs the notion of hybridity to achieve his project and write the transvestite community into the literary history of Chile. There are multiple manifestations of this hybridity, but I will focus on six specific examples, each illustrated in Lemebel's work: 1) the genre of the text itself, the *crónica*, which is an amalgam of many different genres; 2) the notion of gender, a sexual hybridity that is depicted by the transvestites who protagonize the works; 3) multiple urban spaces that resist a centralizing, reductionist tendency; 4) diachronic historical time, which alternates between predictatorship, references to the regime, and the indeterminate current reality of the "transition"; 5) national–transnational hybridity as seen through the interplay between external–internal cultural factors; and, finally, 6) the influence of AIDS, which creates hybrid bodies, blurring the boundaries between illness and health, youth and old age, life and death.

As in the first three chapters of this study, AIDS becomes a marker of both individual and social identity, continually modified and reconceptualized through both the impact and the absence of interpersonal interactions. This shifted identity is ultimately expressed through the process of writing, which becomes a central theme in the majority of the works examined. Lemebel is inherently aware of the act of writing and intentionally chooses the chronicle to best narrate the experience of protagonists facing multiple hybridities. In chapter 3, the diary form utilized by Pérez enables an intimate exploration of the effects of AIDS on the author's identity construction, but, as I explore, Pérez deviates from the traditional genre by explicitly stating his intentions to publish his thoughts and share them with the public. In chapter 2, the act of writing is central to the process of confronting death through a very deliberate choice to celebrate life vis-à-vis narratives that depict the eroticized and often romanticized lives of the protagonists rather than the impending death that each is facing. Chapter 1 is the only chapter in which the act of writing does not enter explicitly into the texts I study. Unlike those in chapters 2–4, these protagonists focus their efforts more on the destruction of others than on the construction of self, choosing to exert the caustic potentials of their altered bodies rather than reflecting on those changes and examining the self. I address the act of writing and the choice of genre as it relates to the different works studied in each chapter, ultimately examining its interconnection with HIV/AIDS as well as the construction of personal and communal identity.

CHAPTER ONE

The Body as Weapon
HIV as Revenge

Otra ruleta rusa
En la manzana
de este imperceptible
revólver,
cargamos
en un sólo casquillo
el virus,
y jugamos en la ruleta
de la cama
apostando a los abismos
pegados
a la sien acuosa
del deseo . . .

[**Another Russian roulette . . .**
In the chamber
of this imperceptible
revolver,
we load
only one shell
the virus,
and we play roulette
in bed
betting on the abyss
pressed
against the watery temple
of desire . . .]
  —Eric Landrón (*POESÍdA* 98)

Narrating Revenge

Revenge as a theme has pervaded both public and private discourses and can be found in areas as diverse as religion, law, psychology, and literature, to name just a few. The motivations for revenge are just as diverse as its manifestations, but underlying all such vengeance narratives is the desire to "get even" or correct a grievance perceived to be committed against the avenger. Cultural theorist Susan Jacoby, in her study on the evolution of revenge, has investigated this desire for retribution in a variety of arenas and has concluded that underlying all such arenas is the cultural belief that justice and revenge are mutually exclusive. Society tends to look at those who seek revenge on their own as renegades who buck the traditional justice system in their personal quests for a distorted form of justice. Given this public perception, the avenger is often left to function alone, under his or her own perceived laws of justice, oftentimes because of fears or the knowledge that society's justice system will not provide the sort of resolution that is so craved or one that would afford a sense of justice for the perceived loss (Jacoby, Introduction).

Such is often the case when one is dealing with the deliberate transmission of HIV and the use of the body as a weapon to exact retribution. Because this transmission can occur via human sexual intercourse,[1] a decidedly private and intimate interaction, it is often shielded from public and legal scrutiny. This fact has inevitably caused a drastic rethinking of interpersonal relationships, sexuality, eroticism, and health itself. Even in committed, monogamous relationships, risk exists because potentially lethal ramifications are involved in a possible previous sexual encounter. This risk increases exponentially when one of the partners decides to manipulate and maximize the fatal potential of the disease as a means of

---

1. Clearly, this not the only method of transmission, but it will serve as the central focus of this chapter. In essence, a person is at risk of contracting the virus whenever she comes into direct contact with infected bodily fluids. It is worth noting, however, that when the virus first appeared in the U.S., it was given the acronym GRID (Gay Related Immune Deficiency) because it appeared to strike only homosexuals (Treichler). As evidence later surfaced that it was possible to contract HIV through means other than homosexual contact, some of the damage had already been done to public perception. There are countless anecdotes about this deep-seated belief, not only in the U.S., that AIDS still predominantly affects homosexuals. Even if one examines the corpus of literature from Latin America in which AIDS and HIV appear, some of the most notable authors and works are from homosexual men. For example, two of the works that have received the majority of critical attention for their treatment of HIV/AIDS are Reinaldo Arenas's *Antes que anochezca* and Severo Sarduy's *Pájaros de la playa*. Both authors were openly homosexual and intertwined the themes of homosexuality and illness into their works. There are still very few works from Latin America either by or about heterosexuals that deal with AIDS. The three works examined in this chapter focus specifically on heterosexual transmission.

exacting revenge. The silent nature of this virus only adds to the sadistic potential for utilizing HIV for revenge. Furthermore, intent is very hard to prove, particularly in situations involving two consenting adults. Because of this delicate scenario, when a person suspects that she or he has been deliberately infected with the HIV retrovirus, she or he often has little judicial recourse. Consequently, revenge becomes one avenue to retaliate for the permanent biological, and ultimately physical and psychological, alterations that will be caused by the progression of the HIV virus.

These themes permeate the literary works that form the backbone of this chapter, in which the protagonists all choose to take matters under their own control and utilize their virus-altered bodies in a search for retribution. While the contemporary reality of sexual relationships in this age of AIDS may resonate in the actions of the characters, these narratives are all fictionalized depictions of the dynamics of revenge within sexual relationships. As such, they will be referred to as **revenge narratives** because the theme of retribution is central to the overall literary product. Furthermore, in each such narrative, the avenger creates his or her own plot for enacting that revenge, thus producing a metarevenge narrative. The three fictional texts that will serve as the backbone of this discussion are El vuelo de la reina by Argentine novelist Tomás Eloy Martínez; the short story "El secreto de Berlín" by Chilean storyteller Ramón Griffero; and "Luna negra de noviembre" by the Uruguayan writer Ana Solari.

During the emplotment of revenge, these three authors recur to a variety of metaphors analyzed by Sontag in *AIDS and Its Metaphors*. According to Sontag, the most prominent, the plague metaphor, has been used to represent diseases throughout history, including syphilis, cholera, and now AIDS. It is linked to fear, xenophobia, and the notion of foreignness, themes that surface not only in the imagining of the origins of the virus, but also in the contradictory reality that faces those who are infected with a disease that they previously viewed as belonging to "others." Eloy Martínez's work shows the strongest tendency to employ this referent. Related to the plague metaphor is the second metaphor, the notion of the apocalypse, which is underlined by fear, judgment, and a preoccupation with an impending doom. This tone sets the stage for Solari's depiction of revenge and the uncertain future facing her protagonist. Finally, there is the military metaphor, which utilizes an aggressive vocabulary of schemes, attacks, mobilization, and ambush as well as the required counterpart, a formidable defense. This metaphor is intimately related to the notion of revenge and the envisioning of the body that seeks it. Because of the aggressive nature of these narratives, militaristic overtones predominate, particularly in relation to the forceful transmission of the virus through rape, other violent and sadistic sexual activity, and sheer force. These aggressive tendencies are evident in both Griffero's and Eloy Martínez's texts, which I will explore in relation to the military metaphors that underline them.

The Body as Weapon
EXACTING REVENGE

Within the arena of the revenge plot and the metaphors that inhabit it, the central focus of this chapter is on the avenger and his or her victims' bodies and on how the narration of retribution is performed by and upon them. The theories of sociologist Arthur W. Frank and his conceptualization of different types of "wounded" storytellers illuminate this discussion. Frank's work *The Wounded Storyteller* critically examines the different manifestations of ill bodies that strive to find a voice in narratives about an illness experience. He focuses specifically on four common "wounded" bodies that resurface in the fictional and nonfictional works he has examined: the **disciplined body,** which is ruled by regimentation and self-control; the **mirroring body,** which depends upon images from popular culture to try to recreate the healthy body within itself; the **dominating body,** defined primarily by force and rage; and finally the **communicative body,** which is the idealized self who accepts its condition and communicates openly with others about that reality. I predominantly focus on the dominating body that exemplifies the protagonists in both Eloy Martínez and Griffero's works, as well as the mirroring body that surfaces tangentially in Griffero's story and centrally in Solari's work. Frank's terminology provides a manner to envision the alterations and reconceptualizations that befall the protagonists of the three fictional works being examined.

Also key to this discussion are the multiple manifestations of the HIV-infected body, at times consumed by an overwhelming association with victimization, while at other moments conceptualized and utilized as a weapon that illuminates the way in which AIDS has provided a deadly way to exacerbate the power differential that can exist in sexual relationships. The deliberate exploitation of HIV to exact revenge can be regarded as a type of physical and psychological torture, particularly in light of the use of violence and rape as an expression of that power. This dynamic is particularly evident in the first work discussed in this chapter, *El vuelo de la reina*. Elaine Scarry's *The Body in Pain* provides a lens through which to better comprehend both this sort of torturous revenge and the manipulative desires of the victimizer to thoroughly dominate his or her conquest.

Scarry argues in her initial chapter, "The Structure of Torture: The Conversion of Real Pain into the Fiction of Power," that during an act of torture, the physical pain being inflicted onto the victim by the torturer is "so incontestably real that it seems to confer its quality of 'incontestable reality' on that power that has brought it into being. It is, of course, precisely because the reality of that power is so highly contestable, the regime so unstable, that torture is being used" (27). While Scarry's work focuses primarily on the connection between an illusive power and the overt use of violence and torture within the realm of war, as well as the use of torture to force confessions, I will utilize her theories to analyze the interpersonal relationship depicted by Eloy Martínez, one that not only exhibits some of the characteristics already highlighted by Scarry but that also involves the use of a weapon to assert the protagonist's agency. As Scarry goes on to explain, "What assists the conversion of pain into the fiction of absolute power is an obsessive, self-conscious display of agency. On the simplest level the agent displayed is the weapon" (27). In the case of these works, the weapon is the HIV-infected body rather than a more tangible form of weaponry.

In Eloy Martínez's text, the protagonist struggles with a faltering sense of agency over his own life and as a result obsessively tries to reassert his power vis-à-vis violence and some of the mechanisms of torture outlined by Scarry. I argue that the deliberate transmission of HIV through rape and other forms of violence is akin to the torture that Scarry examines and theorizes. Although this torture does not occur systematically, as it did during the authoritarian regimes in Argentina, this text, a product from the postdictatorial society of that country, contains unmistakable vestiges of the rhetoric of torture that predominated in the terror-filled regimes of the dictatorship. That torture has been translated into a personal, intimate anguish that is connected to the power differential of the relationship, the desire for revenge, and the fear provoked by conceptualizations about AIDS, which is expressed through the use of plague, militaristic, and apocalyptic metaphors.

Although Scarry's theories on torture and power are most useful for understanding Eloy Martínez's work, Griffero's and Solari's works have also been indirectly imprinted with the marks of the previous authoritarian regimes that ruled the countries—Chile and Uruguay, respectively—which produced their authors. Griffero's story recurs to physical torture, but it is distinct from that occurring during the dictatorships in that it was inflicted postmortem in an elaborate ruse aimed at personal redemption. Furthermore, the protagonist, as an exiled Chilean suffering from AIDS in a faraway country, internalizes the stigmas attached to his condition and perpetuates his own destruction through self-induced psychological torture. The harsh marginalization and stereotyping of anyone perceived to deviate from the norms established by the dictatorship seem to be internalized by the protagonist, who is still carrying with him indelible marks of that regime, particularly given his current plight in exile. Perhaps the text least overtly connected to the previous Southern Cone dictatorships is Solari's work, which is certainly informed by the repressive silence that predominated during the regime, but which is devoid of specific referents to that period in Uruguay's past. Therefore, while all three of these works have varying degrees of markers of the authoritarian regimes that ruled each country during the 1970s and 80s, all three have in common a primary focus on the act of vengeful transmission itself and the operation of the bodies that consummate that act.

One of the central preoccupations of many AIDS narratives is the body itself, both as the site of infection and as an altered being that obtains and loses certain significances. In reality, however, it is inaccurate to speak of just *one* body; the HIV-positive person actually experiences various bodily permutations and manifestations. Furthermore, in the realm of the revenge narratives, it becomes necessary to examine the relationship between a dominant body and a dominated body. These narratives illustrate the bifurcated destinies of the HIV-positive person. Both of these bodies will pass through multiple phases before agency intervenes and sets the course for future action. I will call these phases **infection, realization,** and **action** and will discuss the divergent manner in which these paths progress in the sphere of revenge narratives.

Quite obviously, the first step to acquiring HIV-positive status is infection by the virus, although the significant aspect of that step is *how* one is infected. Common means of transmission are through unprotected intercourse, sharing of needles, transfusion of tainted blood into a healthy person, or transfer from mother to child through the placenta. Each of these modes of transmission carries with it distinctly separate stigmas that can greatly affect the way an HIV-positive person is perceived and subsequently treated. Furthermore, "The link between stigma, discrimination, and HIV/AIDS has long been recognized by several world organizations. . . . They all agree that HIV/AIDS-related stigma is an undermining factor for public health since it not only causes psychological distress but it harms individuals by discouraging those who are at risk, including those who do not know they are infected, from seeking testing and/or counseling, as well as getting antiretroviral treatment at the earliest signs of infection" (Rosati 164). Smallman's work also supports this statement by illustrating how "when the first cases of HIV did appear in Latin America, the reaction was often one of hysteria" (13). He goes on to explain how this "hysteria" took the form of isolating patients and destroying items touched by them, ostracizing them, forcing them into exile, and taking other actions that separated those who were infected from the rest of society (13). In addition, Sontag notes that "to get AIDS is to be revealed, often linked to guilt, scandal, to be a member of a certain risk group, a community of pariahs" (112–13). Many critics have aptly identified the social tendency to divide people with AIDS into two groups: innocent victims and those deserving of the disease.[2] Because of this premature categorization, simply by becoming infected a person is unwittingly entering into a fraternity of sorts with other "sinners" or "innocent victims," both of which, as Sontag concisely extrapolates, carry the burden of significant metaphors and preconceived notions that will affect the future treatment of the person (113). I argue that equally important is the drastic impact that infection has on self-perception. Becoming infected with a disease that carries multiple stigmas means confronting each of those perceptions and reconciling them with one's own vision of self. Any resultant discordance ultimately contributes to an altered sense of self.

Another key element of this phase of transmission, besides the automatic categorization intrinsic to it, is the notion of volition. The rhetoric of blaming the victim tends to penalize those who willingly participated in acts that led to their contagion, particularly if those acts are viewed by society as illegal, deviant, or unsafe. This desire to place blame all but evaporates when considering those infected by tainted blood or those who experienced the sadistic and violent actions of another. Society tends to view the former as unwitting victims of a failed medical system that did not adequately protect its citizens from disease-free blood. In the latter situation, the victim of rape or attack from an HIV-positive person is viewed as just that—a victim. This is the body that characterizes the manipulated characters in revenge narratives. Their attackers envision their victims' bodies as being receptacles for the biological weapon that will ultimately transform them from healthy to ill.

Stephen F. Krueger, in his study on the confluence of gender, sexuality, fiction, and science in AIDS narratives, illustrates the transformation of the ill body by explaining that "the body of the person living with AIDS, its cells under foreign attack and then control, its immune system taken hostage, becomes the body of a victim" (45). In this sense, those who are deliberately infected are initially conceptualized as fragmented enti-

---

2. For an in-depth discussion of this tendency to stigmatize HIV-positive individuals, see Jones; Sontag; and Gilman.

ties whose physicality takes predominance over mental functioning. At the moment of infection, the violators know that the route to their revenge is entirely through the interaction of two bodies—one infected and one soon-to-be infected. The distinction between the two at that moment is volition: the victims either are forcibly overtaken or are not privy to the HIV status of their partners/attackers and therefore are willing participants in the sexual exchange because of false information they have been provided.

The second phase to consider in the transformation of the body of a HIV-positive person is realization. In this phase, the individual is affected both psychologically and physically because of the conflicting realities of psychological realization and physical symptomology. In its early stages, the HIV virus is characterized by a silent, invisible quality that can often go unnoticed without an intervening diagnosis from a physician. On the surface, the self may at first seem to be unaltered, whole, even healthy. However, this conception of self can be drastically altered during this phase and may produce a fragmentation of the mind and body as one fights to comprehend the new reality she faces. In essence, as literary critic Emily Apter has concluded in regard to Hervé Guibert's writing, AIDS is capable of "blurring the boundaries, both mental and physical, of individual personhood" (88).

Being diagnosed as HIV-positive causes the patient to confront an entirely new identity. This phase requires a drastic re-envisioning of the self as the individual contends with images, memories, stereotypes, taboos, and metaphors that have long inhabited the social consciousness in regard to HIV/AIDS. One must reconcile the fact that a disease that for so long seemed foreign, belonging to others, has now taken residence in one's own body. This process is further complicated by the seemingly contradictory body that often continues to appear healthy long after the diagnosis. This conflict can produce a strong sense of denial, something that eventually disintegrates as the body begins to manifest physical symptoms and signs of AIDS, further emphasizing the lack of physical control over the virus. At that point, the mind may fight to regain control over a body that is slowly being destroyed from the inside out. In the disjointed state wherein the realities of the mind seem at odds with the physical asymptomology of the body, either the self becomes more vulnerable to outside forces because of its fragmented state or it fights to regain control and exert its agency.

Part of the process of consciousness-raising regarding HIV-positive status is the recognition of the potentially lethal quality of the virus and the fact that the body carrying it is, in essence, converted into a sort of biological weapon. Consequently, the carriers are thrust into a paradoxical existence in which they are physically weakened and incrementally destroyed by the virus. However, it is precisely through this experience with the destructive potential of the virus that they recognize the power they possess within to wreak that same destruction on another if they so choose. It is in this action phase that the person begins to reintegrate the mind and body to refocus them on the goals ahead. While individual reactions vary wildly, for some, action translates into aggression and domination that are harnessed to seek vengeance on others. As mentioned earlier, Frank defines these victimizers as "dominating bodies," or those who feel rage over the loss of control brought by HIV-positive status and who therefore displace that rage onto others. The dominator's weapon is the infected body itself, utilized in an attempt to force another person to experience the same loss of control that led to the dominator's rage in the first place.

I will examine the divergent ways in which the protagonists of these three texts choose to exert their agency vis-à-vis their infected bodies. In the case of Eloy Martínez, in addition to the obvious manifestation of domination through rape, torture, and murder, I will also analyze the allegorical meaning of dominance as an attempt by Eloy Martínez's protagonist to exert his masculinity by clinging to the vestiges of authority that traditionally accompanied it, particularly in the authoritarian society that lingers in the not-too-distant past of this narrative. Rebecca E. Biron's study on the connection between murder and masculinity enlightens this discussion. Biron focuses on works that "explore the cliché of proving virility through violence" (7). She goes on to argue that "when successful manliness is associated with power over women, and successful male citizenship is associated with obeying laws designed in collective male interest, then the criminal male who kills simultaneously celebrates and undermines hegemonic masculinity" (8).

While Biron succinctly problematizes the duality of masculinity in the social and institutional realms of societies with clearly delineated laws governing behavior, I will explore this association in a text that does not plainly depict an institutional authority that condemns murder, particularly murder of women, thereby examining the residual effects of an omnipotent dictatorship that was complicit in the torture and elimination of thousands of citizens and that provided a model for the convergence of murder and masculinity on the state level. *El vuelo de la reina* is a postdictatorial work, but I argue that the expectation of supreme masculine authority that was seen during the dictatorship continues to inform the behavior of its protagonist. In the end, however, as Biron illustrates in her study, the enactment of murder to assert one's masculinity is indicative of the true lack of power that these individuals possess, both within a society that lacks clear direction and as individuals whose control over their own lives is compromised by AIDS.

In Griffero's narrative, the protagonist's agency is tied to the notion of the "secret" and is enacted via a combination of overt physical and sexual dominance combined with erotic seduction. For this central character, the main motivation for revenge is not power and dominance per se; rather, he attempts to relieve the rage and guilt that accompany the virus that he carries. In that sense, the woman who becomes his victim is an object to whom to express his rage rather than a specific individual chosen for personal reasons.

Last, I will compare these phallocentric versions of revenge narratives with Solari's gynocentric approach in "Luna negra de noviembre," in which her character enacts a pattern of retribution out of wrath toward the man who infected her but is unavailable to her. Instead, she focuses her attention on unsuspecting suitors, functioning as a seductive *femme fatale* rather than a dominating force.

El vuelo de la reina

Eloy Martínez's novel centers on the relationship between Argentinean newspaper editor Camargo and Reina Remis, the reporter with whom he becomes intimately involved and carries on an all-consuming, torrid affair. Camargo, as an older, power-driven man, goes to great lengths throughout the relationship to infiltrate and subtly control nearly every aspect of Reina's life. Slowly, their relationship begins to deteriorate and Camargo suspects that Reina is seeing someone else. His suspicions are soon confirmed when Reina terminates their relationship because she loves another man. As he feels the reins of control begin to slip, Camargo increasingly turns to intimidation and violence, ultimately striking Reina in the face. However, she doesn't succumb to his physical domination but rather continues to rebuff him. This rejection and betrayal prove to be too much for Camargo, catapulting him into a state of extreme, obsessive behavior in which he strives to find a way to once again dominate Reina and prove to her and himself that "Vos sos quien sos, Camargo. Nadie puede dejarte" [You are who you are, Camargo. No one can leave you] (217).

At first, Camargo attempts to manipulate her by denigrating her work at the newspaper and creating a negative perception of her in the industry, all the while plotting the most complete revenge possible. While formulating his plan, he begins to fear that her affair with another man has led to her contraction of a sexually transmitted disease, consequently putting

Camargo at risk. He also, through the perceived affront committed against him through Reina's indiscretions, reasons that he is justified in seeking vengeance. In essence, the revenge plot is set in motion by his paranoid imaginations of a worst-case scenario, imaginations that are never verified but rather become reality in Camargo's mind. In this case, the specter of STD infection, coupled with his fervent desire to regain dominance over Reina, eventually lead him to take action and execute a plan of revenge.

He reasons that he must attack her at the exact point of his loss and her betrayal—her sexuality. Throughout their affair, Reina, and more specifically her body, represents the idealized, sexualized female form: Camargo not only has the pleasure of fantasizing about her, but as her boyfriend also has the privilege of communing with her physically and sexually. When she terminates their relationship, he loses the access he once enjoyed to her body and, consequently, to her sexuality. Therefore, he can no longer tolerate that she continues to be a sexualized being, particularly one who offers her body to another man. Through his plan of revenge, he aims to taint her via a virus that he hopes will complicate (and in his mind eliminate) all future sexual relationships: HIV.

In order to exact his revenge, Camargo must be certain that Reina is indeed exposed to HIV. His desire for certitude is significant because Camargo himself cannot function as a "dominating body," regardless of his sadistic desire to exact revenge on Reina personally. He has never confirmed his own suspicions that Reina infected him with HIV or any other STD, and he therefore wonders whether he lacks the biological weaponry necessary to carry out his plan. Ironically, he is rendered doubly impotent, first by the loss of a sexual partner and second (and consequently) by his inability to physically and sexually dominate Reina as he seeks revenge. Because of this ambiguity about his own health status, he must utilize another's body to infect Reina. To achieve this goal, he turns his focus to the homeless couple who live outside Reina's building.

He has seen them on multiple occasions and has surmised that they are refugees from the war in Kosovo who paid dearly to come to Buenos Aires, only to find themselves living in the street. They desperately want to return to their homeland with the aid of new passports and identities, thus creating an opportunity for Camargo to manipulate them to achieve the revenge that he desires. At first his mental scheme of how to achieve that revenge is imprecise; he only knows he wants to include Momir, the homeless man, in his plan because he intuits that "él puede ser el instrumento de tu castigo. Su hedor, la irredimible suciedad de su cuerpo, el asco de sus manos: eso es lo menos que merece la traición de la mujer" [he could be the instrument of your punishment. His stench, the irredeemable filth of his body, the repugnance of his hands: that is the least that the woman's betrayal deserves] (218). He wants to humiliate Reina and destroy the pleasurable connection between sexuality and her body by having Momir rape Reina. The desire to have Momir carry out this vengeance shows that Camargo wants not only to overpower and dominate her through violation, but also to humiliate and degrade her by planning her violation by someone from a group who, according to Camargo "deberían ser borrados de la Tierra: utilizados para la servidumbre y luego aniquilados" [should be erased from the Earth: utilized for servitude and then annihilated] (237). The fact that he must bribe another man to carry out this act of sexual and physical domination further highlights Camargo's metaphorical impotence. The use of rape here is significant because it accentuates the fact that in order to control another person through her own body, a violent overtaking of that body is used in an attempt to force a fragmentation of self and thus eliminate agency on the part of the victim.

The rhetoric of rape resonates with one of the predominant metaphors described by Sontag: that of the military metaphor. Much of the discussion about HIV and AIDS tends to recur to these metaphors in an attempt to conceptualize the virus. It is not at all uncommon to hear about the "war on AIDS" that many public health ministries have launched to combat the threatening virus that is conceived as an invading force, much like an invading army. It is unwelcome, to say the least, and unexpected, and therefore much of the rhetoric focuses on strategies of defense against this virulent invader. AIDS theorist and commentator Michael S. Sherry, in his article "The Language of War in AIDS Discourse," focuses on this pervasive metaphor and the fact that it is often used in an attempt to paint a dire picture of the current public health situation in order to mobilize either the government or the gay and lesbian community to fight back or, in the language of the war metaphor, stage a counterattack against the invader that is HIV (50).

On the individual level, physiological discourse turns to this same metaphor when describing the way in which the virus enters the body and overtakes the immune system. Much of the medical discourse surrounding HIV transmission recurs to the notion of an ambush carried out by the virus against the cells of the body, ultimately annihilating the healthy defenses of the body and leading to the destruction of the body from the inside out. Sontag illustrates how disease is seen as an invasion of alien organisms. The body must try to use its "immunological defenses" and "aggressive" medicines and therapies to try to combat that invader. This discourse in turn contributes to the stigmatization of those infected with the disease (97–99). In fact, she argues for the destruction and retirement of this metaphor over all others because of this stigmatizing effect and the overzealousness of its descriptive potentials (182). When examining these common discourses in both societal and individual models of infection, one can see how these same metaphors resonate in the image of rape.

Steven F. Krueger deconstructs this metaphorical language of war by showing how the keywords associated with HIV infection can also connote a sexual encounter. He explains how HIV "penetrates" the cell membrane, "attacks" the cell's nucleus, and ultimately "takes over the cellular machinery" (36). He argues that "homosexual imagery is evoked by the description of cellular DNA that is made to 'bend over' so that the virus can sneakily insert itself into the host chromosomes" (39). I would argue that this same imagery also evokes the violent actions of rape, in which the attacked body is invaded by the dominating force of the rapist, ultimately forcing the victim to succumb to the overwhelming power of the attacker. A woman who is attacked is often rendered defenseless, just like the cell that is invaded by HIV. Therefore, we can see that in the case of Eloy Martínez's depiction, the rape committed against Reina is not only a physical and sexual attack, but a biological one as well.

The desire to physically overpower and disgust Reina is only part of the revenge that Camargo hopes to impose on her. Instead, he wants the rape not only to affect her during the act itself, but also to leave a lasting impression for her lifetime. Camargo reasons that "ya que la mujer te ha traicionado . . . no vas a permitir que nada en ella quede sin mancillar ni herir, nada de esa sangre sin infectar" [because the woman has betrayed you . . . you're not going to allow anything in her to remain unsullied or unharmed, none of that blood uninfected] (238). This desire to physically damage Reina internally and externally requires the use of a weapon that, once it enters the body, continues on its destructive path from the inside out. That weapon is HIV, or "el mal," and it is something that Momir, the homeless refugee from a faraway land, carries. "El mal" is never explicitly defined as HIV in this text, but the use of the referent "el mal" to connote HIV is one that can be seen in both literary works and critical studies of HIV.[3] Nonetheless, it is up to the reader to connect the referent to the textual clues provided and ultimately supply the names HIV and AIDS. Eloy Martínez offers these clues, first through visual imagery referencing "la sombra de unas escaras" [the shadow of some ulcers], likely a reference

3. In her article "El mal del siglo veinte: POESíd A y SIDA," Kuhnheim not only utilizes this referent in the title and body of her critical article about elegy and AIDS poetry, but also cross-references the vocabulary "el mal" in Mario Bellatín's novella *Salón de belleza*, where the term is also used in reference to a disease that, through textual clues, is clearly AIDS.

to the telltale Kaposi sarcoma that appears on the skin of AIDS patients (223). "El mal" that Momir carries is also strongly suggested to be HIV after he rapes the drugged Reina and his partner asks, accusingly: "¿Por qué no te cuidaste? ¿No le advertiste que estás enfermo?" [Why didn't you protect yourself? Didn't you warn him that you're sick?], to which Momir responds "lo quiso así" [he wanted it that way] (239).

These opaque references to "la enfermedad" [the illness] and "el mal," along with the apparent deadliness of the virus, are the only clues that Eloy Martínez offers to the readers that the disease in question is indeed AIDS. This silent treatment and refusal to directly name the virus is repeated in a large number of works related to HIV/AIDS, not only in Latin America, but also in the United States.[4] It is also a common characteristic of all of the works discussed in this chapter and will be examined later in this chapter in relation to the short stories to be contrasted with Eloy Martínez's novel.

In addition to the lack of definitive naming of the disease that Momir is infected with, the very use of Momir as the carrier of the HIV virus is significant, given the treatment of AIDS throughout literature. As previously mentioned, a common perception exists that AIDS and HIV attack from outside both the body and the community. This belief is often extrapolated to the extreme by situating the blame outside of the community on "foreigners" or "others" in an attempt to exculpate one's own community and emotionally distance oneself from the reality of the disease. This perception is complicated, however, by the very name given to the refugee: Momir. The suffix of the name (mir) means "peace" in Serbo-Croatian.[5] The juxtaposition of the peaceful moniker and the violent actions enacted by the body inscribed with that name create a sense of dissonance. On the surface, Momir incarnates the disease-carrying foreigner who poses a direct threat to the new society he inhabits, but his name suggests that, to those who have the cultural and linguistic knowledge necessary to "translate" him, he would not have naturally posed the daunting threat that was previously perceived had it not been for Camargo's manipulation. Nevertheless, no one, especially Camargo, takes the time to look past his "foreign" exterior, choosing instead to operate on the xenophobic belief that he incarnates the pernicious "plague" that inhabits his body. He essentially becomes the "foreign" and "deadly" disease that is feared by the modern Argentinean society represented in the novel, thus giving credence to the misconception and further exacerbating the cycle of blaming foreigners and "others" for the maladies of society.

4. For further discussion, see Jones 225–40.
5. Personal correspondence with Ksenija Bilbija, January, 2004.

This representation perpetuates one of the pervading misconceptions surrounding AIDS, namely, that it is from elsewhere rather than in one's own society. Cultural theorist David B. Morris, in *Illness and Culture in the Postmodern Age,* his study on postmodernism and illness, identifies this origin plot as one of the most common plots found in AIDS-related literature. These plots "seize on the exotic, the unfamiliar, and the remote, on some distant site of deviance and otherness" (211). In fact, many theorists define this tendency to situate the origin of AIDS elsewhere, often in the Third World. Paula A. Treichler adds, "The term exotic, sometimes used to describe a virus that appears to have originated 'elsewhere' (but 'elsewhere' like 'other' is not a fixed category) is an important theme running through AIDS literature" (46).

Sander L. Gilman mentions this concept by bringing attention to the groups seen to be most at risk in the 1980s: the 4-H's,[6] that is, homosexuals, heroin addicts, hemophiliacs, and Haitians. Gilman further notes that nations that attempted to trace the origins of HIV invariably turned outward as they pointed their accusatory fingers. To the U.S., AIDS was either an African or a Haitian disease, while in the eyes of France and the former Soviet Union, its origins were placed firmly in the U.S. (100). This tendency to transfer blame and origin to foreigners often leads to a further connection between marginalized members of society and AIDS because foreigners are often lumped into the same subjugated category as society's other outcasts, such as homosexuals, drug users, and prostitutes. In Eloy Martínez's novel, Momir experiences multiple marginalizations: As a refugee from the Serbo-Croatian war, he has been displaced from his native land, being forced to flee to escape the violence and persecution of the war. In his new society, Argentina, he inhabits yet another marginalized space: not only is he a foreigner, but he is a carrier of a deadly disease, leaving him as a homeless outcast of society.

As Momir's condition illustrates, there is a double stigmatization of members of marginalized social groups who are also HIV-positive. As a result of this association, the converse is also often true: those who are HIV-positive are often cast into a subjugated role and assumed to be associated with the perceived outcasts of society, whether that is true or not. Arthur Kleinman, in his work on illness narratives, has defined and emphasized the role that this sort of stigma can play in the subsequent marginalization of certain members of society. He asserts that

> Stigma often carries a religious significance—the afflicted person is viewed as sinful or evil—or a moral connotation of weakness and dis-

---

6. These categories originally were mentioned in Gottlieb and Groopman,

honor. Thus, the stigmatized person is defined as an alien other, upon whose persona are projected the attributes the group regards as opposite to the ones it values. In this sense, stigma helps to define the social identity of the group. (159)

Sontag has also commented on the pervasive link between disease and foreignness in the public imagination, noting the tendency for this perceived link to propagate fear and xenophobia (135–36). She points out that xenophobic propaganda has always rendered immigrants as vectors of illness (149). The perpetuation of this misconception is particularly dangerous because it causes people to become less vigilant and therefore to unnecessarily expose themselves to the virus because of the ignorant belief that it is something exotic, or, as Sontag puts it, "an infestation from the third world" (139) carried only by immigrants or at-risk groups, rather than something endemic to modern society that has the potential to affect all of its members.

The fact that Eloy Martínez situates HIV in a foreign immigrant can be seen in two lights: on the one hand, it exposes this common tendency to transfer blame for epidemics and infestations to outsiders, but on the other hand it continues to problematize this depiction by neglecting to question that representation as one that lacks veracity. In the end, "the desire to locate the origin of a disease is the desire to be assured that we are not at fault, that we have been invaded from without, polluted by some external agent" (Gilman 100). In the mind of an avenger attempting to bring about some sort of sexual justice, this external location of HIV's origin, which continues to perpetuate the military metaphor of an unprovoked attack from external sources, provides justification, albeit skewed, that retaliation is a valid response to the situation. More specifically, Camargo indeed feels that he has been unfairly exposed to a potentially lethal sexually transmitted disease through Reina's infidelity, and he therefore considers himself justified in his desire to retaliate against her, whom he sees as the enemy.

Camargo aims to punish Reina for having an affair with a foreign writer by intentionally exposing her to a disease that is often associated with foreigners and marginalized citizens. He also strives to marginalize her by isolating her from her support network in the days following the rape. When Reina finally awakes from the drug-induced state that Camargo had put her in, she is extremely disoriented, unable to understand what happened to her, how multiple days have passed without her knowledge. She calls for help, but no one comes to her aid, thus isolating her emotionally. She has lost physical control of her body as she stumbles about the apartment. When she finally sees the blood between her legs and feels the excruciating pain in her body, she only has a bodily knowledge of what happened but is unable to connect that feeling with mental certainty. In the words of Elaine Scarry, she has undergone a torturous session of "unmaking" in which Camargo strives to utilize pain and objectification to display what he ultimately believes to be his absolute power over her. This absolute power is in actuality fictitious, but by attacking Reina from multiple angles, Camargo deludes himself into believing it to be real.

These perceptions are key to the idea of the revenge narrative. As Jacoby pointed out in the introduction to her work on revenge, the avengers who strive for retribution following a perceived grievance committed against them often eschew society's normal channels for achieving justice, such as the criminal justice system, and strike out on their own vengeful quests. As avengers often operate independently, their perceived affronts, whether imagined or real, motivate their redemptive actions, all in an attempt to reestablish control and power, not only over their own lives but over the lives of their offenders. In Camargo's case, his desire for revenge originated primarily from being rejected and subsequently losing his influence in Reina's life. How Camargo processed both affronts was central to the type of revenge he eventually plotted. Fearing a loss of control and agency, he created a plan that would give him the feeling of dominance in both his life and Reina's. His obsessive desire for an omniscient presence is also reminiscent of the authoritarian regimes that plagued Argentina from 1976 to 1982. Camargo calls to mind the dictators who refused to tolerate the slightest deviation from their established laws and rules. In an attempt to dominate Reina, Camargo recurs to similar tactics that were used during the authoritarian regime: intimidation, torture, and, ultimately, murder.

In the tactics that Camargo has used to attack and violate Reina, one can see some of the vestiges of torture sessions that Scarry identified. His primary weapon was rape, used for myriad purposes: to humiliate and degrade her, to disgust and frighten her, to physically harm her, to destroy her sexually, and, ultimately, to infect her with a potentially fatal virus. This one act, symbolically one that Camargo lacked the power to carry out, mimicked the primary physical act of torture in that its goal was to inflict pain in its numerous forms. By locating the attack in her own home and, more specifically, in the room and on the bed once used for lovemaking between Camargo and Reina, he aims to reduce her world to that minuscule space, thereby isolating her and converting her once safe and comfortable surroundings into weapons themselves because they no longer function as everyday items but instead have become accomplices in her destruction. Furthermore, she is isolated and cut off from help outside her home, a seclusion that Reina herself recognizes when the doctor she calls for assistance naively suggests that she report the rape to the police, despite her concern that her she will not be taken seriously by authorities who have routinely minimized and dismissed accusations of rape. Consequently, in the hours after the rape, Reina is a fragmented, diseased, physically disintegrated being who seems unable to exert substantial agency over her situation: "Está privada de cuerpo, tal como vos querías, Camargo, no puede estar en sí misma ni tampoco en nadie" [She is deprived of a body, just as you wanted, Camaro, she can't be in herself nor in anyone (else)] (254). In short, she is exactly what Camargo hoped for because he assumes that he can manipulate her at her weakest moment and "rescue" her, thereby reasserting his control over her. In the end, this façade of ultimate power quickly erodes, revealing behind it the agency of Reina and her desires to remake herself.

To Camargo's surprise, Reina's will cannot be broken, as she continually reiterates that she will not reconcile with him. She defies the overriding conception that an HIV-positive person is a victim without agency through her stubborn resistance to Camargo's attempts to further degrade and annihilate her. Shortly after the attack, she consults with a doctor, who immediately conducts tests for various STDs, confirming that the man who raped her was indeed a carrier of several venereal diseases. Furthermore, because the waiting period for HIV-test results is several weeks and the probability of HIV infection is high, the doctor insists that Reina begin to take "el cóctel anti-SIDA" [the anti-AIDS cocktail] (265). However, despite the trauma inflicted on her and the realization of the potential future she may face as an HIV-positive person, Reina chooses to focus her energies on healing from the attack and caring for herself. She is determined to avoid all contact with Camargo. Emblematic of this internal shift in focus is her decision to flee the hectic life of the city and spend time alone at her family's country estate. Initially, she is successful in reintegrating her body and mind and fusing them in a quest to regain control over her life. However, in spite of her efforts to heal and regain agency over her own body and mind through this retreat to her family's estate, she cannot escape the sadistic determination of Camargo. Once he realizes that Reina will not be possessed by him, Camargo completely unravels.

Although he originally recognized the importance of her survival after the rape because he felt that the punishment would matter only if she were forced to live with it, his need to completely dominate her overtakes him, leaving him unable to even allow her to *live* with HIV. In the end, he murders her, realizing that only through the complete destruction of

Reina's entire being is he able to be certain that she will no longer betray him. In the grand scheme of the narrative development, Camargo's quest to control and punish Reina for abandonment and betrayal passes through many phases and levels, as he attacks her mentally (through the destruction of her career), emotionally (through his sadistic manipulation, threats, and isolation), physically (by hitting and drugging her), sexually (through the rape and transmission of HIV), and, ultimately, by murdering her. HIV functions as one of the many weapons Camargo uses to achieve ultimate domination over Reina. Although the use of HIV as a weapon is a relatively new addition to the arsenal in sexual warfare, in the end the destruction wrought by HIV on the body failed to yield the immediate and extreme results that Camargo craved; therefore, his impatience led him to the ultimate weapon of total annihilation: the revolver.

The fact that Camargo recurred to such drastic measures in the end ultimately illustrates his impotence and the façade of power that is rapidly disintegrating. It becomes clear that despite his desperate attempts to assert his own agency and prove his masculine authority over her, each successive action reveals eroding authority on a personal level, which in turn echoes the still unsteady political climate that serves as a backdrop to the novel. Camargo's figurative impotence began when Reina left him, thus shattering the hold that he had over her life. In response, he developed a plan to "reclaim" authority over Reina's body and life, thus revealing his belief that dominance can be achieved over someone seen as subservient, both as an employee and as a lover. However, at every step of the way, the illusive nature of Camargo's power is ultimately revealed. He is unable to conquer her through emotional intimidation and thus quickly progresses to violence and physical threats, yet he enlists the help of another man to carry out his plan. By utilizing another man's body, he undermines his own power and authority, revealing his increasing powerlessness over Reina. When all of his plans fail and Reina still refuses to succumb to his control, Camargo's decision to utilize the phallic weaponry that is the revolver reveals not only his lack of authority, but his lack of *masculine* authority over Reina. In this sense, Eloy Martínez's text shows some of the tendencies that Rebecca E. Biron examines in her study of the confluence of murder and masculinity. One of the conclusions she reached was that the texts she studied "paradoxically resist violence against women by reenacting it, providing staged enjoyment of radical transgression at the same time that they force readers to criticize static and destructive dominant fictions" (150).

One of the primary "destructive dominant fictions" that Eloy Martínez's text reveals is that of absolute masculine authority. Each of Camargo's actions reveals a man still clinging to the promise of what R. W. Connell termed "phallic privilege" (quoted in Biron 8), still convinced of his power simply because he is a male. However, Eloy Martínez, by juxtaposing an imposing female who does not willingly succumb to his power, reveals Camargo to be a vestige of the types of masculinities that operated during the dictatorships of 1976–83 in Argentina's history. Through Camargo's eyes, Reina is a possession rather than an individual, resulting in the devaluation of human life. Throughout the conception and enactment of his plan, Camargo is concerned only with exerting his own power over someone that he views as "his," and he proves a willingness to use any means necessary to exercise that power and reconquer Reina. This complete disregard for human life combined with the acceptance of torturous means to exert power was commonplace during the authoritarian rule, thus creating masculine identities in which violence and intimidation were not only commonplace but also lauded. On an allegorical level, this text seems to posit the question: once the dictatorship ends, what happens to the perceptions of masculinity that were created under authoritarianism? Camargo's actions reveal that to a certain point, these perceptions continue on into the new society, despite the transformation to a democratic system. Essentially, Camargo still exhibits dictatorial behavior despite the lack of authoritarian structure to support it.

The echoes of authoritarianism that can be found in Camargo's vengeful actions against Reina also call to mind one of the common metaphors of the regime, specifically expressed by Admiral César A. Guzetti, that depicted Argentina as a wounded social body being "contaminated by a disease that corrodes its insides and forms antibodies. These antibodies must not be considered in the same way that one considers a germ" (quoted in Graziano 133). The metaphorical use of disease as a means to justify social cleansing capitalizes on the fear associated with real diseases and plagues, thus lending credence to the "need" for a strong government to "cure" the wounded social body, at least in the minds of those in power. Camargo functions in a similar fashion. The corrosive contaminant plaguing him is not the "subversive" elements metaphorically recast as dangerous antibodies by the Argentine government, but a "subversive" girlfriend who refuses to abide by his rules. Like the actual military regimes before him, Camargo, functioning much like a dictator in his own life, recasts Reina as a diseased entity, thus obliterating her individuality by envisioning her as an infested, corroded body carrying a potentially lethal disease (HIV). He then sets out to "cure" her in much the same way that the military junta "cured" those deemed subversive and disruptive to the social body: through torture, manipulation, and a quest for physical and psychological destruction. To attempt to justify his actions, he encapsulates them in a rhetoric of revenge, thus shifting the blame to Reina rather than examining his own role in both the unraveling of their relationship and, ultimately, her destruction.

In essence, Camargo's personal spectacle of revenge mirrors the one played out by his country's government. The combination of these elements in a contemporary political novel functions as a social and civic criticism of a society that once again is mired in corruption and scandal and that on many levels still has not abandoned facets of the authoritarian mentality. The use of the AIDS-infected body as a weapon reveals a society that has yet to completely eradicate the totalitarian mindset, which for some, like Camargo, is still a justifiable way to operate. AIDS becomes yet another weapon to assert a masculine authority that, until 1983, was hailed as a virtue of strong citizens and a strong government. As Eloy Martínez reveals, while the weaponry may have changed and the society is different on the surface, some of underlying conceptions of identity and power dynamics are still lagging behind in their transformation.

The multiple phases of destruction and retaliation seen in *El vuelo de la reina* are also echoed in Ramón Griffero's short story about the confluence of sadism, eroticism, HIV, and revenge: "El secreto de Berlín." It, too, depicts the risks and deception resulting from sexual relationships in the age of AIDS. Like Eloy Martínez, Griffero has chosen to center his story on the intimate interactions within the realm of a heterosexual relationship. This similarity is noteworthy, particularly because of the initial assumption that AIDS was a "gay" disease, one to which heterosexuals were immune.[7] Since the early days in which AIDS was seen to be linked directly with homosexuals, there has been some degree of shift in this misconception, particularly as scientific evidence has clearly shown that the virus is passed through the exchange of male *and* female bodily fluids. However, as Silvana Paternostro shows in her sociological study on sexual attitudes in Latin America, *In the Land of God and Man: Confronting our Sexual Culture*, many heterosexual women still do not see themselves as members of an at-risk group as far as AIDS is concerned. The reality is actually the opposite. According to Dr. Juan Eduardo Céspedes, who has studied sexual practices and attitudes in Latin America and whom Paternostro interviewed regarding these issues, a Latin American housewife is at a higher risk of contracting AIDS than a prostitute because of two main factors: the hidden bisexuality of Latin men and Latin men's refusal to use condoms (Paternostro 28). This risk is heightened when one factors in the

---

7. See note 11 in introduction.

"profound level of denial in relation to sexuality on all fronts" that Paternostro witnessed throughout Latin America (137).

This assertion is also supported by Shawn Smallman's historical and cultural analysis of the AIDS epidemic in Latin America, *The AIDS Pandemic in Latin America*. Through a detailed, region-based approach that takes into consideration such divergent forces as NGOs, religious groups, social activists, and others actively involved in addressing the AIDS epidemic across Latin America, Smallman highlights several common sociocultural factors that have profoundly impacted both the spread of the HIV virus in Latin America and the information circulating about the disease. Smallman's work deconstructs many of the early misconceptions about the epidemic in Latin America, showing precisely why it was and continues to be a risk to the population:

> In truth, there were good reasons to be worried about HIV not only in Brazil but also throughout Latin America: an active sex trade, the large number of men having sex with men, the inability of many wives to negotiate condom use, a significant population injecting drugs, efforts by the Catholic Church to block sex education, and the prejudice that warped the early response to HIV/AIDS. (2)

Smallman's work carefully deconstructs each of these social factors. For the purposes of this chapter and the texts I examine, Smallman's study is particularly important in that it illustrates that "despite significant changes in social practice, extensive research on sexual practices and gender roles in Latin America has found that *machismo* is alive and well" (5). Its counterpart, *marianismo*, or a "power relationship in which the woman is supposed to subordinate her needs to those of the man," is also a significant factor in gender relationships in many countries (5). This power differential, while not inherent in all heterosexual relationships, still persists in many areas and therefore impacts HIV/AIDS transmission in a number of ways. In addition to remaining virgins until marriage, despite early sexual initiation for boys, women are exalted for being good mothers and wives. Women are not supposed to enjoy sex or experiment sexually and must not have extramarital affairs. However, men often experiment sexually outside of marriage, and women are expected to tolerate their affairs. It is not uncommon for this sexual experimentation to occur between two men; as long as a man is the penetrator, he is not perceived as a homosexual. Consequently, despite this knowledge of infidelity, women often cannot ask their husbands to use condoms, therefore putting themselves at risk of infection. Coupled with strong mandates against contraception from the Catholic Church, many women are left vulnerable to infection (5–6).

Returning our focus to the works discussed in this chapter, we see several of these factors at play. The fact that these authors depict the danger of AIDS in heterosexual relationships can be viewed in multiple lights. On the one hand, the sheer fact that these topics have been combined and presented in contemporary literature is one step toward shattering the silence and denial currently operating in much of Latin American society about the real risks involved in unprotected sex between any individuals, heterosexual or not. On this level, these texts ostensibly serve a didactic function, exhibiting a part of society that has been the subject of sharp prejudice by the hegemonic culture (Pastore 3). By dramatizing the risks involved in heterosexual relationships, these authors have the ability to question the current conceptions that perceive heterosexuals to be less at risk than homosexuals, IV drug users, and prostitutes. How they choose to depict those relationships, however, affects the type of reception they will have, ultimately jeopardizing the already fragile readership that exists because of the innately tragic nature of many AIDS narratives. Therefore, while it can be seen as a positive step forward that these authors have chosen to depict heterosexuals as the protagonists for AIDS-related narratives, the violent manner in which they opt to portray those relationships and the dangers associated with them is problematic, particularly in Griffero's case.

"El secreto de Berlín"

This tendency to emphasize the violent elements of risky heterosexual relationships comes to a dramatic head in Griffero's "El secreto de Berlín." By shifting the focus from the lovers themselves onto the violent acts committed during and after intercourse, Griffero's story resonates with the familiar echoes of the plague metaphors that have so infiltrated AIDS narratives since their inception and that have been omnipresent in the treatment of other pernicious diseases throughout the epidemiological history of humankind. Griffero's succinct narrative follows an anonymous Chilean through the streets of Berlin as he undergoes meticulous rituals of preparation—a nearly scientific selection of a suitable partner and a methodical routine of seduction, followed by the final moment of conquer and the parallel destructive resolution whose ritualistic machinations are underscored by a delirium that threatens to unravel the protagonist completely. The text eerily underscores the danger that the HIV virus poses, not only to the individual and the society that comes in contact with the infected body, but also to the carrier himself. Griffero's story tautly manipulates the notion of the body as weapon to such a point that there is confusion as to who the real victim is. The notion of the HIV-positive person as a latent killer is perpetuated until, in this work, he becomes a ritualistic serial killer, seeking vengeance against women and against society in general. However, behind the destructive façade lurks a conflicted self that is unraveling both physically and psychologically under the weight of guilt.

The "wounded" body of the protagonist, to borrow the term from Arthur W. Frank, exhibits numerous qualities that lend themselves to at least two of the categories that Frank has identified. As a serial killer who hunts his prey, the protagonist is clearly a "dominating body" whose rage remains undetected until he violently explodes during an episode of sex. He shows his force as he tyrannizes the woman he is with, making this interaction with her an essential means for him to express his new bodily identity. His violence takes the form of strangulation, biting, and asphyxiation, initiated first during a particularly intense session of intercourse—carried to its murderous extreme.

Despite this overt violence and domination exhibited by the protagonist, he also functions as a "mirroring body," who, according to Frank, is defined by acts that attempt to recreate the body in the images of other, healthy bodies, often taking his images from popular culture (43–44). He exhibits this mirroring tendency in the great care he takes in hiding his disease and presenting a healthy sexual being to the women he seduces. He is aware of his altered presence but chooses a ruse of pseudo-disguises so that he can personify the seductive lover role which he plays to carry out his hunt, attack, and kill of the prey he has targeted. In keeping with the tendencies of a "mirroring body," he relies on popular culture for inspiration. The dual identity as suave lover and brutal killer shows the ambivalence of this protagonist. He recognizes his potential to kill by transferring the virus unto others, but he also clings to his seductive prowess in an attempt to reclaim the sexuality that has been compromised by his HIV-positive status. This duality is exhibited not only in the precursors to the attack, but also in the hours following the murder of the lover.

Griffero's succinct tale begins at the moment of physical contact between the protagonist and his unwitting victim, which at first glance appears to be a typical interaction between two lovers. Yet despite this seemingly normal interaction between a man and a woman, the narrator is certain to inform the reader (and perhaps the woman at risk) that there are signs that "presagiaban un inconmesurable peligro" [foreboded an immeasurable danger] (57), although that risk remains hidden until it is too late. The narrative provides a close-up of this intimate encounter, which takes place in an anonymous hotel room and lasts from dusk until dawn. Only through flashbacks do we learn more about the two people whose bodies remain entwined in lovemaking throughout the evening. Unlike in Eloy Martínez's novel, where the readers were privy to the key self-altering moments of infection, realization, and action affecting both Camargo and Reina, in this narrative we are only privy to the action phase and are only provided clues as to how the victimizer/protagonist arrived at his current plight.

The protagonist first appears as one of two partners in a sexual encounter that by all appearances is consensual and has resulted from time spent in courtship. In reality, the man seems to have fortuitously stumbled upon this woman while spending time comparing one U-Bahn station in Berlin to those of his hometown of Santiago, Chile. She appears in his line of sight, and he immediately notices her and thereafter waits every day in the station to watch her. For several weeks he continues this pattern, keeping a distance in order to learn her patterns, likes, and dislikes. In essence, "observándola fue descubriendo cómo cautivarla [by observing her, he discovered how to captivate her] (60). She slowly takes notice, ignorant of the fact that the man has crafted a carefully planned visage of himself in an attempt to seduce her. Just as Camargo plotted his revenge, so too does this protagonist use his imagination to envision his plan before enacting it. In essence, their plots become metarevenge narratives, because their actions are not fortuitous, but rather are carefully crafted to exact the revenge desired. This protagonist has chosen specific books, clothes, hairstyles, and shoes, all in an effort to present the person that he is certain will most attract this woman. Through all of these details, the reader observes a deliberate stalking of the victim, showing that the victimizer has intentionally chosen to mirror himself based on dominant cultural images of an attractive male to put himself in position to operate as a dominant body, eventually using force in an attempt to avenge the anger he feels over his own plight. How that angst is executed is eventually revealed on the night in question, a night of sex in which the woman decides that "no le importó que ya no usara condones, que su piel se juntara con la de ella y que ambos participaran en el riesgo de la muerte" [it didn't matter to her that he no longer used condoms, that his skin connected with hers and that both participated in the risk of death] (61).

The night that serves as the backdrop of this story begins as one that is unremarkable and could easily befall many couples. As the two lovers explore one another, they yield to their own desires instead of following the careful rules of prophylactic use governing sexual encounters. In the woman's mind, they both consent to risking their health because they are so overwhelmed by passion, thus exposing them to the possibility of contracting an STD such as HIV. Up to this point, the narrative serves the didactic function of representing the inherent dangers of HIV infection that face all sexually active individuals. However, Griffero adds an additional level of sadistic vengeance and violence that amplifies the individual risks involved and catapults the depicted revenge to the social level as well.

In contrast to Reina, the female in this story is seen throughout as an object on whom the protagonist chooses to exert his wrath. She has no name and is not described outside of her physical attributes. The only points when the readers are privy to her thoughts are the moments before her demise, when she thinks that the man she is with reminds her of her first lover, and later in that same sexual encounter, when she no longer cares that they eschew protection during their lovemaking. These small excerpts of the woman's thought processes only serve to show how thoroughly she has been deceived and how willingly she has fallen for the man she is with, without concern for her own safety in the age of AIDS. Her body is simply an object to be seduced and drawn to the destructive force that is the protagonist. When she has been thoroughly entranced by him, she is further objectified in that she only serves as a physical receptacle for the deadly virus that the protagonist passes onto her. Once this mission is complete, he kills her.

It quickly becomes apparent that this protagonist's sadism goes beyond the intentional infection of women with HIV and extends to the most complete destruction possible. While Eloy Martínez's protagonist's decision to kill his victim at the end of the story reveals his obsessive desire to completely dominate *one* individual, Griffero's protagonist is less concerned with avenging a particular affront committed by a specific woman and instead perpetuates a chain of destruction for two specific reasons: to express his rage against a society that has shunned him, at least in part for his HIV status; and to make a futile attempt to exorcise both the physical and psychological traces of the virus from his own being. The first step in that process is to transmit the virus through intercourse, but it is the psychological need to cleanse himself that ultimately drives the protagonist to kill his victim.

In his mind, her role is more important when she is dead, serving as a soul to whom the protagonist tells his story and in the act of telling attempts to expunge his guilt. This additional element of guilt and morality is unique to this story and reveals the bifurcated reality that the protagonist faces. On the one hand, he seems almost compelled to kill, as if it were genetically programmed, something that he must do and over which he can exert no agency. This determinacy suggests that the lethal potentialities of the virus within him have converted him into a killer, an obvious deviation from the realities of this virus. On the other hand, what this does show, however, is the potential that HIV-positive individuals possess to destroy others' lives through the deliberate transmission of HIV and that the realization of that potential is part of the new identity of those affected. This dramatic confluence of HIV-positive person with serial killer suggests that we can look at the protagonist as a simulacrum of HIV itself: he is a silent, stealthy killer who hunts women of all types, he appears healthy with no outward signs of disease, he infiltrates himself into their lives through the seductive power of eroticism, and he kills the women when they repeal the protective barriers that would have prevented him from completely overtaking them. This portion of the protagonist operates according to the physical realities of the disease, choosing to avenge his fate by spreading the disease to unsuspecting women, although he never fully articulates why he has opted for this course of action. Instead, he appears compelled by a force almost beyond his control.

Nevertheless, as heartless as he is during the act of transmission and murder, he shows signs of remorse and has a semblance of a conscience after the murder, when he ritualistically tries to assuage his guilt by explaining his story to the dead woman, forcing her to "listen" before her soul takes flight. He reasons that if he keeps her body warm (through a series of steps that include hot baths and raised thermostats), he will be able to clear his conscience by transmitting his story to her, much as he transmitted the virus before her death. There is a sense of urgency here, because he believes that her soul will depart within three hours of her death. He struggles to make a coherent story, alternately crying and becoming irate when he fears she is not listening. This obsessive urge to expunge himself, both sexually and linguistically, is what drives him. He fears that if he does not satisfactorily narrate his "secret" to this woman, then he will need to continue searching for more victims.

Clearly perturbed, he tries to "relatarle su secreto" [recount his secret to her] (62), but his details and clues are interspersed between further incoherent moments in which he photographs the woman and fights with her corpse, which is rapidly advancing to rigor mortis. Through the hints he offers, it becomes clear that he has fled from Santiago. Although there are no direct references to Pinochet's dictatorship, which ended three years prior to the publication of this story, the sense that the protagonist has unwillingly left the homeland for which he is clearly nostalgic suggests that he is living in exile, perhaps as a result of the persecution committed by the regime. Clearly, he is displaced, not only physically but emotionally, a fact that preempts his attempts to use his new locale to start anew, causing him to rant about his perception that even at this distance from his homeland, he feels he can't flee from "su mala suerte" [his bad luck] (62). At the same time, he feels profound guilt over his actions and starts to apologize to the dead woman. He tries to remedy this guilt by indicating all of the clues that she should have seen to know that he was indeed a murderer, not only literally, but virally as well. His "clues," however, are cryptic and become silent markers that would be impossible for anyone to detect on his exterior, much the same way that HIV silently progresses through the unsuspecting body that it inhabits. Additionally, he silently posits that "él había culpado a Dios por haber creado seres imperfectos, malditos, mutantes, abandonados en esta masa de tierra" [he had blamed God for having created imperfect, damned, mutant beings, abandoned on this land mass] (63) further revealing to his victim that "veía el gene de la maldad posesionándose de su cuerpo y quería destruirlo" [he saw the gene of evil taking possession of his body and he wanted to destroy it] (63). This reference to genetic malfeasance can be read to indicate not only the genetic perturbations that have made him violent, but also the mutations that have occurred because of HIV infection, thus further exacerbating his violent potential.

By insisting that she should have known that he was dangerous, he is in effect utilizing the rhetoric of blaming the victim that so often is repeated in regard to rape victims and in the case of HIV transmission. Society often chastises those who contract the virus by assuming they were participating in risky behaviors and therefore at some level deserved the punishment they received. The protagonist of this story not only functions as the perpetrator of violence and vengeful transmission, but also represents one more victim of modern societies that conflate the connotation of HIV-positive status, catapulting it from a medical condition to a state of being inundated with stigma and embedded meanings that come to so thoroughly dominate the identity of those affected that they often lose part of their own identities in the process. The protagonist in this story has arrived at that point, metamorphosing at will as he continues his desperate attempt to find a woman who will accept his physical and emotional "secret" and finally liberate him from the "profunda claustrofobia" [profound claustrophobia] that entombs him in his existence (64).

The notion of the "secret" in reference to AIDS is one that is connected to the tendency to treat AIDS in an indirect and metaphorical manner, as has been illustrated by these authors' works. In fact, literary critic Paul Julian Smith has concluded that Spanish artists and intellectuals commonly recur to "fatal strategies" of inevitability and mortality when referring to AIDS. Furthermore, they rarely utilize literal language to speak of the disease (103–4). I posit that these same tendencies are true in Latin American writers' and artists' responses to the epidemic. In these three texts, for example, the authors recur to plague, militaristic, and apocalyptic metaphors to discuss AIDS. The authors' references that are more direct are still opaque; they choose instead to use referents such as "el mal" and "el secreto" rather than literally denoting the disease. Smith concludes that this notion of the secret is connected to the larger tendency to choose "fatal strategies" and indirect references rather than recur directly to positive and life-affirming messages, such as those seen in the U.S. or the UK. He refers to Baudrillard when asserting that there is a tendency among Spanish (and, I would add, Spanish American) writers to "seek what is more hidden than the hidden: the secret" (Baudrillard, quoted in Smith 104). This tendency to cover rather than uncover is also associated with the cultural taboos that surround AIDS, as Sontag has affirmed in her landmark essay. According to her, because of the strong negative connotations associated with the illness, many patients keep their diagnoses a secret, even from family, as a way to escape the categorization and stigmas that are attached with the diagnosis (124). Our protagonist exhibits a strong desire to expunge himself of the burden of carrying his secret, but he fails in his mission because it falls on deaf ears. The repetitive quagmire in which the protagonist lives shows his desire to liberate himself of the tremendous burden that he carries, but the destructive compulsions that dominate his actions annihilate his chances for redemption.

The remarkable quality about a secret is its obscure nature, its opacity; secrets are very personal, given a unique imprint by the people they inhabit. Therefore, references to a secret illness connected to sexuality and shame have the ability to create different connotations in the minds of different readers. While the secret is obviously a destructive weight that the protagonist carries, others may see it in different lights. In fact, Griffero himself recognized this mutable quality of the notion of secret, and therefore the multiple manners of interpreting his work, when he affirmed that "los secretos no se nombran, cada lector lo asume como propio" [secrets aren't named, each reader assumes it as (his/her) own].[8] Griffero's conscious manipulation of the notion of the secret highlights precisely the tendency to opt for obfuscated references rather than direct language to narrate AIDS. What it means for readers is a multifaceted text full of interpretive possibilities, both currently and in the future. The

---

8. Personal correspondence, December 2003.

current fears in contemporary culture regarding the transmission of HIV from unprotected sex provide one way of reading the secret as AIDS. Perhaps this interpretation will change when AIDS is no longer so intimately connected with death and therefore invokes less fear in society than it does today. Nonetheless, AIDS still affects millions of people worldwide and imparts a weighty burden on those who carry it. This protagonist, however, fails to find the liberation he so desires.

The desire to be liberated and to begin anew calls to mind one of the positive aspects of plague conditions: to rise up from the destruction that the epidemic has wrought and, with the strength of a survivor, forge a new life and new identity. Here, the protagonist, through his interactions with others and his internal struggles, is emblematic of the plague metaphor that Griffero subtly employs in this story. According to Sontag, the plague metaphor is one of the most insidious, appearing in many of the narratives depicting epidemics through the ages, from syphilis to cholera to AIDS. In the classic script, the plague is invariably from elsewhere, and this script forges a connection between foreignness and illness (133–36). In this story, the protagonist himself is from Santiago, Chile, and while Chile would not be categorized as one of the Third World countries where such "exotic" diseases are believed to have originated, it is still often perceived to be less advanced than Europe, where this narrative takes place. In essence, the protagonist *is* the plague, having come from a faraway land to permeate the sexual and social boundaries of the society he is in, infiltrating both boundaries as he transmits his deadly infection. Part of this plague metaphor, according to Sontag, envisions AIDS as an indicator of both individual and social vulnerabilities. Our protagonist, through his sadistic, vengeful actions, also serves to reveal those weaknesses, as he easily permeates the lives of the woman he has targeted, who succumbs to him physically and sexually, and in the end with her life.

According to Michael Denneny, AIDS as an epidemic has become a social event, and therefore "when death is a social event, both the individual and the community are threatened with irreparable loss" (37). This dual threat can be seen through the protagonist's failure to halt his pattern of destruction at only one woman. Despite his attempts to purify himself both corporeally and mentally through the transmission of both the virus and his "secret" to his victim, he finally realizes that both still inhabit his being and that his victim cannot expunge them. He is undeterred, however, and continues his quest, thereby continuing to try to avenge himself by hunting for more women with whom to share his "secret," intending to return again to the same location where he found his previous victim. His intention to repeat the same pattern of hunt, seduction, transmission, and destruction calls to mind the annihilative potentials of a plague: it does not stop at just one victim, but instead continues on its deadly path until it has worn itself out or finds a force greater than itself. The protagonist seems to be careening down that same path, surely headed toward the obliteration of not only more women, but also, in the end, himself.

"Luna negra de noviembre"

For a final examination of a pattern of vengeful sexual encounters that are carried out as retribution for the diminishing health of the protagonist, we can turn to Ana Solari's short story "Luna negra de noviembre," which appeared in the collection of feminine erotic Uruguayan literature, *Mujeres de mucha monta*. Solari offers a different version of the revenge narratives witnessed in Eloy Martínez's and Griffero's texts; instead of placing both the power and the moral onus in the hands (and, more precisely, the body) of a male protagonist who takes his wrath out on women who have wronged him either personally or by extension of their gender, Solari has turned the tables and chosen to portray a female in the role of dominator, avenger, and victimizer. This portrayal is significant, particularly in light of the conceptualization of women within the cultural narrative of the AIDS epidemic and AIDS transmission.

According to AIDS theorist Steven F. Krueger, there has been a consistent erasure of women from the public discourse on AIDS. Often, women are perceived as exceptions or are seen as *being* their illness, or, more precisely, vectors of the disease (57–59). This vision is particularly applied to prostitutes for whom sex is their career and who therefore embody the risk of HIV transmission. In fact, it is this fallacy that led Solari to write about sexually transmitted diseases in the first place. In both her own life and the society around her, she witnessed an overwhelming sense of denial about HIV and AIDS, leaving people unwilling to admit that their partners might be unfaithful, or preventing families from discussing the topic openly. Additional fodder for this story was an urban legend circulating about a woman who intentionally stalked airports and hotels looking for unsuspecting men with whom to have sex, with the hope of transmitting the HIV virus.[9]

Solari manipulates both of these angles in the story. By situating a female protagonist at the heart of this story, she questions the very rigid categories that have existed in society and have led to the perpetuation of

---

9. Personal interview, May 1997.

myths about the risk of contracting HIV. By painting a picture of a heterosexual woman who vacillates between seductive darkness and moral misgivings, Solari fleshes out a protagonist who embodies parts of many women. She does not belong to an at-risk category, but nevertheless she is just as at risk as any other sexually promiscuous person. This representation successfully challenges the myth that heterosexual women are not in danger of infection, while it simultaneously illustrates the heavy moral charge that burdens those who are carriers. The weight of that burden is something that becomes clear during the realization phase, when the HIV-positive person must take stock of the new reality facing her- or himself and eventually choose a course of action. In that process, the individual realizes the fatal potential of the virus and the subsequent limitation on sexual freedom that comes with abiding by the unwritten code of ethics governing "safe" sex. Trying to find a balance between those two polar opposites, sexual freedom and ethical sex, can prove to be too heavy a burden to bear and can lead to a rage that is directed toward the very individuals that HIV-positive people are "supposed to" protect: their future sexual partners. Such is the case with the female protagonist in Solari's narrative.

Combining the details of her protagonist's own process of corporeal and mental transformation, as well as the formation and enactment of her plan of revenge, Solari weaves a tale that illustrates the complexities facing an HIV-positive woman. Through a series of flashbacks and mental ruminations, the reader learns about the key moments in that process of metamorphosis: infection, realization, and action. Like the majority of people infected with sexually transmitted diseases, and specifically HIV, the protagonist was not aware she was infected until she received the diagnosis that would forever change her future. In essence, her moment of realization occurs via narrative, or the relaying of a verbal diagnosis that codifies a physical disease. Because of the multiple meanings attached to the virus, the communication of the diagnosis becomes a narrative event whose meaning is determined by personal and social connotations that ultimately affect the way the protagonist negotiates how to receive the information, or narrative, that is communicated to her. That moment of realization is shrouded by harsh social criticism, as the nurse-nun who attends to her shows little compassion for the woman's situation. Her memories of that day are encapsulated in short bursts that are characterized by the negativity surrounding her situation. This phase of realization is accentuated by the isolation and marginalization she experiences in the very place where she is supposed to receive treatment: the hospital.

The force of this initial contact with the social connotations of her condition causes her to abandon the one place that could offer her any hope of a relatively healthy future and instead turn her attention to a plan of revenge. She accentuates her departure with a feeble attempt at verbal retaliation against the condemnation of the nurse and the hospital: "¡puta asquerosa, por lo menos yo conocí el placer!" [disgusting whore, at least I knew pleasure!] (125). This retort suggests that what is plaguing her is a sexually transmitted disease, one born from pleasurable encounters that belied their inherent danger.

It is interesting to note that in these quotes, as well as throughout the entire story, Solari does not capitalize any words, even at the beginning of sentences, as grammatical rules would dictate. This syntactic shift suggests the burgeoning narrative project that the protagonist herself is undertaking. Suddenly recast as a newly envisioned version of herself because of the transformative meaning of her diagnosis, she embarks on her own journey, thus directing the flow of her own personal narrative, her life. The destination and ultimate manifestations of her new persona remain cloudy, however, as she reconciles with herself how to digest the current news of her medical condition, respond to the rage she feels over the past that led to her plight, and negotiate her uncertain future. Her dubious future is reflected in the unorthodox syntax of the story. The surrender of traditional rules illustrates a woman trying to write her own story and life, following her own rules. In much the same way, the dearth of details about her identity also reveals a woman trying to figure out how to construct her new self amid the altered reality she faces.

During this phase, she desperately feels the urge to flee her current life and try to forget about her illness. In short, she flees from the lonely realities of her new bodily identity and chooses instead to exert her sexuality and seductive potential to find companionship and to react against the hatred that swells up inside her toward the man she is sure infected her. She ruminates on the man whose selfish, and perhaps sadistic, actions led her to her current status, concluding that

> si un día volvía a cruzarse con aquel maldito . . . no sabía que haría. pero lo más probable es que ya estuviese bajo tierra. la mujer no quería reconocer que estaba haciendo ahora lo mismo que él había hecho cuando lo conoció. quién sabe dónde había comenzado la cadena de odios y venganzas. ella había formado parte de eso sin saberlo y ahora no había manera de cambiar el destino. había jurado matarlo y vengarse. pero el desgraciado había desaparecido sin dejar rastros.

[If one day she crossed paths again with that damn guy . . . she didn't know what she'd do. but most likely he was already under ground. the woman didn't want to recognize that she was doing right now the same thing that he had done when she met him. who knows where the chain of hatred and revenge had begun. she had formed part of it without knowing it and now there wasn't any way to change her destiny. she had sworn to kill him and avenge herself. but the wretch had disappeared without leaving a sign.] (126)

Born of this hatred toward the man who infected her is a plan of action and retaliation. In Griffero's and Eloy Martínez's texts, the man was the one who plotted and ultimately enacted revenge. Here the man becomes the unwitting target of a vengeful female who has chosen to exert her agency and construct her own future. Recognizing the unlikelihood of having the opportunity to carry out her vengeance against the one who was responsible for transmitting the virus to her, she settles for a plan that will not only allow her to avoid the loneliness that haunts her, but seduce unsuspecting men to fall for her, thus enabling the perpetuation of the destructive "cadena de odios y venganzas" [chain of hatred and revenge] within which she unwittingly finds herself and from which she feels she cannot escape.

Once again, however, as was the case in Eloy Martínez's and Griffero's texts, HIV and AIDS are never mentioned in this text, with Solari instead opting for the "fatal strategies" of silent, metaphorical indirectness that Paul Julian Smith theorized in *Vision Machines* (103–4). Solari commented on this omission, noting that she did not want to specify any particular illness, instead allowing people to interpret the disease in multiple ways.[10] As a result of the many hints provided in the text, the protagonist becomes accentuated by her physicality, and her body tells the clues that lead the reader to conclude that AIDS has been inscribed on her body and that it will, through her deliberate acts of transmission, likely be replicated on the bodies of her victims. The first indication that she might be ill come in the form of her own silent musings about her deteriorating physical appearance and the fact that she feels there's little time left to live. These preoccupations about physical appearance cue the reader in to the terminal illness the protagonist faces, one that has started to deteriorate her outward persona. For example, the bartender in the hotel she frequents observes that she is becoming unraveled physically and looks sickly. While these references clearly indicate that the woman is suffer-

---

10. Personal interview, May 1997.

ing from some sort of deteriorating, terminal illness, it is the reference to "las manchas en la piel" [the marks on her skin] that most strongly connote the telltale Kaposi sarcoma that often accompany late stages of AIDS. The sexually transmitted nature of the unnamed disease that leads to those "manchas" is made clear by her sadistic desire that the man she sleeps with "tal vez . . . se acordara luego de ella, cuando empezaran a aparecerle las mismas manchas en todo el cuerpo" [perhaps . . . would remember her, when the same marks began to appear all over his body] (129).

In contrast with the avengers depicted in Eloy Martínez's and Griffero's works, this protagonist does not operate as a "dominating body" while executing her revenge. Instead, she becomes a "mirroring body" who is acutely aware of the outward appearance of her body and works to recreate her image as one that fits with the health prototypes perpetuated by popular culture. According to cultural critic Lee Edelman, the mirror often functions as the specific site of the articulation of AIDS, precisely because it reflects the transformation of the body. Some narrators focus on learning to accept the new body, while others shun the mirror, unable to face the morphed image projected there (32). The protagonist portrayed in this story is acutely aware of her appearance and the literal and figurative mirrors that project that image back onto her. She sees herself reflected like a prism not only in the multiple mirrors that decorate the hotel, but in the eyes of the men who look upon her with lust. To this effect, she accentuates her sexuality and downplays the physical deterioration she is experiencing as a result of her illness.

Despite the secluded location, she keeps her nails manicured, and when she tries to attract the attention of the man she hopes to eventually infect, she is supremely aware of his eyes on her and as a result measures her every move so that it has the desired seductive effect. She uses her body as a seductive weapon that disarms the man she hopes to conquer, all the while monitoring her actions and those of her prey in a mirror in the hotel bar. As she had surmised, he responds exactly as she had expected and allows her to finish the evening upstairs in his room.

Her self-awareness continues as she examines herself in the mirror in his room while she slowly disrobes, thus increasing his desire for her and making him a very willing participant in the sexual encounter that will likely lead to his infection with the virus she carries so discreetly. The mirrors reflect a body that appears firm and attractive. She continues to undress and proceeds to bathe herself while the man becomes more aroused by her nakedness. This action is misleading because she presents herself to him as a seemingly clean body, when in reality she is infected with a virulent disease that lies in wait for the moment of transmission. Nonetheless, the man sees the body he wants to see, not the one that really is, despite the obvious lesions on her skin, which she dismisses by explaining that she has very delicate skin.

When her mission is accomplished, she once again assesses her body, now satisfied not only sexually, but also because her plan has been completed. Despite the repetitive utilization of the mirror to acquaint herself with her mutable body, she does not seem able to accept the new changes that are occurring, but instead meticulously tweaks her image so as to appear healthy to those around her. The mirror becomes a tool in her seduction, one more prop in the plan she is inflicting on her unsuspecting victims. After this latest enactment, she no longer needs the man and moves on, he being merely an object on whom she executes her plan of retribution, one that has apparently been enacted on multiple occasions, as is evidenced by the hotel bartender's comment that she rarely slept in her own hotel room, instead spending the night in the company of the men traveling alone.

It becomes clear that she has arrived at her current location, a semi-deserted hotel, planning to stay "hasta el final" [until the end] because, she reasons, "no le quedaba mucho tiempo, no pasaría demasiado sin que se comenzara a notar las manchas en la piel y el temblor de las piernas; su aspecto se deterioraría y estaría obligada a ocultarse" [she didn't have much time left, it wouldn't be long before she started to notice the marks on her skin and the tremors in her legs; her appearance would deteriorate and she would be forced to hide herself] (126). However, despite her original intention to enact her seductive drama with the various clientele of her selected lodging, the stifling heat and the lack of water resulting from a drought have driven most customers away, leaving the place almost deserted. She realizes that she must modify her plan because she still has time to carry out her vengeance before the disease starts to manifest itself completely on her exterior appearance. By focusing on the plan itself, she is able to avoid thinking about the imminent future and the unwelcome changes it will bring to her body, mind, and lifestyle. This insistent denial of the future translates into an obsessive focus on the present encounters with anonymous men who provide an escape from her own haunting loneliness and bodies ripe for contagion and vengeance. She rails against the double affront received from the man who infected her and subsequently deserted her, mimicking his deceptive, heartless actions. In the end, she succeeds in perpetuating the cycle of anonymous transmission, but fails to drive away the pervasive thoughts that continue to bombard her consciousness despite her ardent attempts to repress them. In fact, memories of the moment she became cognizant of her diagnosis affront her every time she gets in someone else's bed.

This overwhelming sense of dread about a future that is viewed as bleak and certain to end in a premature death illustrates a pervasive metaphor about AIDS that operates throughout this text. The hopelessness attached to HIV-positive status suggests that there is no future and that the world as the protagonist knows it is coming to an end; in other words, it hints at an apocalyptic vision of HIV infection, one that has infiltrated a variety of representations of AIDS,[11] particularly early on in the epidemic. Sontag identifies this apocalyptic depiction of the disease as one of the predominant metaphors that function in literary renderings of AIDS (175–76). The first hint of this trait is the description of the hotel and its locale, conjuring up images of a hell on Earth that prevents life from flourishing. The climate is dry and hot, there is no longer any potable water, the constant wind assails the place, the swimming pool has become a putrid eyesore, and the lack of vegetation makes everything appear to be the same hellish tones of yellows and ochre. Nothing in the description offers any hope of refuge, yet the woman has chosen this place as the final scene in which to enact her retribution before her earthly stay expires.

In her eyes, she has no future, and her diagnosis is a death sentence that slowly ticks by as she waits for her fateful destiny. This vision of AIDS conflicts with the realities of the disease today, particularly given the success many patients have had with the antiretroviral drugs that have become common treatment. Nevertheless, this story was published in 1992, and its desolate view of the disease reflects some of the apocalyptic discourses that have circulated in many societies, often predominated by falsehoods and perpetuated by fear. These characteristics have invaded this text and the protagonist herself, providing a bleak outlook for the future. Her imminent death is viewed as a given, and the focus turns instead to how her last months on Earth are spent. She is able to carry out her plan of revenge, which offers her the slightest bit of solace from her lonely, terrifying existence as a person who knows she will die prematurely yet can do nothing to prevent it. The futility she experiences with her medical condition is translated into the only agency that she can manifest and that is enacted through her carefully plotted seduction and revenge.

Despite the overwhelming negativity and pessimism associated with the condition that appears to be HIV/AIDS, the disease itself is never mentioned explicitly in the text, but rather is alluded to through corporeal

---

11. Another work from the Uruguayan context with an apocalyptic message is Prieto's theatrical work, *Pecados mínimos*, discussed in detail in chapter 3 of this study.

clues and commonly used metaphors (such as the apocalyptic view of life and the future). In not mentioning the virus directly, Solari's work mirrors the predominant tendency found in Spanish American works about AIDS. In the Uruguayan context specifically, Solari believes that the dictatorship (1973–84) caused a pause in the development of the country, resulting in a delay in addressing current topics such as AIDS. She also notes that the conservative, religious values promoted by the dictatorship have carried over and thus culminated in a silencing of the nation in regard to taboo topics such as AIDS. The aversion to this theme is strong in the public discourse, and as a result "escribir sobre este tema es como poner sobre la mesa cuál es la realidad y a nadie le gusta esto" [writing about this topic is like putting reality on the table and no one likes this].[12]

Consequently, in order for many writers like Solari to address sensitive issues such as AIDS, they often resort to subtle textual clues and references to AIDS that will likely be ascertained by an astute reader, but that at the same time will not offend those who have yet to come to grips with the reality of the society in which they live. This technique is evident in Solari's work. On the surface, it can be seen as a traditional *femme fatale* story in which a seductive woman ultimately causes the demise of her conquests. This narrative trope has been seen time and time again in literature from diverse genres and regions, and on the surface, it is familiar to many. However, Solari has woven specific references to a fatal illness that is likely to be HIV into her story, for example, by mentioning the sexual nature of the fatal illness plaguing the protagonist as well as the chancres that appear on her skin, suggesting AIDS-related opportunistic infections. By not directly naming the disease, however, she relies on the reader to make the connection. Joseph Cady, a contributor to the collaborative work *Writing AIDS: Gay Literature, Language and Analysis*, defines this tendency as one of the two main tracks taken by writers dealing with AIDS; he calls it "counter-immersive" writing (as opposed to the other approach, immersive) because it recognizes the problem of denial and protects its readers from too jarring a confrontation by using textual devices that buffer the reader. This approach has the advantage of pulling in readers who would normally be put off by overt references to AIDS, but it runs the risk of further perpetuating and conspiring with the societal denial of the disease by refusing to challenge it (244–45).

In these specific works, there are some tentative attempts to expose and challenge some of the stereotypes routinely associated with people with AIDS, but the overriding theme of retribution and revenge, combined with

12. Personal interview, May 1997.

a pervasively negative, depressing, and fatalistic tone, ultimately undermines whatever good intentions these authors had of uprooting pervasive notions about AIDS. Solari, Griffero, and Eloy Martínez have indeed broken some of the silence that permeates AIDS discourse in Latin America, yet they still refuse to directly name the disease that inhabits their texts. Their narratives do provide an examination of the ever-changing landscape of sexual relationships in the age of AIDS, particularly depicting heterosexuals who were previously believed to be "immune" from contagion, but they indulge rather than challenge some of society's darkest fears about contagion. I believe that by choosing to address the topic, their texts initiate discourse, an action that is far favorable to the continued repression of this cultural taboo. In the end, however, what we see is a tendency to adhere to many of the same debilitating perceptions that have ruinous effects on the lives of those affected by AIDS and to resort to stigma-laden metaphorical language that refuses to challenge cultural stigmas. In essence, the fact that AIDS is being indirectly examined in these works is indeed a positive step in a literary landscape that is characterized by a significant void in this area, but in the end, the methods that are used to portray these HIV-positive individuals do little to actually undermine the persistent stigmas that continue to operate; instead, these portrayals often reinforce them.

The one arena that these authors do explore to a significant degree is a more intimate portrayal of those affected by the virus, particularly during the meaningful moments that I have identified: infection, realization, action. Through these texts, readers are privy to some of the conflicts facing these HIV-positive protagonists. More than mere "types," they have slowly emerged from the traditional mold that tried to encapsulate them at the inception of the epidemic (the 4 H's referenced by Sander L. Gilman: homosexuals, heroin addicts, hemophiliacs, and Haitians). As they confront their conditions, they are given the opportunity to exert some control over their own situations and decide what course of action to follow. While we can accept the agency that each of these protagonists exerts as a positive step toward reasserting control over one's own personhood, the way in which that agency manifests itself is disturbing.

Recognizing the potential to utilize their bodies as the weapons they have become because of their viral infection, all three choose to exert that potential (e.g., Camargo "borrows" the infected body of another because he is uncertain of his own health status), opting to eschew any moral responsibility for their conditions and instead directing their rage toward other, seemingly healthy bodies. What is revealed is the façade of power and control whereby the protagonists steer the course of their lives in the only way they see possible, but in the end, they reveal their powerlessness over the disease that they carry. Despite Camargo's attempts to exert his masculine authority over Reina, each obsessive step forward in his plan ultimately contributes to his own destruction, which in the end is wrought by Eloy Martínez himself as he textually punishes Camargo by inflicting him with Guillain-Barré syndrome. As a result, the Camargo who once envisioned himself as the omnipotent editor-lover-godlike figure not only has ceded his association with the newspaper, but also is reduced to an asexual individual, lacking the libido that once characterized him. All of the power he once believed to possess evaporated when he destroyed the woman whom he used to create that fiction of power.

Griffero's and Solari's protagonists further show the elusiveness of agency, particularly over a disease that continues to progress despite their best intentions to shun its advancement. In both cases, their agency required the destruction of other individuals, all in a quest to assuage the rage and guilt inhabiting Griffero's protagonist and alleviate the loneliness that haunts Solari's. By trying to function as dominating and mirroring bodies, respectively, each individual attempts to assert control over their selves and others through the use of the very bodies that are slowly being hijacked by a virus that progresses despite their protests. The "dominating body" perpetuates the illusion of agency because it operates on the fiction that physical supremacy equals true authority. In the same vein, the "mirroring body" allows the protagonists to delude themselves (and others) into believing that they have control over HIV by covering up and thereby thwarting some of the physical manifestations of the disease. While these projections of self allow all three protagonists to inflict their wrath and destruction on others, they do little to allow them to assert true authority over their own lives or undertake thorough self-reflection, showing that in the end they are powerless to control the fatal virus that has infiltrated their lives.

CHAPTER TWO

Eroticism and AIDS
The Confluence of Desire, Death, and Writing

> Fui exuberante en la felicidad de amar
> y heme aquí, ahora,
> afectado por el castigo de la exuberancia.
>
> [I was exuberant in the happiness of loving
> and here I am, now,
> affected by the punishment of that exuberance.]
> —Husayn Mansur Halladj, cited by Valentín Cózar in POESídA 66
>
> ... It's best not to make
> too much of it.
> Death is only what it is,
> no more and indeed,
> never any less.
> —Ana Castillo, excerpt from "Death Is Only What it Is," POESídA 55

Eroticism and Death

"AIDS is not so much a punishment for promiscuity—the wages of sin—as a brutal material proof of something known but never quite comprehended, namely that death inhabits sexuality: perversely, lethally, ecstatically" (Dollimore xi). Cultural critic Jonathan Dollimore's blatantly honest assertion in *Death, Desire and Loss in Western Culture* serves as a brutal reminder of the drastically altered sexual landscape in the age of the AIDS epidemic. Perhaps more telling than the link between sexuality and death that Dollimore reminds us of is the element of ecstasy that infiltrates and inhabits the complicated realm of potentially lethal sexuality. The link between sexuality and desire is not hard to comprehend, but the forces that bind desire and death challenge some of society's preconceived notions. Most would agree with the assertion that "desire is on the side of life, life is opposed to death, and therefore, desire must also be opposed to death" (xii). However, in his detailed study of philosophical and literary renderings of this pervasive link in Western society, Dollimore deconstructs this apparently logical conclusion, showing instead how death and desire have been intertwined since medieval and Jacobean times. He explains that the underlying connection between the two forces is mutability, which forms the inner dynamic of desire: "mutability animates desire even as it thwarts it. Put somewhat differently, the very nature of desire is what prevents its fulfillment, what makes it impossible" (xvii). That lack and the impossibility of fully satiating desire are linked to death because it "is at once the destiny of the self and what destroys it" (xvii).

Returning now to the realm of AIDS, we can see how it forms a clear example of the inextricable link between sexuality, desire, and the possibility of death. As a disease that can be transmitted sexually and has the potential to be fatal, HIV poses a risk to those who follow their sexual desires without exercising precautions. Once infected, the individual faces a quandary: continuing to operate according to the laws of desire poses a direct threat to unprotected sexual partners, yet ignoring personal desires drastically alters the enjoyment of life, thereby eclipsing life as it was known and catapulting the individual toward a metaphorical death, if not the physical death that advanced stages of AIDS ultimately bring. How, then, can this apparent contradiction be reconciled? Or is it possible to maneuver through the landscape of desire, sexuality, and death despite having an AIDS diagnosis? Put slightly differently, how do those with AIDS confront death while still assenting to their individual sexual desires? What role does the sexualized body play in a protagonist's end-stages of life when faced with an imminent death from AIDS?

These questions, among others, will form the central framework for this chapter and will be used to examine how Puerto Rican poet Manuel Ramos Otero (*Invitación al polvo*) and Uruguayan writer Andrea Blanqué ("Adiós Ten-Ying") navigate this complex triumvirate of human life. *Invitación al polvo* is a collection of poetry that was published posthumously, following Ramos Otero's death from AIDS in 1990. It follows Ramos Otero's other poetic compilation, *El libro de la muerte* (1985)[1] and, taken together, forms the primary corpus of Ramos Otero's poetic works. Ramos Otero's work as a whole is known for its unapologetic examination of

1. This work will not be discussed in this chapter, except through brief commentary.

homosexual life and culture, often recurring to abjection and transvestism to disavow the patriarchal taboos against homosexuality in Puerto Rican society (Cruz-Malavé 156–59).

We can situate Ramos Otero's work against the backdrop of Latin American poetry about AIDS. Jill Kuhnheim, in a study on the relationship between poetry and AIDS, contends that poetry's long relationship with death, combined with its status as a marginalized genre, makes it a particularly apt literary form to confront and discuss AIDS (2). Kuhnheim examines poems by Cristina Peri-Rossi, Néstor Perlongher, and Severo Sarduy, illustrating how "utilizan la indirección de la poesía y su formalidad para ordenar el desorden de la desintegración resultante de la enfermedad y para insertarse en una trayectoria literaria—de la lírica, pero particularmente de la lírica frente a la muerte" [they utilize poetry's indirection and its form to bring order to the disorder of the disintegration that results from the illness and to insert themselves into a literary trajectory—of poetry, but particularly of poetry in the face of death] (5). In addition to these formal tendencies, one also notes that not only in these three poets' work, but in the most explicit poetic anthology published to date about AIDS, POESídA, there is a pronounced emphasis on the connection between homosexuality and AIDS. The majority of well-known poets who have chosen to depict AIDS in their work are also openly homosexual (Arenas, Sarduy, Peri-Rossi, Perlongher, Ramos Otero), and even in the aforementioned collection which brings together works from Latin American and Latino writers, homoeroticism is a common element of the majority of the poems.

Ramos Otero's poetry follows the tendencies seen throughout Latin America. His poetic corpus is considered an important reflection of two very important phases in the homosexual experience in the last two decades: namely, repression and AIDS (Hernández, "Homosexualidad" 226). Additionally, his work utilizes some of the formal elements of traditional amorous poetry, but it subverts them to accommodate both an unapologetic exaltation of homosexual love and an unabashed exploration of the difficulties of AIDS. While *El libro de la muerte* has a few subtle metaphorical references to the emergence of AIDS in the everyday reality of homosexual existence, the opacity is erased in *Invitación al polvo*, where AIDS is referred to directly, particularly in the second section of the collection, where Ramos Otero's poetic voice faces "La víspera del polvo."

The poems, composed over a five-year period, were specifically motivated by Ramos Otero's personal struggle with the virus (Hernández, "Política" 87). The collection is divided into three parts: "De polvo enamorado," which comprises twenty-nine poems; "La víspera del polvo" (thirteen poems); and "La nada de nuestros nunca cuerpos" (one poem). Taken as a whole, the collection narrates the amorous relationship between the poetic persona and José, a Cuban painter, and the subsequent abandonment suffered when the relationship ends. Other escapades occupy his attention, as does the reality of AIDS surrounding those relationships, which incrementally inhabits more of the poetic space in the second and third sections of the collection, when the poetic persona has confirmed his own diagnosis.

Ramos Otero deftly balances the dynamic forces of love/sexuality with the impending death facing his poetic voice, also a poet in its own right. The poetry articulates the quest for love to escape the solitary reality that the fictionalized poet begins to see as his condition in life. Despite the heart-rending struggles and abandonment experienced in his romantic relationship with José, the poetic voice repeatedly celebrates love and sexuality as a perpetual fountain of possibility and inspiration. As death inhabits the portrait of his life more insistently, his solitary condition is accentuated. Still, he refuses to reject the life he has led, choosing instead to commemorate his life and sexuality through his writing and ultimately seeing the writing process itself, rather than eroticism and relationships, as the true way to transcend his perpetual solitude and, in the end, accept his demise with both a jubilant reflection and an obstinate refusal simply to quietly disappear. Ramos Otero illustrates how sexuality and eroticism, combined with the powerfully indelible force of writing, allow his poetic persona (and perhaps himself?) to accept death on his own terms, without erasing or negating the pleasurable experiences that led him to his final moments in life.

This decision to celebrate life and sexuality rather than dwell on the protagonist's impending death is also apparent in Andrea Blanqué's short story "Adiós Ten-Ying." Blanqué's story depicts a thirty-year-old woman who is dying of AIDS in Hong Kong and who spends her remaining days relating her life story to one of the physicians caring for her. The narrative flashes back to her upbringing in Ciudad Vieja[2] in Montevideo, Uruguay, where her sequestered childhood fueled an ardent desire to explore the world outside her sheltered existence. At age fifteen, Ten-Ying flees from home and goes to the port to offer herself as a prostitute to the multitude of sailors stationed there. The subsequent years are spent fulfilling both her own wanderlust and the sexual desires of the sailors around her, ultimately leading to her contraction of HIV from her multiple unprotected sexual encounters.

---

2. Ciudad Vieja is situated near the port of Montevideo and historically was dilapidated and frequented by sailors and prostitutes. It has since undergone significant transformations.

The depiction of a young, naïve girl enclosed in a patriarchal household with little or no contact with the outside world calls to mind popular fairy tales such as "Rapunzel." Ten-Ying, like her fairy-tale counterpart, dreams of an escape from her cloistered existence and a Prince Charming (in the form of virile sailors) to unlock her horizons, both geographically and sexually. Blanqué's use of this familiar plot has certainly been subverted by the subsequent prostitution and infection with HIV that befalls the princess figure. I will examine why and how that subversion occurs, using cultural critic Christina Bacchilega's *Postmodern Fairy Tales* to illuminate the ways that Blanqué's story manipulates the familiar tropes found in fairy tales. By manipulating these tropes, she produces a story that is comfortingly familiar on the surface, but, through its shocking deviations from the expected plot, forces readers to face and ultimately reevaluate their preconceived notions about prostitution, overt sexuality, and AIDS. This narrative strategy is particularly useful given the uncommonly open treatment of AIDS found in this story because it breaks the silence surrounding AIDS without altogether alienating the reader.

Bacchilega's text melds the traditionalist, time-honored narrative project of the fairy tale—which has existed cross-culturally for centuries—with postmodernist theory to illustrate the ways in which contemporary revisions of fairy tales and their specific manipulations of voice, narrative framework, focalization, and agency "make visible ... gendered patterns of complicity and resistance, differing socio-economic and historical dynamics of gender representations, the making or unmaking of a heterosexual project, and the varying impulse to enact fleshed knowledge in narrative" (140). The product of that strategy is an enlightening work that sheds a unique perspective on contemporary literature and the continual reappearance of familiar tales and tropes that have been twisted and distorted to achieve the various narrative projects. Bacchilega illustrates the power that these seemingly simple tales hold. She focuses on postmodernist rewritings that consciously manipulate the traditional elements of a fairy tale to subvert their original messages and instead produce innovative versions that tend to question the patriarchal societies that led to their production and promulgation in the first place.

In Blanqué's situation, the postmodern rewriting of the Grimm Brothers' classic tale "Rapunzel" has dual functions: on the one hand, it provides the moribund protagonist with a pleasant, escapist narrative that allows her to remember her life as a prostitute, not through the taboo-ridden narrative that society would prefer, but through a romanticized version of her life, thus enabling her to construct her own vision of self as she prepares for death. It is important to note that Blanqué employs an indirect narrative style by which she relays Ten-Ying's story through an omniscient narrator, a technique that I will examine in regard to the narrative project that Blanqué undertakes. Additionally, the use of familiar elements of this international fairy tale softens the presentation of a topic that is still largely relegated to the margins of public discourse in Uruguay and Spanish America and is often silenced because it is still viewed as taboo.

Like Ramos Otero, Blanqué has chosen to situate her protagonist at the untimely end of a life shortened by the progression of AIDS, which was contracted through pleasurable sexual encounters chosen by the protagonist's acting on her own volition. Despite the impending death facing both Ten-Ying and the poetic voice in Ramos Otero, the retrospective examinations of the years leading up to the end are imbued with an insistence on celebrating the life that was lived, rather than dreading the death that awaits on the horizon. Central to that celebration is the recognition of the importance of sexuality and eroticism to the protagonists, both of whom have yielded to their corporeal desires to achieve happiness, albeit short-lived at times. As such, their bodies become co-protagonists in their narratives, accentuating the centrality that eroticism has played in their lives. While there are some mentions of the ravages of AIDS on those bodies, the vast majority of these two texts focus instead on the exploration, expression, and communion of the bodies in sensuality rather than in disease. I will examine how that sexuality is emplotted as well as its relation to the current plight of the protagonists and their stoic acceptance of their impending deaths.

While these two works differ in many ways, in the end they converge in their exalted treatment of human sexuality as a celebration of life, even in the face of death. Georges Bataille has critically examined this connection between life and death, and his classic work *Eroticism* provides a theoretical framework from which to examine the insistence of "assenting to life even in death" (11). Bataille's work expounds upon his theory of the three main types of eroticism (physical, emotional, and religious), including how each is concerned with the isolated, discontinuous individual's quest to find a sense of continuity, which according to Bataille is provided through death itself (15). He purports that taboo is the limiting factor of eroticism and that much of the joy and pleasure experienced through erotic activity derives from the transgression of accepted taboos (256).

Bataille's work provides several stimulating tenets that I will examine critically in relation to Ramos Otero's and Blanqué's works. It must be said that while many aspects of his postulations are thought-provoking, others are difficult to accept, particularly in light of the sensibilities of this modern era. In particular, his glorification of sexual violence, and of violence in general, flies in the face of our contemporary legal and ethical norms that proscribe it. Nonetheless, it is precisely because of Bataille's renegade views and willingness to run counter to society's accepted norms that contemporary critics have such a useful tool with which to analyze so-called taboo-laden depictions of human sexuality and eroticism. Because of AIDS' intimate relation to taboo, sexuality, and death in many societies, Bataille's thinking has a renewed pertinence and, as such, will be utilized to inform this investigation.

Invitación al polvo

Of particular interest in relation to Ramos Otero's *Invitación al polvo* are two key facets of Bataille's theories: the notion of the taboo and the pleasure derived from transgressing that which is prohibited or condemned by society; and the expectation that sexuality and eroticism can remedy the profound discontinuity that defines the human experience in Bataille's mind. Both of these elements are explored and manipulated by Ramos Otero as he depicts the interaction of desire, love, solitude, AIDS, and death in the life of the poet who protagonizes his collection.

The title of the collection offers a glimpse into the primary factors at play; although the word "polvo" literally means "dust," according to José Luis Vega, *polvo* can be read in two lights—in popular speech, it is a vulgar term for the sexual act itself, while in Christian discourse, it refers to the disintegrated body that remains after death, thus connoting death itself (35). In this way, Ramos Otero alternates between the erotic and the elegiac. It also can be read as a reference to Quevedo's verse, which serves as an epigraph to the first section of Ramos Otero's work: "Su cuerpo dejarán, no su cuidado; / Serán ceniza, mas tendrán sentido; / Polvo serán, mas polvo enamorado" (8). By beginning with a reference to one of Quevedo's classic love poems, Ramos Otero is inserting himself in this tradition of celebrating love as a way to achieve transcendence. He situates his work against the backdrop of traditional *heterosexual* love poems, and by doing so establishes an intertextual dialogue of sorts with Quevedo, employing some of the same techniques that "metaforizan la ausencia del ser amado" [create a metaphor for the absence of a beloved] (Hernández 236), but subverting them by portraying them in homosexual relations. In fact, his second epigraph essentially announces his intention of combining these two elements. It is a quote from Luis Cernuda, taken from *La realidad y el deseo*, which displays clear references to unabashed homosexuality. Hernández views Cernuda as a clear influence in the work of Ramos

Otero: "Cernuda asumió valientemente su condición, tanto en su vida privada como en la pública y, para nuestros efectos, lo más importante, también lo convirtió en uno de los temas claves en su escritura poética" [Cernuda bravely assumed his condition, both in his private and public lives and, for our purposes, the most important part, (is that) he also made it into one of the key themes in his poetic writing] (234). Ramos Otero reflects the influence of both poets in his work, but he presents his own unique view on the relation between eroticism and death.

Throughout the three parts of the book, there is a constant confluence of love, sexuality, and death, mediated by the recognition of the solitude that the poet inhabits. At different moments of enunciation, the focus shifts between erotic reminiscing about a key relationship in the poet's life and the solitary musings of a man facing a premature death because of AIDS. The alternate foci provide different avenues through which the poetic persona searches for transcendence and for an escape from solitude. At times, love provides that illusion of interconnectedness, but in the end, the only ally that remains is his vocation, writing. The book as a whole shows the continuum of emotional experiences offered from the valuable perspective of one who is contemplating his existence before death (both literally, as was the case for Ramos Otero while writing these poems, and figuratively, as depicted by his poetic voice). Along the way, the erotic body is first celebrated and then slowly deconstructed, leaving behind a solitary *hombre de papel* [man on paper] who will surely disintegrate into *polvo*. The metaphor of the hombre de papel is utilized by Ramos Otero himself and aptly summarizes the ultimate destiny of the poetic voice and the importance of literature and writing above all else.

For the purposes of this discussion, we can note three key moments in the metaphorical journey embarked upon by the poetic persona: erotic celebration of his former relationships; the burgeoning realization of HIV-positive status and impending death; and, finally, the emergence of writing as a true marker of identity and the ultimate way in which he celebrates the past and prepares himself for the future. In short, while eroticism itself initially provides the illusion of a means to achieve continuity in the face of death, in the end, writing *about* sexuality and death enables the poetic persona to construct his own identity and evade the solitude that continually haunts him. In this sense, he returns to the traditional concept of using writing as a way to confront, and perhaps overcome, death, illustrating yet another way in which Quevedo's work and the reference to "polvo enamorado" preceding Ramos Otero's first section of poetry have influenced his own outlook on the confluence of sexuality, writing, and death.

The first part of the collection, "De polvo enamorado," memorializes the poetic persona's experiences with love and eroticism. He reflects back on his romantic relationship with José, presenting a flashback to their erotic relationship. There is a primacy of the healthy, vibrant, eroticized body whose desires transgress societal taboos in these poems. There is also a very conscious celebration of homosexual identity, to the point that they condemn José for being a "bugarrón," or a homosexual living in the closet under the guise of a heterosexual relationship. This section is also invaded by imagery depicting the pain and sadness that accompany abandonment and lost love, often metaphorically referred to as a type of death. This "death of love" also serves to foreshadow the very real death that awaits him from AIDS. However, despite the hardships that the poetic persona encounters in the romantic realm, he still expresses a view of love and sexuality that suggests the possibility of achieving a "continuity of existence," which Colin McCabe, in his introduction to Bataille's *Eroticism*, explains "in the world of sex and death . . . the individual and discontinuous beings that we are taste the terrifying pleasure of the continuity of existence" (xi).

The first poem of section 1 sets the tone for this key moment in the poetic persona's journey of recollections. In it, he refers to himself and José metaphorically through their countries of origin: "Cuba y Puerto Rico son / las dos efímeras alas del ángel del amor" [Cuba and Puerto Rico are / the two ephemeral wings of the angel of love . . .] and later in that same poem, "Cuba ama a Puerto Rico por todo" [Cuba loves Puerto Rico for every reason" (9). The confluence of identities and countries here suggests a transcendent power of their love, something capable of enduring far beyond the lives of the two men hailing from those respective homelands. Like the islands that share some geographical and cultural traditions, the lovers find common ground in their love for one another and their common Caribbean heritage. This first poem clearly indicates the protagonist's hope for love and his belief in its ability to remedy the discontinuous state of being. According to Puerto Rican writer and literary critic Daniel Torres, Ramos Otero appears to be drawing on *bolero* verses by Lola Rodríguez de Tió,[3] much in the same way that Ramos Otero's poem portrays a union between the two lovers. By projecting the ideal of Caribbean unity, Ramos Otero extends that to the individual level, providing the possibility of transcending loneliness and discontinuity through the connection with others. Love and sexuality, through the communion of

---

3. For a detailed discussion of the intertextuality between Ramos Otero's collection and popular boleros that are referenced in his poems, see Torres's discussion of what he calls "la crónica de cuatro amores en tiempo de bolero" (33).

two amorous bodies, metonymically portrayed as their countries of origin, provide the allure of infinite pleasure, extending beyond this life—beyond death itself. This belief in love and its corporeal expression continues in a number of other poems as well.

The image of the erotic body predominates in many of those poems, and its pleasure is linked to the openly homosexual identity of the poetic persona, despite the acknowledged societal prohibitions against it. There is a wealth of explicit sexual imagery, often focusing on the male sexual organ and its function. The second poem of the collection is openly erotic, offering an apparent intermingling of sexual pleasure with what is seen as the inevitable suffering that accompanies it. Here the poetic voice reiterates his quest for love, fearing suffering and disillusionment in its absence. That fear, however, is not enough to dissuade him from his search for love and companionship. It serves instead to solidify his gratitude for the relationship he does have with José, despite the constant possibility of lost love. The poem's imagery serves as an ecstatic celebration of that relationship, one that is expressed through details of their erotic escapades. The body of the lover is explored and their sexual encounters are chronicled as the two men strive for a connection that will allow them to avoid the unpleasant feelings that accompany solitude.

This theme is revisited in yet another poem (#10), where Ramos Otero recurs to a traditional *petrarquista* portrait of the lover, but the traditional formula is subverted because the object of affection and admiration is a man, admired by a man:

> Tus manos José tus dedos José
> tus brazos José tus hombros
> tus labios José tus besos José
> tus ojos José tu pelo
> todo en mis manos José
> todo tu cuerpo en mis manos . . .
>
> [Your hands José your fingers José
> your arms José your shoulders
> your lips José your kisses José
> your eyes José your hair
> all in my hands José
> your whole body in my hands . . .] (19)

The imagery paints a homoerotic representation of love, refusing to apologize for or hide that which comes naturally to the poetic voice. He is well aware of society's views of homosexuality ("habrá quien diga, corazón, que nuestro amor / traiciona la familia" [there will be those who say, my love, that our love / betrays the family], but concludes (in poem #25) that "¡No hay nada, corazón, mejor que estar contigo!" [There is nothing, my love, better than being with you!] (35). Love is life for the poetic persona, and being in love and connecting physically supersedes even the prejudice and persecution he faces from the society that disallows his sexuality.

The open acknowledgment of the societal taboos regarding homosexuality and the willing and pleasurable decision to transgress those taboos provide an additional level of desire and pleasure for the poetic persona. According to Bataille, human sexuality is defined by secrecy and taboos, and the domain of eroticism resides precisely in the transgression of those taboos. This overt eschewing of societal convention is, in Bataille's thinking, the heart of desire that fuels eroticism (252–56). In the poems in this collection, there is a very conscious recognition of the moral prohibitions against homosexuality in Puerto Rican society, but the poetic persona instead explicitly details and celebrates the very actions considered taboo. The poems have been considered "una imagen física y gráfica del sexo homosexual rayando casi en la pornografía fina de una erótica más sugestiva que vulgar" [a physical and graphic image of homosexual sex almost verging on refined pornography of an erotica that is more suggestive than vulgar] (Torres 36). The poetic voice is ecstatic over his sexual and amorous relationship with José, and his graphic depictions of that love represent the early phase in his journey toward accepting the life he has led (despite the society that condemns him) and the death that awaits him. He happily transgresses the boundaries proposed by the hegemony, sharing details that assert rather than apologize for his homosexual identity.

The centrality of the homosexual experience to Ramos Otero's work has been well documented by critics.[4] Hernández has focused specifically on Ramos Otero's poetic corpus to further illuminate the important contribution these works have in expressing the experiences of homosexuals not only in Puerto Rico, but also in New York (where Ramos Otero lived for a great deal of his adult life) and elsewhere. In fact, Hernández argues that these two collections mark two very important phases in the "la experiencia homosexual de las últimas dos décadas" [the homosexual experience of the last two decades] ("Homosexualidad" 225),[5] suggesting a universality of his work that extends beyond the geographical boundaries that Ramos Otero inhabited. Those two phases are defined by Hernández as the period of sexual liberation and assertion of gay rights following Stone-

---

4. See Figueroa; Hernández (also see note 6); Cruz-Malavé; and Torres, among others.
5. Unless otherwise noted, all future references to Hernández will come from this work.

wall in the 1970s and early 80s, and the AIDS epidemic of the 80s until today. Both events were formative factors in the homosexual experience and have found their way into both collections of poetry composed by the openly gay Ramos Otero, where "su obra rebela contra la represión de su orientación sexual" [his work rebels against the repression of his sexual orientation] ("Homosexualidad" 226).

That rebellious nature is clearly evident in the unapologetic way in which homosexual love is celebrated in these poems, particularly in the first section of the collection. Although there is a clear recognition of the prejudices existing in society against homosexuality, the poetic persona refuses to alter his actions to appease society. In fact, despite the love he feels for José, he is increasingly perturbed that José refuses to live his homosexuality openly, opting instead for a closeted existence hidden behind the façade of heterosexuality. Ramos Otero's contempt for this dishonest existence causes him to use the word "bugarrón" to further criticize his lover, hoping that the shame connected with the regional word describing José's dual existence will motivate José to accept his true homosexual identity. According to Torres, a bugarrón is the active partner in a homosexual relationship who doesn't consider himself homosexual (40). The desire on the part of the poetic persona to "out" his lover again reinforces his insistence on being honest about sexuality, despite the societal pressures that exist. This brave refusal to bow down to societal taboos is also evident in the direct treatment that HIV and AIDS receive in the latter portion of the collection.

In fact, when "Nobleza de sangre" was published in the newspaper *El Mundo* a few days after Ramos Otero's death, per his own request before death, it was the first time that a poem published in Puerto Rico spoke openly about the ills associated with AIDS (Hernández 225). In this sense, Ramos Otero is a pioneer in his native Puerto Rico for breaking the taboo-laden silence that previously existed regarding AIDS. Even so, as we have seen, the disease does not inhabit the entire poetic space. Instead, a large portion of the collection focuses on the sexuality and eroticism that eventually led to the disease. This primacy of the physical that we have seen thus far slowly gives way to a transcendental quality attributed to love that enables the poetic persona to face death having exalted in his life's pleasures, namely, sexuality and eroticism.

Eroticism provides a way for him to avoid the discontinuity of being that a solitary death brings. Bataille explains that "we are discontinuous beings, individuals who perish in isolation in the midst of an incomprehensible adventure, but we yearn for our lost continuity" (15). Through physical, emotional, and/or religious eroticism, Bataille asserts, the individual occupies himself with substituting a feeling of profound continuity for the isolation he experiences in individuality (15). This sense of continuity is provided by communing with others in erotic experiences. Therefore, the poetic persona's relationship with José offers a way to escape his personal isolation and experience a continuity of existence that approximates death itself. In fact, Colin MacCabe explains that for Bataille, "the aim of sexual pleasure is . . . the losing of control" (MacCabe in Bataille xiii). This occurs at "the moment of orgasm with the rending of the separate and unified self into a physicality that can no longer be located in one body" (xiii). In a sense, orgasm is a type of death whereby the individual ceases to exist and becomes one with the partner. Bataille views this metaphorical death as fleeting but argues that it provides a way in life to experience and understand the continuity that is achieved permanently through death (106).

The poetic persona is aware of the ability of his finite body and its terrestrial experiences to supersede his own existence and enter an infinite realm. In this phase of his journey toward literal death, love and sexuality provide him with the only possibility of achieving transcendence and escaping his perpetual loneliness. In poem #9, he readily acknowledges "La tierra te tragará completo todo" [The earth will swallow you up completely] (18) because his body is a finite entity that will eventually become the *polvo* alluded to in the collection's title. Nonetheless, the love and eroticism experienced by that body provide a glimpse of the infinite: "Pero hay amores / infinitos, hay reglas que ni el tiempo se atreve / a deshacer, y tu mundo es un eterno paraíso" [But there are infinite loves, there are rules that not even time dares to undo, and your world is an eternal paradise] (18). The individual bodily limits are corroded and instead replaced by a unified force that appears capable of achieving eternity. This nebulous state of continuity is further expressed in poem #11, in which the poetic voice once again expresses his desire for a transcendent love achieved through and with José.

Corporeal death is hardly a preoccupation in the midst of an all-encompassing love that provides the hope of an eternal continuity that supersedes death. It is important to note the lack of religious connotation of eternity. The infinite experience that the poetic voice seeks is achieved not through heaven or hell, but through earthly interactions of the body. This defiance toward religion repeats itself later in the collection when the poetic voice is faced with his imminent demise. Even then, God does not provide solace but becomes an interlocutor for his poetic musings about the disease with which he has been afflicted. Instead, he seeks solace in love, eroticism, and the writing process itself.

This early optimism belies the tragic reality that faces the poetic persona in his advanced stages of AIDS. Even in this collection, which as a whole serves as a retrospective glance at the poet's reflections and experiences as an HIV-positive person, eroticism and love initially override all fears of the premature death he faces, a death wrought by a sexually transmitted disease contracted through the very actions from which he derived such a wealth of joy and pleasure. Throughout this initial phase of exuberant sexuality and overt eroticism, the poetic persona seems to exist in a utopic space where the dangers associated with promiscuity do not enter into his consciousness. It is clear that the two men enjoyed many sexual encounters in which prophylactics were not used. On multiple occasions, the poetic persona exalts the *leche* (slang for "semen") that is shared between the two, clearly suggesting that despite the threat of sexually transmitted diseases, the two partners chose to forgo protection. In this first section of the collection, AIDS and HIV are not referred to explicitly, despite the fact that Ramos Otero eventually dies from the disease and his poetic persona will befall that same fate in later sections of the collection. Sex is enjoyed for the pleasure it begets, with little regard for the consequences after the fact.

Despite the initial irreverence toward venereal diseases when the relationship is flourishing, there is a growing preoccupation over the possible loss of a sexual partner and lover and the resultant solitude that will likely ensue. This concern does surface tangentially in some early poems, but it is often downplayed because of the overwhelming pleasure that the two experience. However, as the poetic persona begins to feel the gradual disintegration of their relationship, the imagery of loss becomes more tangible. When the poems are read exclusively within the realm of the individual poems of the first section, the notions of loss and solitude are recast metaphorically as a type of death, both of the relationship and of the erotic body of the poetic persona. However, when these poems are read in relation to the collection as a whole, a second reading is possible: the multiple macabre references provide a foreshadowing of the death that the poetic persona (and author) will be facing because of the virus that has been transmitted through the previously celebrated erotic encounters.

The first allusions to a fast-approaching end of life appear in poem #3, in which the protagonist celebrates his love with José despite the fact that "llega cuando la vida es tarde" [it arrives late in life] and "Tenemos poco tiempo" [We have little time] (12). These allusions to a "reloj sin horas que nos seduce" [an hour-less clock that seduces us] (12) depict the contradictions that face them: on the one hand, their love and infatuation with each other's bodies allows them the illusion of evading death, feeling as though time stands still while they are together. However, even the power of that love fails to truly halt the hands of time, reminding them that in reality, each day together brings them another day closer to the end of their lives. What is telling is that despite the temporary dissociation from reality and time which eroticism provides the lovers, the poetic persona is inherently aware of the progression of "el lento funeral de nuestra dicha" [the slow death of our happiness] (12) that continues to march forward despite their wishes to suspend or supersede time.

The preoccupation with the ephemeral quality of life and time illustrates the dual forces affecting the poetic persona: On the one hand he is a lover who wants to encapsulate the moment he is currently living and imbibe the pleasures associated with it without the destructive force of time eroding the connection he is experiencing with José. His sexualized body and erotic pleasures take precedence over all else. On the other hand, he cannot ignore his entire existence. He is a writer as well as a man, and, as such, not only do his poems serve to memorialize his life and love, but they are also a recognition of the end that is not revealed to the readers until later in the collection: a life truncated by AIDS. This aspect subtly surfaces in this and other poems, through references to an untimely death that lurks around the corner despite his apparent youth and vitality. Slowly, it is revealed that AIDS is the culprit, stealing precious time from the poetic persona and inhabiting his body with what essentially is a ticking time bomb, flashing private reminders of the seconds of his life that are rapidly disintegrating despite his attempts to evade time and death through carnal interludes which mask the terrors that lurk in the future. His resolve against the future seems solid when fortified by companionship, but when his relationship with José ends, the mourning over that lost love quickly shifts to greater preoccupation with his loneliness and impending demise.

The transition to this next phase is accentuated by a gradual dissolution of the eroticized body that predominated in the first phase. That body is replaced by the absence of a corporeal presence that comes to define the solitude facing the poetic persona. That absence is twofold: it represents the loss of José as a partner and lover, and it creates the feeling of loss resulting from that abandonment. The notion of death is one of the multiple metaphors utilized in this phase wherein the poetic persona flounders in an interstitial space until he ultimately emerges in his next permutation, as an HIV-positive man facing his literal death.

The catalyst for this transitional phase is the loss of love and the end of the poetic persona's relationship with José. The sense of mourning that he experiences is presented in multiple poems. Initially, he curses love itself, railing against his earlier illusion that love was everlasting, depicting instead the brooding alterations that have befallen his world now that love and José have disappeared. The image of a united "nosotros" [us] echoes mournfully in the repetition of "éramos" [we were] that appears in poem #23, in which the poetic voice tries to fill the void once inhabited by their intertwined bodies with words commemorating their love, words that he wanted to write "con lágrimas de sangre" [with tears of blood] but instead composes "con tinta sangre, del corazón" [with blood ink, from the heart] (33).

These early indications of abandonment suggest a voluntary departure on the part of José, leaving behind the poetic persona as an unwitting victim of romance squandered. Growing allusions to death, however, suggest the possibility that José's departure was due to his own death rather than abandonment. In fact, in poem #14, the poetic voice announces "Un poema ese muerto pide ahora / que de alguna manera justifique / la carne que fue amor de cada hora" [that dead one asks for a poem now / which in some way justifies / the flesh that was hourly love] (23). All indications are that the "muerto" is José himself, explaining his seemingly abrupt departure. This interpretation becomes more plausible when one considers the specter of AIDS that enters the arena through subtle allusions to the lasting remnants of the relationship they shared. In fact, Hernández affirms that these clues do indeed suggest that José died of AIDS and ultimately passed the virus on to the poetic persona (237).

The first of these suggestions appears in poem #12, where the poetic voice speaks directly about *polvo,* which connotes not only the erotic experiences the two men shared, but also death itself. These dual meanings intertwine, particularly as the poetic voice muses about the "fugaz amante del veneno en las venas" [fleeting lover of the poison in the veins] (21). The overt reference to "veneno" certainly calls to mind the destructive potentialities of the HIV virus, which remains behind after the erotic trysts have ended. Furthermore, Ramos Otero uses the image of the rose, which, according to Torres, "es la enfermedad misma como metáfora de la llaga (o la carne enferma que se hace verbo)" [it is the illness itself as a metaphor of the wound (or the ill flesh that becomes a verb)] (46). One can read this scorched rose as the once erotically beautiful body that has been tainted by the virulent invader which has hijacked the lovers' bodies and traveled freely from one to the next in the midst of their ecstatic communing. The lovers' bodies, like the rose, have been caustically altered by the invisible marauder that corrupted the beauty of their eroticism, forever tainting its memory. Now, as the poetic voice reflects back on his relationship, much of the utopic ecstasy has subsided, replaced by ominous signs that, in retrospect, prophesize the eventual disintegration of the relationship, such as the thoughts "de aquel beso final que fuera un rito / profecía infernal de tu partida" [of that final kiss that was a rite / hellish prophecy of your departure] (24).

No longer finding solace in the memories of the erotic union of the two amorous bodies, the poetic persona slips into varying degrees of solitude, exploring first the fleeting comfort he finds in three Puerto Rican lovers, all referred to as women, but given Ramos Otero's penchant for exploring the fetishism of transvestism through the frequent assumption of the drag queen as an authorial persona (Cruz-Malavé 156–57) and the protagonist's assertion of being an "irremediable maricón de cuna" [irreparable queer since birth] (26), the "women" are more than likely transvestites. The brief romantic interludes hardly replace José, as is evidenced by the continuing lack of overtly erotic imagery and the persistent absence of the sexualized body that was omnipresent when referencing José.

Consequently, the sense of isolation increases, eventually, at poem #19, becoming a personal hell. The poetic persona desperately seeks a way to escape the confinement of suffering and desolation, ultimately concluding that the "antídoto de luz es mi poesía" [the antidote of light is my poetry] (25). While writing holds an important position throughout the collection, it is after the devastating loss of José that the poetic persona focuses his energies on his passion for writing rather than for his erotic passions, ultimately exhibiting the way his writing has always been a salve on the wounds of his unsuccessful amorous exploits. The confluence of literary and erotic desires, underscored by the persistent solitude that has haunted the poetic persona throughout his existence, forms the backbone of the last poem of the first section of the collection (#29). The poem serves as a transition from an erotic body to an hombre de papel [literary body] whose desires and whims are memorialized on paper rather than through interactions with lovers.

Poem #29 has a parallel structure in which the poetic voice harkens back to his adolescent days in Puerto Rico, experiencing lost love even at the young age of fourteen. Even then he understood loneliness, and he makes a pact with himself, one that he will ultimately break time and again: "juras que no amarás jamás, / tu escritura será la salvación o el castigo" [you swear that you will never love again, / your writing will be your salvation or punishment] (39). This pact to eschew love and opt instead for the solitary existence of a writer was one that became more complex as the poetic persona experienced a life in exile in New York, a life commemorated in the later stanzas of this same poem. The geographical transition is abrupt, perhaps mimicking the sense of uprooting that a life in exile causes. Nevertheless, he continues to examine his identity crisis, still failing to remedy completely the dueling forces of erotic love and literary passion that seem to pull at him from opposing directions:

> Tienes miedo al amor
> o a la pasión que amenaza
> tu pasión por la escritura.
> La soledad del verso es bálsamo seguro
> de todas esas otras soledades . . .
>
> [You are afraid of love
> or of the passion that threatens
> your passion for writing
> the solitude of the verse is a safe balm
> for all of those other solitudes . . .] (40)

Despite the affirmation of the passion he feels toward poetry and the apparent hands of fate that made him a poet, regardless of his conscious desire—("Tú no escogiste la poesía. / La luna te volvió poeta." [You didn't choose poetry. / The moon made you a poet."] (40)—the poetic persona continually struggles with his current loveless state and the loneliness he embodies. He mourns the loss of past lovers, especially José, and the corporeal connections he experienced with each. He recognizes, however, that his time is running out, an ironic statement considering that he is only thirty-eight years old at that point. The contradiction here between a relatively young age and the sense of time accelerating, thus obliterating his opportunities to find another lover, suggest that he is already aware of the virus that is shortening his life and will lead to an untimely death. That virus, HIV, long inhabiting the darkest recesses of his fears, has slowly emerged to the forefront of his existence and will assume a central position in the second section of the collection, "La víspera del polvo," in which he abandons the erotic body that predominated the first section of the collection, using, instead, his poetry to face his untimely death and create a literary body, which he refers to as the hombre de papel.

It is important to note that the connotation of *polvo* shifts in this second section, in that it refers to the inevitable disintegration of the terrestrial body that will result from death. In the previous section, it was a reference to the colloquial jargon that uses the same vocabulary to refer to the sexual and erotic activity that dominated the poetic persona's thoughts and actions. The shift in connotation also represents the alteration in the conceptualization of his body between these two sections, leaving behind the physical, sexualized body in favor of the figurative body he can create through his pen. In essence, the literal phallus of the first section has been abandoned for the metaphorical tool that will be wielded in the remaining poems of the collection.

It is this literary rendering of himself that will ultimately allow him to confront his illness and death, continuing the process that was begun through his previous erotic celebration of the life he had led. However, instead of reflecting back on the past, he turns his pen toward the present, realizing that

> El presente es perfecto. Es todo lo que tienes.
> Has descubierto el puente que da sentido al tiempo
> que pensabas perdido. La prueba es el poema
> que has escrito.
>
> [The present is perfect. It is all you have.
> You have discovered the bridge that gives meaning to time
> you thought was lost. The proof is the poem
> you have written.] (41)

The bittersweet memories of the romantic relationship with José are left in the past, and the poetic persona instead uses the power of his poetry to confront the present head-on.

This poetic force is one that has occupied an important position throughout the collection, but until this point, it took a backseat to the power of eroticism. However, the poetic voice makes numerous references to the creative process and the fact that poetry has the power to outlast sexuality, love, and even life itself. One of the metaphors used to express this notion occurs early in the collection in poem #4, in which he celebrates his current love for José and the mystery of his body. Even in the midst of the rapture he was experiencing, he was aware of the uncertain future of the lovers, musing about that time "cuando te vayas sin plena ni bolero / cuando regrese al silencio de otra sinfonía/cuando te vuelvas un hombre de papel / un espíritu atrapado en el poema" [when you leave without plena nor bolero / when I return to the silence of another symphony / when you become a man on paper /a spirit trapped in the poem] (13). Here the physical body that was so celebrated in life will be converted into a literary rendering of that body in absence. The poem becomes the absent body, its words the spirit and embodiment of the person it captures for posterity. This allusion to the hombre de papel that was initially used in reference to José is an apt descriptor of the transformation that befalls the poetic persona in the "Víspera del polvo." He constructs his own visage through the poems, mediating the transformation from a healthy, eroticized body to the solitary, progressively incapacitated one that finally succumbs to AIDS. The body that once was whole becomes fragmented as it faces the cascading effects of the illness. Through it all, the mind and the voice predominate, converting the poetic persona into "la dulce mensajera de una plaga" [the sweet messenger of a plague] (47).[6]

In this sense, he becomes a voice and constructed body of not just his own suffering, but that of many individuals facing the deconstructive capacity of AIDS. Torres noted that the idea of the hombre de papel that is elaborated in the second part of the collection "accede a una universalización del cuerpo más allá del deseo y del placer" [accesses a universalization of the body that goes beyond desire and pleasure] (43). Although he was not referring specifically to the universalization of the experience of the AIDS-afflicted body, I would argue that Ramos Otero's poetic persona does indeed write and construct the experience in a way that supersedes the individual level and connects with other sufferers, all the while unabashedly exploring the links between sexuality, life, AIDS, and death.

Compared to the first section, this section has a marked change in approach and strategy. Instead of striving for and celebrating the continuity achieved through erotic communion with others, the poetic persona once again reverts to the discontinuous state that, according to Bataille, is remedied only through eroticism or death (MacCabe, Introduction x). While acknowledging that solitude, the poetic voice uses the thirteen poems of this section in order to achieve a variety of goals. First, he slowly deconstructs his life and self, as well as the utopic vision of love that he previously held while with José. This section harkens the return of the true self—the poet. Because of the centrality of the mind and voice to poetic expression, the body that was so visible in the first section slowly disappears, allowing the poetic persona to use his pen to confront the virus that is eroding his corporeal existence. HIV and AIDS occupy many of the poems of this section, both directly and indirectly. Although there are moments of reflection on the past and projection toward the future in this section, one notices a preoccupation with the present that takes precedence over all other temporal references. After reconciling his solitary condition and the necessity to face his death alone, he uses his writing to deal with the present reality he faces: AIDS and the variety of fears and alterations it brings. The last preoccupation of this section is a preparation

6. Note the shift to a transvestite identity (the feminine form "la mensajera" vs. the masculine form "el mensajero"), which Cruz-Malavé has identified as one of Ramos Otero's most frequently assumed authorial personas (157).

for death [polvo] and, with it, the poetic persona's lasting impressions he will leave behind: his words.

Before he can find comfort and transcendence in his words, he must deconstruct the erotic body and existence that held so much promise for him in the past. In contrast to the idealistic expectations toward love during his romance with José, here he bitterly renounces love as he realizes that his world has changed and that love no longer is the axis around which he revolves. Part of this distorted reality is reflected in the slow decay of his eroticized body, once a vital part of his self-portrait, but now becoming unrecognizable even to himself: "¿Soy yo el retrato de perfil?" [Am I the profile portrait?] (57). The harsh reality is finally before him, forcing him to face his lack of companionship and the onus that is on him to face his death alone, without the love or sexuality that provided him with utopic visions of life and death. This final renunciation comes when he concludes in the poem entitled "Entre paréntesis": "Dejemos a los otros con la vida / soñando la utopía de la muerte" (Tú y Yo, para nunca, entre paréntesis) [Let's leave the others to life / dreaming about the utopia of death. (You and I, for never, in parentheses)] (49).

With his amorous past behind him and his previous thoughts about love shattered by his current reality, the poetic persona must once again reconstruct himself and reconcile his own identity that for so long depended on the love of others. This quandary and the final transition he makes from lover back to poet are expressed in the poem "La caja china," where he concludes that "quise volver a ser un cruel poeta / dejar que se escurriera la cálida leche del vacío / para volver a ser el personaje que ya me sabía de memoria: / el solitario" [I wanted to go back to being a cruel poet / allow the flow of warm semen from the void / to become once again the character that I knew by heart: / the solitary one] (52–53).

Once this identity has been affirmed, poetry takes center stage, providing the poetic persona with the tools to face his present battle with AIDS and prepare for death. He enters a suspended state in which he must hold vigil for his own impending demise. He envisions himself as "esa mujer que solitaria espera / cualquier invitación al polvo que venga por correo" [that woman who waits alone / for any invitation to death that may come in the mail] (47). The past is left behind and the future is given consideration, but causes little perturbation: "Yo soy la sin memoria y el destino tampoco me apresura" [I am the one without memory and destiny also does not hurry me] (47). He recognizes the soothing capacity of his vocation, which gives him the ability to explore his rapidly changing reality through his self-reflective poetry. Although he readily acknowledges and does not mask the pain and angst that AIDS has wrought upon his life, poetry provides an outlet that makes the suffering more bearable. He concludes that other people cannot ease his pain, but that poetry moderates it. However, the poetic snapshot of the struggles with AIDS depicts a harsh reality revealed with brutal honesty that at times uncovers the bitterness he feels, particularly toward God and religion, criticized sharply in this section and seen as the culprit for inflicting the wrath of AIDS on society. Most of these poems are personal reflections on the intimate struggle he confronts as he prepares for death. However, in the poem "Nobleza de sangre," the poem in the collection that is the pinnacle of verbal retaliation against the virus, the poetic persona strives to provide a voice for all homosexuals who are suffering from AIDS. The poetic persona's individual journey as an HIV-positive individual begins as he anxiously awaits the results of his tests, an excruciating state of ambivalence that causes severe insomnia and is commemorated in the poem of the same name. Night, once the scene of the erotic adventures shared with passionate lovers, has been converted into an encapsulating tomb of solitary anxiety as he awaits "los resultados de mi muerte" [the results of my death] (46). When dawn breaks and the letter arrives, he hesitates before opening the envelope (which he refers to as "el ataúd" [the coffin]), allowing himself to explore the range of emotions confronting him and the consequences of the news contained in the letter that will largely determine his future. As he ponders the mystery and ambiguity of life and the circumstances that have carried him to this point, he allows himself to examine his fears and thoughts about the very real possibility of an early death, something that will be suggested by the powerful letter he possesses. The results function as a narrative in the life of the writer, effectively constructing a version of the future that is vastly different from the one that the poetic persona envisioned and tried, through poetry, to construct for himself. Gone are the eroticism and joy, replaced instead by the virtual promise of a painful, solitary death, particularly when one considers the terminal nature of AIDS in the time period in which this poem was written (1990).

The time between receiving the letter containing the results and the moment that he opens and reads the results functions as a suspended moment, an interstitial space in which the poetic persona straddles that space as he lets go of memories of the past and tries to brace for the future. The past self has been locked away in his memories and poetry of those moments, while his future self, the one soon-to-be-defined by the illness that is inhabiting his body, has yet to be born, allowing him to simply exist in that moment before his life will be altered forever. Instead of focusing on the upcoming self, he allows himself to fret over death and the afterlife, connecting his fears about the voids in death to the pleasures he experienced in life. While the poetic voice seems to have reconciled his current lack of love and isolation, the thought of eternal solitude without corporeal pleasures such as sex and cigarettes is unbearable.

Still, death becomes a constant in this new phase in his life, harkening to him from every corner, inhabiting his thoughts and his writing. In much the same way, the virus itself enters his consciousness, and he explores it in this section, first in reference to the persistent metaphors that characterized it as the "gay cancer," extrapolated and manipulated in the poem "Metáfora contagiosa." An inherent awareness exists of the metaphors surrounding AIDS, metaphors that are manipulated in this poem in which Ramos Otero even references Susan Sontag. Metaphors about death and AIDS inhabit Ramos Otero's work to some extent, although they are intermingled with direct references to the malady and its effects. The most pervasive of the metaphors for death is the titular referent *polvo* [dust], which is the substitute for the word "death" in poems such as "Puerta de polvo" and "Invitación al polvo." Death is envisioned as a disintegration of the body, a reduction of the formerly eroticized elements to nothing more than a heap of dust. As we have seen throughout the collection, the closer the poetic persona gets to his own death, the less visible his body is through his poetry. The lover has become the poet, and the body of the lover has become his poetry. Soon the only vestige of either will be *polvo*: the disintegrated body of the deceased and the dustlike etchings of pencil lead left behind on the page, the only visible remains. For the poetic persona, his poetry and words are his passage through death, allowing him to navigate the unknown territory of his final days, particularly as his body becomes less viable. Poetry is the "puerta de polvo," and he summons his words to permit him passage through the door which is death. Poetry not only provides a vehicle to maneuver between this transitional phase, but also soothes the pain of living with AIDS.

The anguish that AIDS produces becomes more tangible in these later poems, reaching a crescendo in "Nobleza de sangre," the poem that was published on its own in *El Mundo* a few days after Ramos Otero's death (Hernández 225). Because of the dissemination of this poem through the press, it has become one of the better-known works from this collection. Even without the additional publicity it received, it is certainly the most direct poem of the collection in reference to HIV/AIDS and the way it has ravaged not only the poetic persona (and the poet himself), but the homosexual community for which Ramos Otero serves as a type of spokesperson. He sheds all euphemistic tendencies, boldly unveiling both the disease-ravaged body that remains and the emotional ire that the epidemic has provoked. Instead of using a solitary "yo/I" as the enunciator of this poem, Ramos Otero presents a multitude, choosing the plural "nosotros/us" over the singular "yo/I" that predominates throughout the collection.

This shift is significant, for when the poem first appeared in *El Mundo*, it was "la primera vez que un poema publicado en Puerto Rico hablaba sin tapujos de los males asociados con el SIDA" [the first time that a poem published in Puerto Rico spoke openly of the ills associated with AIDS] (Hernández 225), making it a groundbreaking work in 1990. The fact that the poetic voices of the poem represent a marginalized multitude made up of HIV-positive homosexuals and transvestites spanning various locales (New York, San Francisco, Puerto Rico, and Haiti) makes the work even more remarkable. Talking about AIDS publicly without any metaphorical language is bold enough, but talking about it from the perspective of society's outcasts, as Ramos Otero has so keenly demonstrated throughout this collection, is sure to draw attention—which is exactly what this poem did. It opened a critical dialogue and catapulted Ramos Otero's poetry to a new level.[7] By appearing first in a daily newspaper, rather than in an eclectic collection of poetry, it also reached the masses, thus forcing Puerto Ricans of all walks of life to ponder the reality he was presenting. That presentation is made even more extraordinary by the unabashed language used and, ultimately, the critical words directed at God himself. Thus, Ramos Otero boldly transgresses cultural and religious conventions in his quest to break the silence surrounding AIDS in Puerto Rico. The language reaches a pinnacle of critical and emotive language, brashly depicting a reality that had been hitherto ensconced.

The poem commences with the well-known opening lines of countless prayers giving thanks to God ("Gracias, Señor"). That familiar language is quickly subverted as Ramos Otero thanks the Lord "por habernos enviado el SIDA" [for having sent us AIDS] (62). The satirical tone of this subversive prayer heightens, as he speaks on behalf of "Todos los tecatos y los maricones de New York, San Francisco, Puerto Rico y Haití" [all of the junkies and queers of New York, San Francisco, Puerto Rico and Haiti] (62), denouncing the ingratitude of the heterosexuals of Africa, who haven't recognized that "SIDA les ha permitido entrar a la modernidad sin prejuicios" [AIDS has allowed them to enter modernity without prejudice] (62). He continues his oration, asking the Lord to pardon the bisexuals for their "confusión innata" [innate confusion] and then using false praise to demonstrate his criticism of the Church's greed and deception. The "prayer" shifts to the specific suffering of "los sidosos" [AIDS patients] (63), portraying through vibrant imagery the drastic corporeal

---

7. See Hernández; and Torres.

transformations that have befallen those suffering from AIDS: "esos sudores o escalofríos" [those sweats or chills]. "ese cansancio eterno" [that eternal exhaustion], "ese asco colectivo al Kaposi Sarcoma y a la tuberculosis" [that collective repugnance toward Kaposi Sarcoma and tuberculosis] (63). By openly writing about these maladies, Ramos Otero is continuing to challenge the oppressive silence surrounding AIDS, a silence that has subjected its patients to "esa marginación sin límite" [that limitless marginalization] (63). Just as he refused to hide the ardent sexuality of his poetic persona's body in the first section of this collection, here, too, Ramos Otero forces the readers to visualize his suffering—how it has been imprinted on his body and the bodies of his new compatriots. Well aware that his body will soon decay and decompose into *polvo*, he continues to explore his reality through his bodily transformations and his literary production.

This focus on personal and social suffering in the context of a pseudo-prayer to God eventually reaches what Hernández calls a sacrilegious level (225), when Ramos Otero situates AIDS patients on the same level of suffering experienced by Jesus Christ through crucifixion. This sacrilegious tone continues as Ramos Otero continues to question the motivation for creating such a vile illness, seemingly wondering whether "la enfermedad que sufre fue una vengaza del dios cristiano por sentirse aislado, incapaz o sexualmente insatisfecho" [the illness he suffers from was the Christian God's revenge for (himself) feeling isolated, incapable, or sexually unsatisfied] (225).

Having effectively exorcized some of his wrath toward God through his pen, Ramos Otero shifts back to a solitary subject facing his imminent death in the last poem of the second section, "La rosa" [The rose]. Hernández believes this poem to be the logical end to the entire collection as well, despite the existence of a final poem, "La nada de nuestros nunca cuerpos" in its own section (229). I tend to concur with that analysis because "La rosa" depicts the waning days before death, whereas "La nada . . ." seems to serve as a continuation of a distinct poetic project in which he wrote poetic epitaphs for famous writers (Vega 25). As such, my analysis will focus on "La rosa" as the conclusion to the poetic voice's reflective foray into the dynamics of eroticism, love, poetry, solitude, and AIDS which eventually added up to nothing, absence, death, and *polvo*.

In this poem, the poetic voice accepts his plight and anticipates his upcoming "viaje" [trip] from this world. The voyage he is about to take calls to mind the voyage he has completed throughout his poetic reflection in this collection. While his erotic body captivated his attention and is his primary representation of self in the first section of the collection, that physicality slowly erodes as solitude wears him down emotionally and AIDS attacks him biologically. The body that became so familiar gradually disappears from the text, replaced instead by the mind and the pen of the poet, the true identity of the poetic persona. Through his pen, he creates a new self, an hombre de papel composed of words, memories, reflections, and anticipations. Through poetry and the creation of a literary body, the poetic persona (and to a large degree Ramos Otero, through the autobiographical threads that weave through these works), faces his physical demise by exalting his creative potential. The pen provides the means to confront AIDS, combat solitude, rail against God, say goodbye to friends, and in the end prepare for death.

Although this hombre de papel lacks the physical attributes that once defined the poetic persona, he still has retained important elements of his being, ultimately reaffirming himself through his insistence on experiencing erotic pleasures and exerting his marginalized (at times taboo) existence despite the reactions of others. The pleasures he has experienced through his relationship with José, and the false promise of continuity and the infinite pleasure they provided, have been cemented through poetry, thus providing the poetic voice with a distinct type of transcendence, one offered through the words that have constructed his history, his love, his life, and, ultimately, his death. Although the experience of eroticism fails to provide an escape from his solitary, discontinuous condition, writing about those experiences and leaving an indelible mark through his poetry provides a connection with all those who experience that work, thus eclipsing the constraints of time and geography and providing the ultimate way of transcending the untimely death wrought by AIDS.

"Adiós, Ten-Ying"

The confluence of eroticism and narrative can also be seen in Andrea Blanqué's treatment of AIDS in her short story "Adiós Ten-Ying" from her collection *Querida muerte*. Blanqué's story portrays the final days of thirty-year-old Ten-Ying, a prostitute who is dying in a hospital in Hong Kong. Throughout, Blanqué focuses overwhelmingly on the positive aspects of her past sexuality and eroticism, choosing instead to gloss over the current demise that the protagonist is facing. Although the narrator reveals to us that Ten-Ying is actually narrating her own story to a young doctor who frequently spends time in her room, the readers are not privy to Ten-Ying's own words or voice. Instead, what is heard is an omniscient narrator's retelling of that story.

The narrative is very symmetrical, dividing Ten-Ying's thirty years into the fifteen years of purity and virginity *before* she fled her family's cloistered home in Ciudad Vieja, Montevideo, to traverse the globe on huge ships, and the fifteen years *after*, those years filled with desire, adventure, countless sexual partners, prostitution, and, ultimately, AIDS, which is clearly named in the first page of the story: "Pero hoy acontece que Ten-Ying tiene Sida" [But today it so happens that Ten-Ying has AIDS] (27). Furthermore, there is a contrast between the two bodies of Ten-Ying; the majority of the narrative occupies itself with the young, beautiful, sexualized body. It is this body that she offered up to the sailors during her years as a wanderlust-stricken prostitute, a body that contrasts starkly with the present body she inhabits. The withering, weak body that wastes away in the hospital room is the current manifestation of that transformed body, one that has become unrecognizable. The ravages of AIDS are the cause of this second body, but it is viewed as simply a part of an erotic past that is romanticized through the current retelling. Ten-Ying is conscious of her drastically altered physical state and the causes of it, but she does not complain. Despite being confined to her hospital bed because of her increasingly weakened body, Ten-Ying confronts her current situation through an emphasis on her previous existence, one that was characterized by sexuality, adventure, and freedom. The romanticized eroticism of the past masks the physical and emotional pain of the present and future, thus allowing Ten-Ying to confront her death peacefully and without fear. Death becomes part of her life, one spent expressing and exploring her sexuality. As such, death becomes a natural part of eroticism itself. Bataille reminds us that by assenting to life fully, even in the face of death, one challenges death itself through one's very indifference to it (23). Life and her life choices are highly romanticized in the memory of Ten-Ying, but they function to allow her to disavow death itself and focus only on life.

This romanticization occurs through a narrative that is a postmodern retelling of the classic fairy tale "Rapunzel." Through this innovative rendering, Blanqué not only provides a positive tone that allows her protagonist to face death in peace, but also confronts and challenges some of the existing notions regarding sexuality and AIDS, thus allowing her to break the silence regarding this virus, openly acknowledging it as part of sexuality and intimately linked to both life and death. In the original version of "Rapunzel," as told by the Brothers Grimm, a beautiful pubescent girl is shut away in a tower in the woods to protect her from possible suitors. There are no doors or steps to her tower, only a window. The only access to the tower is Rapunzel's long hair, which serves as a ladder and allows her caregiver[8] to climb up to visit. While cloistered away from society, Rapunzel passes her lonely days singing. One day her song is heard by a young prince, who by chance learns how to gain access to the tower. He uses her long locks as a ladder to access the tower she inhabits and woos the young beauty with the promise of marriage. They plan their escape. However, Rapunzel's caregiver discovers her plan because she notices that Rapunzel's dress has grown tighter with her swollen belly,[9] and as a punishment, she cuts her hair and puts her in a deserted locale. The prince, upon learning about her destiny, leaps from the tower and is blinded by a thorny bush. He wanders alone through the desert for years, ultimately stumbling upon Rapunzel and the twin children she had borne. Of course, following the traditional rules for fairy-tale endings, they lived happily ever after.

Blanqué's story of Ten-Ying's early years echoes this familiar narrative, but the tale has been altered through her postmodern retelling. Literary critic Christina Bacchilega studies the narrative and ideological foundations of these revisions to show the images of women that these writings project (4). Bacchilega's work provides a sound argument for the importance of fairy tales to many narrative projects:

> As a hybrid/transitional genre, the fairy tale also magically grants writers/tellers and readers/listeners access to the collective, if fictionalized past of social communing, an access that allows for an apparently limitless, highly idiosyncratic re-creation of that "once there was." (5)

This ability to access a collective narrative proves useful for Blanqué as she strives to overcome the societal taboos that have silenced open expression about sexuality and AIDS. Through her revamping of this traditional genre, Blanqué imparts her young protagonist with a burgeoning sexuality, whose expression allows Ten-Ying to forge her own identity and life path despite the hardships that befall her precisely because of that liberated sexuality. In liberating herself from her dominating father, she strives for independence and self-determinacy. Ironically, she finds the emancipation

---

8. In the original version, Rapunzel's father gives her away to a witch in exchange for a wild herb that grows in the witch's yard, an herb that his pregnant wife craves excessively throughout her pregnancy. Desperate to placate his wife, he hastily agrees to exchange his unborn daughter for unlimited access to this herb, which is alternately called rampion or rapunzel. The witch cares for the girl as if she were her own, ultimately enclosing her in the tower to protect her from young men. In updated versions of this tale, Rapunzel is locked away by her own parents, still with the intention of protecting her from the dangers of the world.

9. In another version, the secret is revealed by Rapunzel's own inadvertent slip of the tongue.

she craves in a career traditionally viewed as one that subjugates women by forcing them to earn a living by sexually servicing men who often take advantage of them: prostitution.

The fact that Ten-Ying feels liberated through such a problematic career illustrates one way in which Blanqué attempts to manipulate and question the social order and the rules prescribed to women. She creates a confluence between two supposedly contradictory concepts—women's liberation and prostitution—and, in doing so, essentially creates an acceptable space in her literature for a character like Ten-Ying, one who consciously chooses to prostitute herself and rejoices rather than mourns when that choice leads to AIDS. One way to understand this perspective is to recur to feminist theory. Sarah Bromberg produced an enlightening study of different types of feminism and their views on prostitution. Tracing her argument through five different forms of feminism that have articulated strong opinions on the issue of prostitution (Marxist, liberal, existentialist, socialist, and radical feminism), Bromberg shows divergent opinions of the topic (1).

While Marxist, radical, and socialist feminism all oppose prostitution on the grounds that it degrades and oppresses women, liberal and existentialist feminism have a more favorable view of the sex trade. For liberal feminists, "prostitution is conceived of in the contractarian sense of being a private business transaction" and, furthermore, "the liberal feminist wants to free women from oppressive gender roles" (Bromberg, "Liberal Feminism" 1). Existentialist feminists posit that "prostitution allows women an avenue of escape from dependency on men in a way that does not leave them victims, but empowered women." They further argue that "prostitution can provide women with the kind of liberty that is immediate, affirming, and temporally rewarding" (Bromberg, "Existentialist Feminism" 1) In the case of Blanqué's text, there is a notable lack of moral commentary on Ten-Ying's decision to prostitute herself; instead, prostitution is depicted as one way for her to break free of some of her family's and society's expectations. I undertake a liberal-existentialist feminist reading of Blanqué's work to argue that prostitution is indeed a way by which Blanqué bestows agency on her protagonist; it is the agency and pleasure derived from her liberated sexuality that in the end allows her to face the premature death that it has wrought. By subverting traditional societal dynamics, particularly the view of female sexual liberation and independence, Blanqué also, by extension, questions the traditional representations of sexuality and AIDS within that society, forging a unique perspective and a fresh dialogue.

Blanqué's narrative begins with a familiar storyline: a young girl born to protective parents, in this case, a Chinese shopkeeper living on a street filled with brothels in Montevideo. Because of the ill-repute of this section of Montevideo (Ciudad Vieja) that is frequented by lustful, sea-worn sailors in search of nubile women willing to offer themselves up for sex, Ten-Ying's father strives to protect her from her environment, shutting her away in the attic to protect her virginity. Her father despises the sailors but feels confident that by cloistering his daughter high up in an impenetrable tower, he will keep her safe from the sailors who venture inland with the vigorous winds that buffet that part of the city. In his mind's eye, he envisions his daughter as a pure, virginal child, but Blanqué contorts this virginal image of a modern-day Rapunzel as she reveals to the readers the true Ten-Ying, the fifteen-year-old girl whose protected, solitary existence only fuels her desires and helps her recognize her dreams. The setting sun shining through her window transforms into the face of countless sailors who embody her dreams and become the image of her own sexual and physical liberation and her rebellion against her father.

With quickly multiplying fantasies filling her mind and a strengthening will to flee her home and disobey her father, Ten-Ying also begins to claim her body as her own. Her father's plan backfires, and instead of protecting Ten-Ying from the sexual desires of others, the confinement and endless time to daydream awaken her libido. As she continues to explore and discover her burgeoning sexuality in her endless hours alone, her desire to commune sexually with the objects of her dreams grows, finally propelling her to escape from her house, fleeing over the rooftops to the sea and its innumerable sailors that beckon. Blanqué's version of this tale diverges from the original "Rapunzel." Ten-Ying-as-Rapunzel refuses to wait for a Prince Charming to rescue her from her castle, and she refuses to accept the fate that her caregivers impose on her. Instead, this heroine claims her body and life as her own and exerts her own agency in a quest for adventure, freedom, and pleasure.

How she chooses to live that life after she leaves home deviates from the traditional notions of proper comportment for young women. As such, it represents a rebellion against a prescribed set of permissible behaviors for women. According to Dr. Bernardo Camacho, a Colombian doctor working with AIDS patients in Latin America, "In our [Latin American] society, women attach punitive attitudes to their sexuality. They associate sex with sin, so they carry a negative emotional burden. For a man, sex is the opposite. . . . Our society does not allow an adjusted sexual development, and so it is one of great distortions" (86). Ten-Ying rejects the notion that she should not be a sexualized being, choosing the other extreme as she offers herself up to the whims of the captains and sailors of a multitude of ships. Sexuality becomes the route to freedom, independence, pleasure, adventure—and, eventually, infection (from shunning prophylactics), AIDS, and death. According to Blanqué, part of her motivation for writing this story was to explore promiscuity from a perspective of fear of what could happen to those who live that sort of life.[10] Ironically, despite this stated intention, the tone she projects is not one of fear, but acceptance. She refuses to dwell on the many possible repercussions of promiscuity and focuses instead on the joy that her protagonist derived from that choice in spite of the disease it caused her.

Bataille's theories on eroticism and the pleasures derived from it provide a lens through which to view this text and its exuberant celebration of sexuality. Bataille reminds us that much of the joy and pleasure experienced through erotic activity derives from the transgression of accepted taboos (256). The notion of taboo is key in this work and is closely related to the actions of the protagonist. Ten-Yin transgresses multiple taboos: the loss of virginity at such a young age; the willing sexual interactions with men who, according to her upbringing, are not proper suitors; the willing participation in sex with countless men, most of whom were strangers; prostitution itself; the contraction of AIDS; and finally the unabashed discussion of the above topics without the slightest hint of shame or remorse. Blanqué, through her protagonist's actions, carefully deconstructs these limits and propels her liberated protagonist across societal boundaries into territory that is often relegated to hushed conversations, but rarely becomes part of public discourse.

In fact, during a field study in Montevideo, Uruguay, in June, 1997, I had the occasion to speak with Andrea Blanqué and several other contemporary writers[11] about the lack of overt discussion of sexuality, AIDS, and other sexually transmitted diseases in contemporary Uruguayan literature. All of the writers agreed that these topics have largely been ignored by recent writers in Uruguay, not because AIDS and HIV do not present a problem in the country,[12] but because the topics themselves are shrouded in taboo-laden secrecy. As a result, these topics became ones that are rarely discussed by mainstream writers. Even during my interviews with prominent Uruguayan scholars and journalists,[13] I was repeatedly directed

10. Personal interview, June 8, 1997.
11. Some of the writers I had the opportunity to interview are Andrea Blanqué, Roberto Echevarren, Alvaro Fernández Pagliano, Hugo Giovanetti Viola, María Gravina, Ricardo Prieto, Leonardo Rossiello, and Ana Solari.
12. According to UNICEF, at the end of 2007 (the most recent year for which they have compiled statistics), approximately 0.6 percent of the adult population (between ages 15–49) is living with HIV/AIDS. http://www.unicef.org/infobycountry/uruguay_statistics.html#4
13. I met with and interviewed Teresa Porzecanski, Fernando Butazzoni, Horacio Xaubet, Margarita Serra (the Minister of Health at the time), Lauro Maraudo, Hugo Achugar, Ana Inez

to writers who are openly gay or somehow perceived to be connected to a more marginalized lifestyle. The predominant perception was that heterosexual writers (and seemingly most members of society) simply preferred not to talk about AIDS or the types of sexual behavior that could lead to its contraction. Seen in this light, one can understand the impact of Blanqué's story and the multiple ways in which it works to open a dialogue about sexuality and AIDS and combat the persistent taboos that work to prevent such discourse.

One of the most notable qualities of this particular work is the manner in which AIDS and sexuality themselves are portrayed. Instead of being judgmental or prescriptive, Blanqué portrays a woman who is allowed to "escape" from the confining presence of her father and the community that supports his opinions, opting instead to exist in a liminal space, devoid of citizenship, allegiances, or even personal connections. Ten-Ying becomes her own island, happily floating from country to country on whatever vessel willingly takes her along. As the sole "citizen" of that island, she sets her own rules and functions as her own ruler. *She* decides how she would like to comport herself, choosing prostitution as the economic system that will allow her the freedom she desires. The notion of prostitution as a means to freedom may seem like an oxymoron given the negative connotations currently connected to it in many modern societies; but Blanqué exhibits a liberal-existentialist feminist perspective, opting to portray prostitution as a liberating career that affords Ten-Ying pleasure and the ability to cross all types of boundaries with a currency that speaks many different languages. This belief is expressed through the omniscient narrator's affirmation in reference to Ten-Ying: "Quien no ha sido puta o al menos mujer no conoce placer semejante" [Anyone who has not been a whore or at least a woman doesn't know a similar pleasure] (30).

Blanqué's inherently positive depiction of prostitution affords her protagonist the agency necessary to liberate herself from her family and create a life that satisfies her desires. However, her disregard for the harsh realities of the world of prostitution further contributes to the fairy-tale-like quality of the story. Without any rigid plans in mind, Ten-Ying chooses an occupation that affords her the flexibility to literally follow the wind, becoming one with the elements that inhabited life at sea. Eroticism and sex have provided Ten-Ying with fifteen pleasurable years of incomparable adventure and freedom. They have also led her to the contraction of HIV,

---

Larre Borges, Carlos Basilio Muñoz, Juan José Quintans, and Hilia Moreira, in addition to those mentioned above (June 1997).

which in its advanced stages as AIDS has finally forced her to leave the sea that she loves and retire her body, her sexuality, and eventually her life. While AIDS is clearly a result of Ten-Ying's chosen career of prostitution, this connection is not overemphasized. Blanqué steers clear of metaphor-laden descriptions to talk about AIDS. AIDS is clearly mentioned in the first page of the text. It is what it is: it is neither minimized nor conflated into something more than a disease that Ten-Ying contracted through unprotected sex. It is clear that the disease is connected to sexuality, and it is also clear that it signifies an untimely death for Ten-Ying. Yet it is still just a disease, which, according to Sontag, is the desired representation (181); the elimination of metaphorical language divorces AIDS from many of its taboo-laden significances that have perpetuated through stylistic language that ignores the realities of AIDS and instead turns it into something more than what it actually is. Here, Blanqué recognizes the virus's power to alter the course of someone's life, but she refuses to multiply its significance by attaching it to heavily charged metaphors.

Instead, the central focus is on Ten-Ying herself, on the *person* behind the disease and on the body that it inhabits. Ironically, the very activity that led Ten-Ying to the contraction of HIV, sex, becomes the subject of the narrative that provides her with a way to create a lasting image of her life and proceed toward death in peace. It is important to remember that the entire narrative of this story is a retelling (by an omniscient narrator) of the memories that Ten-Ying is sharing with the doctor who attends to her. The central focus on a healthy, exuberant, sexually energized young woman (both before she flees home and during the subsequent fifteen years that led up to her becoming HIV-positive) reflects the manner in which Ten-Ying has chosen to portray herself to her interlocutor. In order for her to have arrived at such an advanced stage of AIDS, she has inevitably passed through many AIDS-related infections, significant pain and suffering, and the gradual loss of a recognizable body. Nevertheless, Ten-Ying chooses not to dwell on those images, opting instead to project herself through the prism of her memory; there she can remain for eternity as the beautiful, erotic young woman who was desired by men across the globe. As such, through the process of narrating her erotic past, Ten-Ying (through the voice of the narrator) constructs an immortal body, one that is vastly different from the current one she inhabits. This process is very similar to the one carried out by Ramos Otero in which his poetic voice transformed himself into an hombre de papel, thus transcending his current suffering and constructing his identity through the process of narrative. For Ten-Ying, in the final moments before death,

Las palabras surgen y entonces prolongan el cuerpo de Ten-Ying. Ella está a cada minuto más escuálida, pero pareciera que su carne se transformara en palabras, palabras que andan sueltas por la Tierra. El cuerpo se evanesce y se convierte en vocablos, que no son llevados por el viento, sino que se quedan allí, instalados. Allí, entre Ten-Ying y el médico, encima de la cama que huele a enfermedad y a limpio. La historia de Ten-Ying flota en una habitación de un hospital de Hong-Kong. Resiste a las bacterias, a los virus, a los diminutísimos monstruos que consumen el cuerpo de una mujer pero no su memoria.

[The words rise up and then prolong Ten-Ying's body. She is more squalid by the minute, but it seems as if her flesh transformed itself into words, words that run loose over the Earth. The body evanesces and it turns into words, that aren't carried away by the wind, but rather stay there settled. There, between Ten-Ying and the doctor, on top of the bed that smells of sickness and cleanliness. Ten-Ying's story/history floats in a hospital room in Hong Kong. It resists the bacteria, the virus and the minuscule monsters that consume the body of a woman, but not her memory.] (34)

While this process of reconstructing a healthy identity through memory and narrative indeed echoes that carried out by Ramos Otero, here the progression has been truncated and Ten-Ying's authority curtailed because she does not function as a first-person narrator. Blanqué's story has crafted a situation in which Ten-Ying is able to construct herself to a very limited interlocutor—the doctor who attends to her. Therefore, the version that is transmitted to the reader has passed through different filters: first, the male doctor who, by circumstance, is the one person privy to her collection of personal narrative; and then the unknown omniscient narrator who ultimately relates the entire tale. Instead of allowing the doctor to retell Ten-Ying's story and manipulate it to his own end, Blanqué has chosen instead to put the complete narrative in the purview of an omniscient narrator, who has access to the external words transmitted to the doctor and the internal dialogue known only to Ten-Ying. It is this narrator who shares the story with the readers. While the tone the narrator projects is certainly sympathetic to Ten-Ying and her desires, the fact remains that Ten-Ying has been denied the full authorial powers that Ramos Otero granted his poetic voice.

This issue raises quite a few questions about authorial agency and the possibility of censorship. In the most optimistic sense, we might hope that the omniscient narrator (and perhaps the doctor himself) has served

Ten-Ying faithfully in the transmission of her message. In this scenario, Ten-Ying has indeed been afforded the ability to indirectly construct herself and her life through a romanticized retelling of her past, ultimately cementing that life in the written word. However, it can also be seen as problematic that a male doctor (as a representative of the dominant patriarchal society that Ten-Ying has spent her life fleeing) is the unwitting recipient of Ten-Ying's unconventional life story. Because of the indirect style of the narrative, there are bound to be unidentified gaps, mediations, and perhaps censorship of the true tale that Ten-Ying relayed to the doctor. While the inclusion of an omniscient narrator who provides access to Ten-Ying's thought processes gives the illusion that the reader is truly privy to her complete narrative, the fact that Ten-Ying was not granted first-person narrative authority raises questions that will forever remain unanswered about how inclusive that narrative really was. Despite the problematic nature of the narrative technique, the process of storytelling did indeed have a positive impact on the protagonist. Narrative, specifically about sexuality, indirectly allows Ten-Ying to preserve, through words and memories, the exuberant, healthy body she prefers to remember.

Blanqué's decision to weave Ten-Ying's narrative with the familiar strands of a traditional fairy tale follows the pattern set by others who have reworked fairy tales, giving them a postmodern update. By choosing to use this trope, Blanqué is able to capitalize on material that is well-known to the public, while manipulating it for her own political, erotic, or narrative ends (Bacchilega 3). Establishing this level of familiarity for her audience is key, particularly because she goes on to subvert the anticipated tale, converting it into one of sexual independence and freedom. Like Rapunzel, Ten-Ying rebelled against her situation, the former pliable to the desires and suggestions of a handsome young prince, the latter selecting her own suitors by going to them instead of waiting for rescue. Furthermore, the two young women give in to sexual temptation. In one version of Rapunzel's case, her yielding to temptation is merely hinted at through her burgeoning belly and ill-fitting clothes, while Blanqué spares no details in her exploration of this new-found pleasure in Ten-Ying's life. Rapunzel suffers punishment for her improprieties, being forcibly separated from her prince and banished to solitude until her prince is able to reunite with her. In Ten-Ying's case, her "punishment" could at first glance be seen as HIV itself, invading her body in retribution for her overly liberal sexuality. Where Blanqué deviates from the expected is in her positive treatment of this turn of events. AIDS is portrayed not as a punishment, but merely as a realistic consequence of Ten-Ying's actions. The tone stays positive, and all negativity is overshadowed by the pleasant memories that allow Ten-Ying to mentally detach herself from her ailing body and inhabit the lands that signified freedom and independence for her.

Blanqué maintains the fairy-tale motif to the end; the doctor that has listened to Ten-Ying's tales becomes a type of Prince Charming, offering to Ten-Ying a caring, nonjudgmental ear and refusing to abandon her in her time of need. He serves Ten-Ying, attending to her every need and whim, even complying with her dying wish: to breathe the sea air and feel the wind on her face. He disregards medical protocol, secretly helping Ten-Ying leave the hospital and carrying her in his arms to the edge of the ocean, where she dies peacefully in his arms. The ships that provided the space for her sexual exploration now become silent witnesses as her body succumbs to the disease she contracted while aboard them. In this last scene, the doctor (and the ships themselves), in the silent, nonjudgmental manner of accompanying Ten-Ying in her final moments, can be seen as the ideal reader for this text as well—one who is open to the thought-provoking ideas and nonconformist representations of sexuality but who refrains from judging, instead opting to hear the narrative to the end. In a nation where much of the discourse about AIDS remains shrouded in stigmas, the portrayal of this type of reception propels Blanqué's text further on its project toward overthrowing the taboos and silences that have reigned for so long. Like her protagonist, Blanqué challenges existing notions about sexuality and presents a new way of viewing life, eroticism, HIV/AIDS, and death itself.

BOTH OF THESE WORKS challenge some of the conservative, hegemonic discourses regarding AIDS, opting to thrust the illness into the light—removing many of the damaging metaphors, shattering silences, and creating their own definitions of the notion of people with AIDS. Through Ramos Otero's erotically defiant poetry and Blanqué's romantically sexualized tale, these authors explore, navigate, inhabit, and ultimately subvert the classic notions about sexuality, AIDS, and death. They provide their protagonists with the tools (poetry and fairy tales) to essentially construct their own biographies, giving them the freedom to portray their sexuality in any light they choose. Both choose to direct their gazes backwards, toward the memories of lives filled with sexual adventure and defiant freedom. Their bodies were their portals to pleasure, and this image dominates over the ones they currently face. Through the interplay of two moments of enunciation, the authors portray healthy, sexualized bodies that predominate over the drastically altered, debilitated bodies that the protagonists inhabit. These protagonists effectively distort their current images and reflect back to the reader the identities that they prefer to remember. In the process they disavow punitive images of sexuality and instead celebrate it and life to the fullest, not *because of* AIDS and their approaching deaths, but *in spite of* them.

CHAPTER THREE

Isolation and Exile
AIDS and the Solitary Body

> AQUÍ ESTOY
> En la ciudad de los ajenos
> el viento ruge feroz
> se borra la memoria
> mueren los amigos
> los mata el tiempo . . .
> Aquí estoy
> tras la puerta del mundo.
>
> [HERE I AM
> In the unfamiliar city
> the wind roars ferociously
> memory is erased
> friends die
> time kills them . . .
> here I am
> behind the door of the world.]
>   —Miguel Miranda, POESídA 111

THE PREVIOUS two chapters focused on the AIDS-infected body in its interactions with other bodies in the arena of retribution and revenge, as well as erotic escapism. Despite their drastic differences, those bodies and their experiences with AIDS were in large part defined by their interactions with other bodies—before contracting HIV, then grappling with the ramifications of the diagnosis, and finally in engaging in subsequent sexual encounters, both sadistic and erotic. The "other" served as a reflection of the self, providing a prismatic view of past, present, and future variations of that infirm body through the imagined and real interactions with other bodies. The revenge narratives examined in chapter 1 would not have been fathomable were there no other bodies on which to enact sadistic machinations. Without another to infect, the perpetrators' power would have diminished, leaving them impotent to fulfill their plots of retribution. The communion with other bodies also proved vital to the protagonists in chapter 2 by fueling their erotic fantasies; they were able to eclipse the pain associated with impending death through the heightened pleasure experienced through their erotic interactions with numerous lovers. AIDS in these chapters was always a component of the self, but was magnified when the individual interacted with others. That interaction accentuated the conflated meaning of the virus, whether as a potentially lethal weapon carried silently in the body or as a constant figure in the altered landscape of contemporary eroticism. The very interaction of two bodies, with at least one of those bodies infected with the virus, called into question the impact of AIDS on both individuals, thereby eliminating the possibility of ignoring its existence.

Despite the perspective that the authors I examined in chapters 1 and 2 provided about the complexities of interpersonal relationships in the age of AIDS, the fact still remains that before an individual can make the decision to enter into a communion with another, he or she must first face the meaning of his or her HIV-positive condition alone. While multiple possible gradations exist in the types of responses to such an alteration in self-identity, one that has reappeared in many literary renderings is a profound isolationism, bordering on self-imposed exile. This decision at times is a response to the pervasiveness of lingering fears and misconceptions about HIV/AIDS, namely, that people with AIDS (PWAs) pose a risk to society and must be identified and categorized, and therefore subtly separated from the "rest" of society, so that society can protect itself from them. This message has been internalized by the protagonists in the narratives examined in this chapter, who, in essence, choose to attempt to erase themselves from the social body either by fleeing society or the social group they are part of, or by self-destruction.

This chapter explores three such depictions—Nelson Mallach's "Elefante," Ricardo Prieto's *Pecados mínimos*, and Pablo Pérez's *Un año sin amor*—divided into what I call **radical isolation** and **solitary separation.** These terms draw largely on some of the existent theories regarding self-imposed exile, but they differ most notably in the fact that none of the protagonists' governments have overtly forced their separation from the rest of the population. That does not mean, however, that the social attitudes surrounding PWAs, particularly in the early days of the disease, did not influence the internalized shame, guilt, and listlessness that these protagonists exhibit in their varying degrees of social withdrawal. This chapter, then, will examine the individual AIDS-infected body as it purposely separates itself from the social body, whether physically or emotionally. The focus will be on the new markers of identity from this position of isolation and the altered perception of the body as viewed from the protagonists' positions on the physical and psychological margins of society.

The term "exile" has a long and varied history in literary criticism and in the realm of Latin American literature in particular. Most critics firmly link it to the multiple forced dislocations of thousands of citizens from war-torn or authoritarian countries, such as those which occurred in Argentina, Uruguay, and Chile in the 1970s and 1980s.[1] Some critics, on the other hand, envision the state of exile as a more philosophical existence that plays out in both literal and figurative border crossings. Among these latter theorists, Mae Henderson, quoting Edward Said in his essay "Mind of Winter," reminds us,

> In a secular and contingent world, homes are always provisional. Borders and barriers which enclose us within the safety of familiar territory can also become prisons, and are often defended beyond reason or necessity. Exiles cross borders, break barriers of thought and experience. (4)

Many factors can motivate such translocations, not the least of which are the brutal dictatorships that forced thousands of citizens to flee their homelands in search of safety, to escape persecution and often torture and death.

While this reason is one of the most apparent to enter into exile, and it certainly should not be underestimated for its critical impact on the formation of countless displaced individuals, I aim to present and elucidate a distinct type of exile experience that is affecting many citizens of diverse countries in Latin America: the desire to flee or isolate oneself because of the mental and physical burdens of HIV/AIDS resulting from both internal and external forces. I do not propose a comparison between this and more traditional forms of exile, but rather I will show how some of the facets of both forced and self-imposed exile can be found in the three narratives cited above about the isolating experience wrought by AIDS.

Even a cursory examination of Spanish American literature reveals many instances in which the notion of exile is used metaphorically in an attempt to capture the struggles of individuals living a marginalized existence. In fact, Guillermina Rosenkrantz's study examines this very idea of

---

1. See Rosenkrantz; McClennen; and Kaminsky, among others.

multiple forms of exile related to the notion of homosexuality in the works of Manuel Puig, while Amy Kaminsky delves into the concept of "radical alienation" as it appears in Sylvia Molloy's novel, *En breve cárcel*. In the latter work, the protagonist finds herself doubly disconnected from her surroundings based not only on sexual preference, but on gender as well. In the above examples, the authors manipulate the notion of metaphorical exile to show how individuals can feel exiled because of the alienation they experience as a result of certain characteristics that set them apart from others—in these cases, sexual orientation and gender, both connected to the body.

My study borrows from this same approach by showing how the protagonists in these three works feel alienated from others based on the virus inhabiting their bodies (and, in some cases, "announcing" itself through obvious physical signs) and the connotations associated with it. As a result, they enter into different versions of exile, separating themselves in varying degrees from the rest of society. The narratives are as diverse in form and origin as are the experiences they portray. Two of these works present a more radical departure from society, accentuating both the physical and social distancing that the protagonists undergo. Perhaps the most dramatic example of this tendency is seen in Ricardo Prieto's (Uruguay) play, *Pecados mínimos*. The protagonist's feverish quest to isolate his mother from AIDS, while at the same time completely separating himself from the exterior world, results in the destruction of self, family, and home. Society is absent in this play, whereas it is altered and foreign in Nelson Mallach's (Argentina) short story "Elefante," which depicts a physical departure from familiar surroundings into an unknown land devoid of friends, family, and other markers of the previously known self.

Radical Isolation
"ELEFANTE" AND *PECADOS MÍNIMOS*

I refer to these two works as exemplary of radical isolation because both of the protagonists take extreme measures to cloister themselves from the society and the world they had known prior to becoming HIV-positive. They take radical steps, imposing a version of exile on themselves (and in the case of Prieto's play, on loved ones), motivated by the fear and shame associated with their health status. This concept of radical isolation, as I posit it, is distinct in some ways from the traditional exile imposed by a governing body as a way of punishing an offending citizen. In the texts I study, while there is indeed a physical departure from one's current society, the departure is not mandated and therefore retains some degree of volition on the part of the protagonists. Nonetheless, I will argue that the harsh cultural climate surrounding AIDS, particularly in the early days of the epidemic, contributed to a heightened fear and sense of shame about the affliction, and therefore served as a coercive factor in these protagonists' decision to exile themselves from their homes and/or daily lives.

I am certainly sensitive to the concerns raised by Amy K. Kaminsky and, to some degree, Sophia A. McClennen, regarding the tendency to co-opt the term "exile" for situations that "tended to disregard the condition's necessary association with anguish and loss" (McClennen 1), such as the appropriation by U.S. feminists that invoked the notion of exile to describe a situation of "cultural disenfranchisement" which "included a prohibition against leaving the home" (Kaminsky xi). However, I believe the term to be an apt descriptor of the departures undertaken in the texts I study, as it functions as a way to conceptualize both physical departures from society and psychological angst and disconnect as a result of health status. In the case of Prieto's and Mallach's works, I feel that the term "exile" is an appropriate referent because both protagonists are tormented by the consequences of their infection, experience a great deal of anguish over the pain and shame that they have caused their families, and struggle with the necessity to confront the loss of the self they knew and the altered future ahead. I will furthermore draw upon characteristics of exile to reference the situation depicted by Pérez, particularly because his protagonist experiences a metaphorical exile as he struggles against the disease that is effectively imprisoning his body as well as causing psychological anguish and isolation.

Solitary Separation
UN AÑO SIN AMOR

In contrast with the radical departure that Prieto's and Mallach's protagonists make from their respective surroundings and the drastic alterations in their day-to-day existence that they undertake as a response to AIDS, Un año sin amor provides a subtler vision of the solitude that can befall the HIV-positive individual as he struggles to re-semanticize life and self, all while facing myriad symptoms associated with AIDS. This work proves to be more introspective than Prieto's and Mallach's works, providing the reader with a notion of the emotional and mental struggles that accompany the physical changes associated with AIDS. Pablo Pérez (Argentina), the author and protagonist of the testimonial-like diary Un año sin amor, displays a contemplative attempt to comprehend his own personal struggle with AIDS on a day-by-day basis. True to the varied existence that it serves to textualize, the diary at times can be rather mundane and repetitive, as its author finds himself stuck in various ruts, often related to his deteriorating health. At other times, it creatively depicts the potential for rapidly shifting changes that AIDS causes in the lives of the individuals it infects. The reader is privy to the innermost thoughts and preoccupations of the author/protagonist, through which the solitude of his existence becomes abundantly clear. Despite occasional interactions with friends and countless anonymous sexual encounters, Pérez is alone, facing his disease by himself, gradually deteriorating without the presence of others, all the while wishing for a connection with another individual, but continually making choices that further alienate him from those around him.

I propose that this ambivalent, semi-internal state of exile in which Pérez's narrator ambles and struggles to exist can be titled "solitary separation" because there is an illusion that he continues to coexist and interact within his home environments. However, upon closer examination, the void in his everyday existence becomes apparent. It is as if there is an invisible barrier separating the protagonist from those around him, resulting in an ever-increasing solitude that characterizes his existence. As a result, he has withdrawn into himself, isolating from family and friends and primarily seeking anonymous interactions, but rarely divulging personal information or investing time and energy in the exterior world. He feels that the world is overwhelming, tiring, and alienating, and thus is motivated toward an inward shift in which he does not actually leave his environment.

This notion of solitary separation is reminiscent of similar theories regarding "internal exile," which literary critic Guillermina Rosenkrantz expounds upon as one of the forms of exile present in Manuel Puig's literary corpus, which she studies in detail in her work *El cuerpo indómito: Espacios del exilio en la literatura de Manuel Puig*. Some of the main traits inherent to an internal exile are self-censorship and alienation, both of which are seen to varying degrees in *Un año sin amor*. Critic Bettina L. Knapp, in her study of Jungian psychology and its relation to exile affirms that, according to Jung, exile can be exoteric, as mentioned in relation to radical isolation, or it can be "esoteric." This private exile "suggests a withdrawal on the part of individuals from the empirical realm and a desire or need to live predominantly in their inner world" (1). However, Amy Kaminsky reminds us that the notion of inner exile "necessarily remains a metaphor in one real sense. Exile is a removal in space as well as in spirit. It is a physical uprooting, an individual's removal from a familiar place to a new space that has, at least at the beginning, no recognizable coordinates" (10–11). It is this central characteristic, the physical location of the body, which on the most basic level will differentiate the radical isolationist narratives from Pérez's depiction of solitary separation and inner refuge.

"Elefante"

Of the three narratives to be discussed in this chapter, Nelson Mallach's "Elefante" (Argentina, 2000) examines the idea of space, home, and location more than any other. In this sense, it is the most overt example of a self-imposed exile in which one uproots oneself and leaves home, in this case, ostensibly to protect his family from discovering the truth of his existence: that he is a homosexual man slowly dying of AIDS. As the narrative progresses, it becomes obvious that each translocation is a further attempt to pull the blinders over his own eyes and avoid having to face his own corporeal reality. He intentionally averts his gaze from his body by first dislocating himself from familiar surroundings (and anyone who would notice his deteriorating self) and subsequently avoiding the reflection of that gaze during the vast portion of his travels.

This notion of the gaze and its depth that Jacques Lacan has imparted to critics through his conceptualization of its role in identity construction will resurface on multiple occasions throughout the story as Rodrigo struggles to form his new identity. Lacan has posited that the mirror stage is part of the normal development of an individual, occurring between ages six and eighteen months.[2] During that time, the child first catches a glimpse of him- or herself in a mirror and subsequently experiences conflicting emotions, which Linda S. Maier, in her analysis of mirror imagery in Onetti's *La vida breve*, succinctly summarizes as "anguish and intense rapture" in her application of Lacan's theories (228). The "intense rapture" that Maier notes is related to the narcissistic libido experienced by the subject, who is in awe of the ideal image reflected back and the perception of a unified body that appears there. The anguish derives from the separation between the individual and the reflected self, a gap that is eternally insurmountable. Throughout life, the individual continues to seek out others in whom she sees that idealized self mirrored and reflected back in their gaze. Although Lacan focuses on the early childhood period for the initial mirror stage, I would posit that this phase is duplicated for Rodrigo as he struggles to adapt to a new identity as an HIV-positive individual. In

2. *Écrits: A Selection.*

this sense, the radical isolation and subsequent reemergence experienced at the end, combined with the multiple mirrors and gazes that reflect back his changing self, serve as a second mirror phase for Rodrigo, one that will force him to abandon his old idealized vision of self and face the new reflection that is emerging.

The narrative of this transformation is circular, as it follows Rodrigo from the preparatory stages of his radical departure from life as he knows it, to his abrupt fleeing, silently without warning to friends or family, and to the moment he reappears, almost two years later, on the front steps of his family home. During his time away from home, Rodrigo wanders, seemingly without direction, from civilization to nature and back again, in what Guillermina Rosenkrantz identifies as one of the elements of exile: "dado que nos retrotrae a un punto de origen . . . pone en cuestionamiento nociones tales como las de identidad individual, cultural y nacional" [since it takes us back to a point of origin . . . it puts into question notions such as individual, cultural, and national identity] (14). Rodrigo's exilic journey surreptitiously traces some of the roots of Latin American civilization as he wanders into the Amazon and ponders a pilgrimage to Macchu Picchu.

Throughout the story, Rodrigo's physical location (and the subsequent spaces he *should* be filling) are related to the central theme he carries throughout his journey: "I can't forget," which is replayed over and over in his head (and his ears) on the one possession he kept from his previous life, a CD. Location is linked to body, which is linked to memory, which is linked to identity. By exiling himself from his original location and thus uprooting his body, Rodrigo tries in vain to disconnect himself from painful memories, thus avoiding the new HIV-positive identity that is his reality. The physical uprooting and the decision to go into exile begin with a process of ridding the self of all material possessions, thereby disconnecting himself from that which binds him to a particular existence. The reader is introduced to this initially anonymous protagonist as he is preparing to sell his clothes, books, and other domestic possessions, and plans to leave his music (except his disc player and one CD by Leonard Cohen) to his brother Fran. This unloading of belongings differs from an unloading by one who is simply preparing to move: Rodrigo is severing (almost) all ties to his past and thus stripping himself of the items that previously defined his interests, tastes, and hobbies. He is not planning on simply moving to another city or country to start anew; he is trying to obliterate his past existence, a process that begins with the purging of belongings and terminates with quitting his job and essentially bequeathing his cat to his brother in a departing letter to his mother and brother.

With the past effectively erased, Rodrigo launches into an unknown and uncertain future in a location undisclosed to his family and friends, but revealed to the reader: Bolivia and, eventually, portions of the Amazon. Despite attempts by friends, coworkers and family to learn of his plans, Rodrigo reveals nothing, saying that he is going to Europe or simply refusing to tell his mother, despite her requests to know why he has been acting so strangely lately. By severing his relationship with his immediate family, he is effectively shattering the reflective potential they held for his identity; without their presence, he has no one to gauge the transformation from the self "before" the journey (and presumably outwardly healthy) and "after." His true plans are never revealed, and his family does not know of his decision to leave until they are confronted with his final letter, which is somewhat akin to a suicide note and last will, comforting them with

> Voy a estar bien, o al menos mejor. Por favor no me busquen, igual ya no me van a poder encontrar. Mamá, esto es una decisión personal, pensá que hay madres en peores condiciones. Fran, te regalo los compactos. . . . Si no lo quieren cuidar a Gómez prefiero que lo envenenen antes de regalarlo. Yo sé Fran que vos me entendés, matalo tranquilo pero que no sufra y después enterralo junto a la foto que dejo en el escritorio. Dispongan del resto de las cosas como les parezca. Los quiero más que nunca.—Rodrigo

> [I am going to be fine, or at least better. Please don't look for me, since you won't be able to find me. Mom, this is a personal decision, think that there are mothers in worse conditions. Fran, I give you my CDs . . . If you don't want to take care of Gomez (the cat), I prefer that you poison him before giving him away. I know, Fran, that you understand me, kill him calmly so that he doesn't suffer and then bury him next to the picture I'm leaving on my desk. Do with the rest of the things as you see fit. I love you more than ever.—Rodrigo] (271)

This letter accentuates Rodrigo's desire to simply disappear. At the outset of his journey, he clearly wants to be "lost" and not found, shunning in advance any attempts by his family to help him face his health crisis. This initial wish can be contrasted at the end of the story with the fact that he does indeed return, but readers are left to surmise the degree to which the family becomes involved in his care. In fact, throughout the story, Rodrigo never verbally reveals his HIV-positive status to his family and acquaintances, or even to the reader. Instead, it is suggested through references to Rodrigo's clandestine homosexuality,[3] his relatively young age and the standard of health that generally accompanies such youth, and, finally, the progressively decaying body that seems to affront Rodrigo and evoke a painful reality every time he catches a glimpse of it in his reflection. The silence regarding his disease mirrors the shrouding of his physical location, both of which serve to hide his present reality from those around him and, as we slowly learn, ultimately from himself.

The voluntary physical dislocation that Rodrigo undergoes is compounded by the confusion and loss imposed on those left behind. Although he tries to function as if he were an island, he cannot ignore them. Rodrigo is obviously cognizant of the impact his absence will have on his mother above all, but he seems convinced that his departure will actually protect her from the unpleasantness of his true identity, including his closeted homosexuality and AIDS. This desire to protect both those left behind and the self by not revealing his location mimics the carefully guarded sites to which other exiles have fled, enshrouding their new existences in secrecy. Here, again, Rodrigo's absence is a manner of fleeing the prejudice and persecution that he will likely face once his disease announces itself in its various physical symptoms, as well as preventing his family from undergoing the shocking revelations associated with that identity. This cloistering of the truth initially provides the illusion of a solution to the dilemma that Rodrigo faces, but, as he learns in his nearly two years of self-imposed exile, he cannot hide from the truth of his identity and eventually must admit it to both himself and his family.

However, this confrontation with true identity is postponed by the radical isolation Rodrigo imposes on himself and the multiple locations he traverses. Mallach introduces, reinforces, and eventually fully reveals to the reader that, despite Rodrigo's best efforts to forget his past and identity, he cannot forget, a fact that is constantly replayed in Rodrigo's mind and spelled out to the reader in reference to the song that serves as a soundtrack not only to Rodrigo's adventure, but also to the text itself. As I mentioned above, when Rodrigo left home he rid himself of all possessions, less a CD by Leonard Cohen with the title track "I can't forget." Rodrigo himself suggests the two possible intonations of this phrase: "no puedo permitirme olvidar . . . , quiero olvidar pero no puedo" [I can't allow

---

3. This is made clear when Rodrigo blackmails an ex-lover, Guille, in an attempt to convince him to repay money Rodrigo needs for his travels. Rodrigo manipulates the secrecy of their homosexuality and affair, threatening to tell his mother who he is and reveal Guille's sexual orientation. This scheme provides the reader with a strong hint regarding Rodrigo's sexuality, something that is later confirmed through his near-sexual encounter with another man while in isolation.

myself to forget . . . , I want to forget but I can't] (274). As both Rodrigo and the reader learn, try as he may to use different environments to erase his memory and with it, the reality of his impending death, he simply cannot forget and cannot escape what awaits him, no matter how far he runs.

This does not mean, however, that he does not try. As he departs, he muses about this anthem of "I can't forget," reiterating his intention to leave the past behind and revealing a conscious attempt to forget, erase, discard, and disappear all that is connected to his previous identity and disease. Part and parcel to this new mission in life are a profound isolation and a high degree of anonymity, as Rodrigo consistently shuns meaningful contact with others, refuses to think about or communicate with those at home, and delves deeper and deeper into an environment that helps in this process of erasure and isolation, ultimately leaving civilization itself and ending up in the isolating land of the jungle.

Rodrigo's journey from his home and away from his country and the friends and family who inhabit it first lands him in Bolivia, where he is subjected to a very thorough and invasive cavity search on the border by the patrolmen who "hablan tal vez en quechua" [they speak perhaps in Quechua] and "no entienden mi nombre" [they don't understand my name] (272). This communication gap and the ensuing discomfort that arises from the strip search are simply the beginning of the subtle and overt layers of unease that Rodrigo will be subjecting himself to by virtue of his self-imposed isolation. McClennen reminds us that language is one of the central dialectics involved in the exile experience, whereby the individual encounters a new existence codified by a language that is often foreign, thus further accelerating the sense of isolation that those separated from home feel. In her studies of Hispanic literature that reflects various exile experiences, language is often portrayed as "both a source of power and pain" (3). This is particularly true for those whose writing was one of the motivating factors for their forced exodus from their homelands. It also applies to the individuals who use language and writing to come to terms with the meaning of exile.

However, the depiction of language barriers in "Elefante" is ironic for multiple reasons. First, Rodrigo has not been forcibly removed from his country for anything he has said or written, but rather has left to avoid the possible prejudice that would arise if his disease begins to reveal his HIV status and his homosexuality. In essence, AIDS, through its telltale signs in later stages, will begin to write itself on Rodrigo's body, thus betraying his silence and revealing his identity not through written or spoken language, but through the unique language of illness. This biological language will ultimately be the source of Rodrigo's pain, both literal (as his body succumbs to the many maladies associated with advanced-stage AIDS) and figurative (as Rodrigo endures the stares, questions, prejudices, and marginalizations of those who connect the code of his bodily language with its cultural significance).

Apart from the messages his body will ultimately send, the communication mix-up at the border is also ironic because it implies a larger degree of separation from his homeland than is the case. It is likely that Rodrigo is from Argentina: Mallach's own nationality is Argentine; the title of the collection in which this story was published (*Historia de un deseo: El erotismo homosexual en 28 relatos **argentinos** contemporaneous/ History of a desire: Homosexual eroticism in 28 contemporary Argentine stories* [emphasis mine]) refers to citizens of Argentina; and the first border crossing is into Bolivia, Argentina's direct neighbor to the north. We know that Rodrigo, being an Argentine, speaks Spanish (and presumably, based on his music selection, understands some English). Nevertheless, Bolivia, where Spanish is also spoken, among other indigenous languages, is immediately depicted as less civilized and more primitive because those guarding its borders do not understand the more cosmopolitan Spanish and function only in what Rodrigo assumes to be Quechua. The result is an immediate sense of dislocation for the protagonist and a journey that is no longer simply a departure from home, but also a jolting confrontation with a land that is immediately construed as foreign and different. Thus, the reader is informed that Rodrigo is no longer in his element and that he is bound to be thrust into situations that will further challenge his comfort level. His position still stands in stark contrast to those of political exiles who have chosen to leave the continent entirely and live in Europe or other areas, often where Spanish is not even spoken. As a result, even though Rodrigo is initially reminded of his new location through a language other than Spanish, he is able to function throughout the rest of his journey in his native tongue, thus giving him a potential tool to connect with others, if he so chooses.

This situation at the border also reminds us that Rodrigo did choose to exile himself from his own society owing to his fears about perceived reactions to his conditions. His comment when faced with the overzealous border agents highlights the distinctions between his exile and that facing thousands of other Argentines just a few decades ago: "Me doy cuenta que no quiero estar dos minutos más en ese lugar lleno de milicos" [I realize I don't want to spend two more minutes in that place full of soldiers] (272). This reference to "milicos" calls to mind the successive military dictatorships that ruled Argentina from 1976 to 1983 with cruel brutality, forcing thousands of Argentines to go into exile to preserve their own lives or those of their family and friends, all of whom were very much at risk. This distinction reminds us that although Rodrigo faces fears surrounding his illness and his sexual orientation, his exile is as much about fleeing from himself as it is about fleeing from social stigma and persecution.

What these actions do is raise a question that is similar to that asked by literary critic Karl Posso in his study on homosexuality and exile, *Artful Seduction: Homosexuality and the Problematics of Exile*. Posso astutely asks, in reference to the many homosexuals who felt the need to go into exile because of their sexual orientations: Did they leave society because it rejected them or because they chose to reject society? I believe the same could be asked of the protagonists in this chapter: Did they leave society and enter into voluntary exile because society shunned them or because they were shunning society? To be certain, the answer is very complex, but what Mallach's story illustrates is that there is often a combination of factors that contribute to the AIDS-induced exile that Rodrigo and the other protagonists studied in this chapter impose upon themselves. That does not mean, however, that the fear of persecution is not often a very strong factor in that drastic decision, but the sources of that persecution can be multiple. What we note in this story is that Rodrigo seems to be fleeing from himself as much as from society, internalizing a perceived persecutory atmosphere that never quite manifests itself anywhere other than in Rodrigo's own mind, but that nevertheless, is strong enough to prove to be a motivator for his flight.

This aversion to the possible repercussions of his true identity leads him to isolate himself even while in Bolivia. He does not reestablish a life in his new location, but rather embarks on a journey that ultimately leads him right back to his point of departure. No new community is created, but rather a continued distancing from all civilizations he confronts. In the early days of his radical isolation, Rodrigo does encounter various other people and has brief interactions with them while still managing not to reveal anything personal about himself. The first of these incidents occurs right after the one with the border patrolmen when Rodrigo buys some coca leaves from a young boy, using drugs as an additional level of escape. The boy requests a ride on Rodrigo's motorbike as payment. As Rodrigo and the boy travel further on the road to Potosí, the bike almost gets stuck in a river. It is at this juncture that he meets Sandra, a woman who needs a ride to Potosí. The inclusion of a name for this new individual suggests the possibility of an interpersonal interaction and the gradual relief of his profound isolation, but Rodrigo simply takes additional steps to avoid engaging her. When she wants to talk, he puts on his headphones. When she begins to ask questions, he asks that "por favor trate de no hablar porque me gusta el silencio" [please try to not talk because I like silence] (273). Again, by shunning "others," he is able to avoid the reflective gazes that they could offer him and the subsequent evidence of the body that is surely changing as the story progresses. Instead, Rodrigo remains blind to his own image, focusing his gaze outward on his adventures to avoid having to see himself. The less people know about him and the less he sees of himself in their gazes, the safer he seems to feel.

This level of safety is challenged by an additional encounter that he has in Potosí, where he meets an artist named Eduardo, who invites him to his studio. While there, Eduardo seduces Rodrigo by playing his favorite song, "I can't forget," on the piano. Rodrigo momentarily loses himself in the seduction. However, as if awakened from the trance of seduction, the mantra of "I can't forget," which is uttered by Eduardo in an effort to seduce, combined with the locked gazes and the potential reflection of self that could ensue, become for Rodrigo a reminder of that which he is trying to flee: AIDS. This memory rushes back to him like an apparition, evidently reminding him of his resolution for isolation and solitude, and therefore causing him to evade Eduardo's advances with an abruptness that reveals his utter fear of intimacy.

The moniker of his next destination, La Paz, reveals what Rodrigo is desperately seeking: peace with himself and his condition. Nonetheless, Rodrigo's departure and the transformative peace he hopes to find within it are elusive, particularly in the void that Rodrigo inhabits. None of the places he frequents represents the possibility of refuge, nor do they even merit description. Besides the names, the locales become as anonymous as Rodrigo. They are mere spaces in which he tries to disappear. Finding it impossible to disappear in the city, Rodrigo journeys into a more anonymous space—the Amazon.

The departure from civilization, a process that really began when he left his homeland, takes a more extreme turn as he sells his motorcycle (his last connection to city life) and buys a canoe with which to traverse the river. His ultimate goal is to eventually end in Macchu Picchu to mark the two-year "anniversary" of his disappearance from home. The purported journey to Macchu Picchu can certainly be read as a return to one of the origins of Latin American culture and spirituality, a solitary, peaceful place that offers a communion with nature and a presence that is much larger than Rodrigo. This site offers him the allure of being able to discard his problems in the face of such an impressive location so infused with meaning that it seemingly would have the power to dwarf his existence and the disturbances that have affected him.

As he navigates the river, he finds that the exit from the city seems to have benefited him. He seems to relish the solitude and the anonymity that accompanies it: "No hay nadie para preguntarme nada. Salvo los que viajan por el río pero ellos no me conocen de antes y no pueden notar las diferencias" [There is no one to ask me anything. Except for those who travel down the river, but they don't know me from before and can't notice the differences] (274). This quote reveals the external changes that have been befalling the protagonist throughout his isolation, but that have been largely withheld from the reader up until this point. More importantly, it further illustrates the complete absence of his image reflected anywhere in the text. By departing from society, fleeing those familiar to him, shunning all new relationships, and avoiding all potential reflections of self, Rodrigo has managed to avoid facing his emerging reality. He has postponed the mirror stage that he eventually will pass through on his way to constructing his new identity. As long as he avoids his reflection, he will never accept his new self. It is during this time on the river that both the reader and Rodrigo begin to envision the new image that has emerged. We slowly learn that AIDS is catching up with him and is making its appearance on his person. There are subtle references to "diarrea" (273) as well as a more revealing mention of his notable physical changes when Rodrigo see his reflection in the river. Still, without others to constantly monitor his changes, and, while shunning any sort of true self-reflection, Rodrigo initially avoids this new reality.

However, the river that offered the promise of solace and a fleeting peace eventually betrays him: "Pero este sitio extraño y ajeno acaba de traicionarme. Justamente el río que creía que me protegía, cuando tiraba de una línea que había picado, me mostró mi cuerpo" [But this strange and foreign place has just betrayed me. Precisely the river, which I thought protected me, when I pulled in a line that had a bite, showed me my body] (274). This betrayal—the revelation of the body—is the first moment when Rodrigo truly starts to face his new version of self. His experience calls to mind the myth of Narcissus. Here, Rodrigo experiences the polar opposite of Narcissus: this first encounter with a "mirror," as an initiation into a second mirror stage, evokes a sensation of betrayal and aversion rather than awe and longing. Rodrigo feels the urge to flee the reflection he sees in the river, thus initiating a further separation between the notion of "I" and "self." Although this confrontation with his visage is important in his new process of identity construction, it immediately becomes clear that he is not yet ready to accept it, but at the same time he can no longer deny that he is not the same individual, neither internally nor externally, who left Argentina less than two years ago. This confrontation with self causes him to deviate from his destination, returning briefly to La Paz where he struggles desperately to control the wild temperature fluctuations that his ill body is bestowing upon him. There he reencounters Sandra, the woman to whom he offered a ride awhile back. Upon seeing him she says that "es imposible que yo sea la misma persona" [it's impossible that you're the same person] because of his shocking physical changes (274). Thus, Rodrigo is forced once again to face the reflective surface and the new self that is being reflected in the gaze of others.

This seems to be the last straw, for without warning and with a similar abruptness as when he left home, Rodrigo returns home, completing the circularity that characterized his self-imposed isolation. It becomes clear that the multiple locations of self-imposed exile, while physically moving the body from place to place, only temporarily achieved the desired effect of turning the gaze outward and avoiding the reflection of the body which he tried to ignore and which, on the whole, was largely absent from the narrative. In the end, however, similarly to being unable to forget his health status, Rodrigo also cannot continue to be blind to his own deterioration and must finally reconnect his internal self with the body that represents him to the outside world.

This homecoming is a reckoning in which he must finally present himself to his family without the illusion that his healthy façade provided, and ultimately he must face his own death. As Rodrigo approaches the house, his brother Fran is visible through the window. After a while Fran peers through the window and sees Rodrigo, but, as Rodrigo notes, "no parece reconocerme, más bien se asusta" [doesn't seem to recognize me, rather he gets scared] (274–75). Fran's frightened gaze clearly discloses the altered body that Rodrigo has become. The reaction itself proves to be one of the more potent markers of the drastic changes that have occurred, particularly because Fran is the only mirroring entity that provides the reader with a sense of "before" and "after." Thus, with any vestiges of disguise now stripped away by his advanced stages of disease, Rodrigo finally confronts himself in the place that he tried so hard to flee, but where he has ultimately come to live out his last days, perhaps accepting the companionship of the family he avoided while in hiding. Unlike the river that surprised him with his reflection, this time Rodrigo seems prepared as he sees his visage reflected back in his home's window: "En el vidrio también estoy yo, una cara sólo de huesos. Me siento un elefante moribundo encontrando por fin el último lugar" [In the glass is also me, a face of only bones. I feel like a moribund elephant finally finding its last resting place] (275). Rather than fleeing from his reflection as he did in the river, Rodrigo advances toward it, much like the toddler confronting his image for the first time, with a mixture of anguish and awe. Rodrigo seems drawn toward that reflection as he nears his former home, each step forward becoming another step toward his new identity.

Notably, his mother, whom he was so concerned about protecting and from whom he intentionally withheld his secrets and his intention to flee, is never mentioned in this homecoming scene, thus leaving the reader (and Rodrigo himself) with a reminder of the turbulence that still awaits the protagonist. His ultimate fate, however, is broadcast to all in the last scene of the story: as he follows his brother's eyes and subtle smile, he sees the small cross marking the gravestone of the cat he left behind, the cat that apparently no one was willing or able to take care of and therefore was euthanized instead. While clearly demarcating the death that awaits Rodrigo, this final scene raises the question about the type of care Rodrigo will be able to receive in a household that kills cats instead of caring for them. Quite possibly he will once again be on his own to face the final days of his life, but presumably his absence has provided him with some of the tools to do so. It has clearly shown him that the notion of place is illusive, providing only as much refuge as one can provide for oneself.

Pecados mínimos

The interplay of place, home, disease, and family are also at work in Ricardo Prieto's play about AIDS,[4] *Pecados mínimos* (Uruguay 1993). This work differs in quite a few aspects from Mallach's rendering of AIDS, including the choice of genre (short story versus theater), the dates when the two works were composed (2000 vs. 1981[5])—and thus the perspective on AIDS that is represented in both. Despite these differences, which certainly contribute meaningful uniqueness to each narrative, the works share similar approaches to the notion of AIDS, even though they are separated by nearly two decades and a wealth of information regarding HIV transmission, protection, and progression. Interestingly enough, they both depict a form of radical isolation on the part of the protagonists in response to their own HIV-positive status. Furthermore, AIDS is portrayed as a direct route to death, with the possibility of living happily and healthily with AIDS (as

---

4. I will be analyzing the written text of this theatrical piece; it has been performed in Montevideo, Uruguay, but I have not seen those representations. According to Ricardo Prieto, the production did not garner critical praise when it was performed, something he attributes to the harsh reality that his work addresses (personal interview, June 1997).

5. Although the play was written in 1981 at the outset of the epidemic (personal interview with Ricardo Prieto, June 1997), the version referenced in this work was published as part of an anthology of Prieto's theatrical works in 1993.

many people indeed do in this current era) not even mentioned. This view is certainly understandable from the perspective of Prieto's 1981 play, written at the inception of the AIDS crisis when spotty information was available about the disease and it was generally accepted to be a death sentence. However, what Mallach's work has shown is how pervasive that belief has been, despite growing evidence that it is indeed possible to live a fulfilling life despite AIDS, particularly since the advent of antiretroviral drugs that effectively inhibit much of the progression of the disease.

In addition to the similar viewpoint that AIDS = death and that it is connected to societal and familial shame, Prieto's work also echoes Mallach's in the depiction of the complex interplay between the AIDS-inflicted male protagonist and his family, in this case, specifically the mother, Julia. While Mallach shows an attempt to separate the self from the family and the past and go into anonymous exile, Prieto depicts the exact opposite: his protagonist, Marcos, isolates himself in his family's home, cloistering himself from the outside world and living within the physical foundation of his life, his childhood home. This does not mean to suggest, however, that home equals comfort for Marcos, because he has turned his home into his own cell. Inside this cell, he has imprisoned his own mother and himself behind cement walls and iron locks while furiously working to precipitate his own demise through the construction of his own coffin and the planning of his own suicide (and, by association and proximity, his mother's murder). Marcos exhibits an extreme level of sadism toward his mother. I will examine that attitude in relation to the apocalyptic theme that runs through the work as well as the apparent attempt by Prieto to fully shock and scandalize his audience through such a raw depiction of what was then a new and terrifying epidemic.

The temporal organization of the play is such that the action focuses on the short period of time before "the end" for Marcos and Julia, a nonspecific amount of time that is composed of anxious conversations between mother and son. Julia desperately tries to convince Marcos to free her from her decade-long imprisonment, using a variety of tactics and approaches, but ultimately failing. She also responds to his growing anxiety and gradual revelations of the history and actuality of his condition by begging him to allow her to help, comfort, and accompany him in his anguishing battle. The crescendo of her pleas matches the manic fury of Marcos's unraveling as he nears the completion of his "project" and, thus, the end of his life. AIDS is given a larger-than-life position in the play as Prieto seemingly attempts to reveal the perils associated with this new threat to global health (ca. 1981, when the play was written). Severino Albuquerque, in *Tentative Transgressions: Homosexuality, AIDS and the*

Theater in Brazil, notes, "In many ways, all plays about AIDS show some degree of didacticism, regardless of authorial intent; even when a play was not meant to be a vehicle for teaching (or preaching), its depiction of living with HIV may come across as such" (123). Prieto's work contains an undercurrent of didacticism, as it seems to strive to reveal, very early on in the AIDS epidemic, not only some of the modes of transmission but also the threat the disease poses on a global level. Prieto himself sees AIDS as a topic that is "tremendamente dramático, con una historia oscura" [tremendously dramatic, with a dark history]. He chose to highlight this disease because "quería denunciarlo" [he wanted to denounce it], asserting that in Uruguay "la gente no tiene consciencia sobre SIDA; creen que es algo ajeno" [people don't have an awareness about AIDS; they believe it is something foreign].[6]

Recognizing that "lo que importa a la gente es lo práctico y realista" [what matters to people is the practical and realistic],[7] his dramatic representation of AIDS has some elements of what Albuquerque has labeled "The Neorealist Paradigm," which "identifies those theatrical representations of HIV and AIDS that most closely parallel the often grim realities of the condition for those who have had to confront the social and personal crisis triggered by the virus" (125). But it also strays into the symbolic realm, or "The "Neoexpressionist Paradigm"[8] that "is characterized," according to Albuquerque, "by a strong reliance on images and metaphors to express internal conflict as they conjure up the HIV and AIDS experience" (130). Most notably, the apocalyptic rhetoric identified by Susan Sontag is an undercurrent of the fatalistic vision presented by Prieto, as are the weakly symbolic references to AIDS as "Sr. Sida," a direct referent and personification of the illness that in later editions of the work was changed to a Sanskrit word to symbolize "el vacío total" [the complete

---

6. Personal interview, June 1997.

7. All direct quotes from Prieto regarding this work are from that same personal interview from June 1997 in Montevideo, Uruguay.

8. Albuquerque presents six different paradigms for categorizing the Brazilian theater depicting AIDS: 1) The Neorealist Paradigm, defined above; 2) The Neoexpressionist Paradigm, defined above; 3) the Collective Theater Paradigm, "Representations based on collective action to resist otherness" (138); 4) The Allegorical Paradigm, "Investigate meanings that tend to become apparent only with careful scrutiny" (145); 5) The Evocative Paradigm, "Plays in this category are laden with mental depictions and lyrical recollections of other places and times" (152); 6) The Postmodern Paradigm, "connected with a postmodern sensibility of ambiguity, instability, and rupture" (155).

They are the only categories that I have encountered in my research that relate directly to theater from Latin America, specifically Brazil. As such, I believe they warrant a brief description, taken from Albuquerque's own descriptions. Each is elaborated upon in his study, with examples to illustrate the different tendencies.

void], which Prieto believes made the subsequent versions of this work stronger and enabled his audience to envision all the bad in the world, not just AIDS.

The original version is already very dark and paints a bleak picture of AIDS and its aftermath. The suggestion is that it is not possible to live with AIDS, but rather that one must surrender to the impending death that looms. In this case, Marcos is the one afflicted, and his strategy of complete isolation results in an imprisonment more than a version of exile, for he stays not only within his own country and city, but also within his own home. His rage toward his condition is so extreme that he loathes the fact that he is alive and has been born into an age in which AIDS is a threat. Instead of reconciling this situation within himself, he has sadistically chosen to take out that rage on his mother, seemingly rebelling against the fact that she gave him life in such a hate-filled world (in his view) by imposing on her the type of life and death that he sees fit. He has gone to great extremes to completely withdraw himself and his mother from society and the world. In fact, as Prieto has depicted it, it is impossible for the spectator to find any sort of points of reference or orientation with the outside world. The sense of claustrophobia is strong as the two characters are confined (by Marcos's choice) to two rooms in a nondescript house. All windows and doors have been boarded up and locked, so there is neither natural light in the scene nor ambient sounds or visions interjecting their presence and the suggestion of civilization. Instead, the focus is on Julia, who lies imprisoned in her own bed, in the house that she and her deceased husband carefully constructed and maintained, and in which they tried to raise their son Marcos, with love and affection. Marcos is never seen (except for his hand), but his presence is felt through his voice, as he responds to Julia's pleas, and his repetitive hammering as he ominously crafts his own coffin. In essence, he is present through disparate parts of the body (the hand and his voice), but absent as a whole individual. This dichotomy of presence–absence is also an apt depiction of his location: although he is still surreptitiously present in society by virtue of the fact that he is alive (although living as a mere fraction of what it means to live), he is truly absent from all meaningful interactions, having removed himself from the world and sequestered himself in his home.

Julia, in her physical suffering and emotional anguish, becomes a mirror for the spectator, reflecting the torturous physical decay and mental anguish that Marcos feels but has opted to act out, viciously, on her. Marcos envisions AIDS as his own tormenter, causing endless suffering and isolation. His role of victim to the tyrant of AIDS is subverted as he sadistically wreaks havoc on his own mother, converting her into his prisoner and subjecting her to isolation, tied to her own bed, forced to endure fetid conditions, and withheld food and water at whim. While Marcos's decaying body is mentioned through his own discourse, Julia's rotting flesh is displayed to the audience. One is caused by AIDS, the other by sadistic neglect. While Marcos's body is frail and thin, Julia's starving and parched shell is projected for all to see. Again, Marco has succumbed to AIDS-related opportunistic infections, while Julia is starving because her son refuses to feed her. While Marcos's voice and his fervent actions betray his psychological torture, the audience reads it on Julia's face and sees it in the tears she weeps for the son who continues to punish her for trying to help and love him. Marcos's absence is heard in his voice and felt in the reverberations of his hammer, and it is seen, most dramatically, reflected in the pain he has inflicted on his mother, using her as an extension of his own destruction.

Not only does Julia serve as a potent visual image of Marcos's pain, but her dialogue with him reveals the history of Marcos's illness, the systematic steps he has taken to enter into the radical isolation in which he currently lives, the way in which he has acted his desperation out on his mother, and the drastic way in which he has tried to alienate all those who could have provided help. That dialogue begins with Julia complaining to Marcos about his incessant hammering, but it soon reveals all of the intricacies that have led up to this current moment. Although the revelations are uncovered in nonchronological order, taken together, they offer a more comprehensive sketch of Marcos's particular situation and a general commentary on the state of AIDS in 1981, when this play was written.

Set at the inception of the worldwide AIDS epidemic, Prieto's work and the particular history of disease that is offered to explain Marcos's situation show some reliance on predominant metaphors, particularly the notion of the apocalypse, but they also reveal a marked break from the stereotypical representation of PWAs. Marcos slowly launches into his personal narrative, recounting his happy childhood in a wonderful home with loving parents. This personal story immediately shatters the perception that those infected with AIDS are somehow "others," outside of the realm of normalcy, relegated to the margins. Instead, this man came from a traditional home and was supported by loving parents who encouraged him to follow his dreams, a fact that makes the despicable treatment of his mother all the more incomprehensible. Again, Prieto is more shocking in the "normalcy" of his representation of Marcos's history. Several years ago, Marcos had fallen in love with a beautiful woman, who broke his heart by sleeping with his best friend. He is not one of the "4 Hs" (homosexuals, heroin addicts, hemophiliacs, and Haitians) referred to by Sander Gilman. Rather, Marcos is a heterosexual male from a seemingly middle-class upbringing, a far cry from the stereotypical people who were regarded as the only ones struck by the virus.

After having his heart broken, Marcos decides to study medicine to help others, but instead discovers within the walls of the hospital and the world of health care unending human suffering. Stripped of the protection of his home, having already lost his father and been betrayed by his lover and friend, Marcos has a hard time facing the harsh realities of the world. In response to the disillusionment and heartbreak he encounters, Marcos withdraws from meaningful pursuits and instead "se dedicó al placer. Se acostaba con todas las mujeres. Las usaba un instante y salía a la búsqueda de otras, acosado por un incontrolable deseo de goce y olvido" [he dedicated himself to pleasure. He slept with all of the women. He used them for an instant and left searching for others, accosted by an uncontrollable desire for pleasure and to forget] (177–78). In this world of indiscriminate sex, albeit (and notably for the time period) heterosexual sex, "Un día, sin saber cómo ni dónde, el señor Sida se apoderó de él" [One day, without knowing how nor where, Mr. AIDS took control of him] (178). Prieto thus strips away all pretense about the supposed "homosexual cancer" of the 1980s that was euphemistically used to refer to AIDS, and instead presents the heart of the issue of risk to his early audiences: sexual promiscuity increases the risk of contracting HIV and eventually succumbing to AIDS, regardless of sexual orientation, gender, race, nationality, or class. This reality was a harsh one, particularly for Marcos himself, who was overcome by shame and indignity and chose to flee society and sequester himself and his mother in their home rather than continuing to live in the world around him.

It is important to note the way that blame is situated in this story. Although Marcos admits to being overtly promiscuous, acting with little regard for the health or emotions of his sexual partners, he places the blame for his behavior and the subsequent virus that he contracted on the one woman whom he loved and who left him. Instead of accepting responsibility for his own behavior, Marcos blames the woman, heaping all of the ill that he has experienced on her decision to leave him. This portrayal of woman = evil is subsequently reflected in the overtly misogynistic treatment that Marcos has consciously decided to act out on his own mother. It appears that in order to exact revenge on the woman who left him, Marcos indiscriminately uses any woman he can find. When his actions result in his contraction of HIV, he hones his vengeful actions in on his mother, the one he blames for bringing him into the world in the first place. In both cases, the women are Marcos's scapegoats, his girlfriend being blamed for causing Marcos to abandon his career and eventually contract HIV, and his mother serving as the unwitting recipient of his overwhelming anger and guilt. What is also interesting is the reference to the father in this work. Julia refers to him once, when she notes that Marcos never mentions his father and has destroyed all physical reminders of him. Interestingly, Marcos enacted his rage only on his father's possessions and not on the man while he was alive. On the contrary, the sort of destruction that Marcos saw fit for his father's items has been amplified as he acts to destroy a real person, his own mother. In essence, he symbolically destroys the male figure in his life while physically destroying the female. The escalation of violence and its direction toward the only female present in his life suggests a targeted revenge for the perceived injustice caused to him by the only other female he loved: his ex-girlfriend.

This gender dichotomy is also present in the depiction of AIDS itself. It is first referred to as "él/he." While this reference is logical given the fact that the noun "sida" in Spanish is a masculine noun, Prieto augments its signification by personifying the disease, particularly by representing it as an all-powerful man capable of destroying the world. Through the use of this moniker, Prieto seems to be suggesting that it is more than simply a virus that invades bodies; rather, it is a being capable of traversing the globe and wreaking destruction in its path: "Tiene todas las nacionalidades. Y se llama Sida" [It is every nationality. And it's called AIDS]; "Es más que inteligente: es incomprensible, abismal" [It is more than intelligent: it is incomprehensible, abysmal]; "Es más poderoso que los estados" [It is more powerful than the states]; "Aterroriza al mundo" [It terrorizes the world]; "Es bastante joven" [It is rather young] (174–75). According to Marcos, in light of this new global menace, "por culpa de él vamos a desaparecer todos" [because of him we are all going to disappear] (174).

The omnipotence granted to the disease and the masculine signifier attached to it present the image of a patriarch capable of controlling, and ultimately destroying, everyone. The underlying tone is one of reverence, much like the silent refusal to denigrate the memory of the father, while willfully destroying the mother. Instead of fighting the father figure (both the literal one and the disease that masquerades as a patriarch), Marcos has chosen instead to exploit those deemed weaker than he (namely, his mother), thus exacerbating the destructive potential of the virus by creating a chain of annihilation.

The fact that Prieto has chosen to situate Julia as the central focal point in his work (and the production of it) merits further discussion. As was previously mentioned, Prieto deliberately wrote and produced this play to reveal a disease that had not yet entered into the public consciousness.

He stated that the piece was his attempt to denounce the disease and force people to open their eyes to what was then a new epidemic. According to Martin Esslin, theater critic and author of *An Anatomy of Drama*, theater, as an institution, "will inevitably be an instrument of social innovation" because it is "subversive of the status quo" (104). In this sense, Prieto's decision to use this medium to challenge society's views of AIDS follows a long tradition of dramatists who have tackled social problems vis-à-vis their productions. Esslin cautions, however, against making that message too explicit because "what matters is the posing of the problem in a way which will compel the audience to think for themselves, rather than drumming some message into their heads" (99). This is one of the problems with Prieto's presentation of his message: it is devoid of all subtlety and is akin to hitting his audience over the head with the hammer that Marcos incessantly uses to construct his coffin. We can examine this approach in light of the role of the audience in drama.

While I have been analyzing the text as a piece of literature, we cannot forget that this work was indeed performed, meaning that it came alive when enacted before a real audience. Esslin reminds us that drama is a collective experience, with the spectators reacting not only to the action on stage, but also to the responses of other members of the audience (23–25). Part of this process is the fact that the "spectator is made to experience what the character on the stage undergoes. And he will very soon be able to judge whether that experience feels right" (24). With whom do the spectators identify in Prieto's work? Although the play is about AIDS' destructive potential, it is nearly impossible to identify with Marcos for multiple reasons. First, he is never seen, but is only represented through a hand, a voice, and his continual hammering. Second, and I believe more important, he is so completely sadistic and perverse in his treatment of his mother that identifying with him becomes akin to empathizing with a sociopath. As a result, Julia becomes the focus of both visual attention and empathy. However, referring to Esslin's quote, does this identification "feel right"? In other words, can the audience members envision themselves in her role and then allow Prieto to navigate them to his final message? I would argue that what Julia is made to endure is so repulsive that it prevents spectators from envisioning themselves in her place. Perhaps this is one of the reasons that, according to Prieto, the play was not successful when performed. An additional cause could stem from the lack of catharsis in the play.

Traditionally, once the playwright has captured the audience's attention and established an empathic connection with one or more of the characters, "in drama the aim is an enhanced level of consciousness, a memorable insight into the nature of existence, a renewal of strength in the individual to face the world. In dramatic terms: catharsis" (28). This is where Prieto's work deviates from dramatic convention: although it is a tragedy, it fails to provide a cathartic release at the end. There is neither resolution nor insight into the human experience. Instead, the effect is shocking and scandalous rather than eye-opening and thought-provoking. Rather than focusing the portrayal on the individual actually affected by AIDS and offering insight into his condition and possibly enlightening the audience about AIDS, Prieto's work instead propagates the notion of AIDS as apocalypse, showing the destruction of not only the individual, but those surrounding him.

This vision of the virus is entirely negative, suggesting that the end of humanity is fast approaching and therefore inciting the sort of paranoid isolationism that Marcos embarks upon by completely shuttering the house with himself and his mother in it. This fatalistic mindset calls to mind what Sontag has signaled as one of the principal metaphors operating in AIDS narratives: the apocalyptic rhetoric and the military metaphors that often go with it (175–76). Sontag illustrates that the disease "obliges people to think of sex as having the direst consequence: suicide, or murder. AIDS reveals all but long term monogamous sex as promiscuous" (160–61). This notion of sex = suicide can be capitulated to a global scale and thus suggests an end-of-mankind type of scenario if the virus is left to propagate unchecked. It is within this paranoid realm that Marcos dwells, ultimately forsaking society itself to prevent further infiltration of "Sr. Sida" into his and his mother's lives. In doing so, he takes elaborate steps to physically separate them from their surroundings as well as emotionally and psychologically isolating them from any possible sources of assistance or redemption.

The physical space that is Marcos's self-imposed exile from the outside world is in actuality an amalgam of multiple layers of isolation and separation from others. The outside world does not exist as a physical entity in this play. It is rendered only through the memories that Marcos shares regarding his failed love affair, multiple sexual exploits, and disheartening career that he has rejected. Because of this nameless, faceless representation of society, Prieto's work becomes more global in its depictions of suffering because it is unleashed from particular markers of nation that would alter its reception. In fact, he has created a work in which the protagonists attempt to survive within a sort of void that is cut off from the surrounding community, society, city, state, nation, and world. Marcos's world is composed of the four walls of his parents' home, the doors and windows shuttered to prevent the infiltration by any outside factors.

Even within the walls of his family home, Marcos insists on creating increasingly smaller spaces in which he forces his mother and himself to exist. This ever-shrinking ambient becomes akin to Russian dolls, with each successive doll representing yet another layer of self-cloistering that Marcos undertakes. One of those chambers becomes his mother's cell, in which he forces her to live, bound to her bed and secured behind locked doors. For Julia, the space of her existence has shrunk drastically: while she once was a citizen of her community and could come and go freely from her own home, she has become a prisoner not only in her home, but in her bedroom, in her bed, and, because of the heightened accentuation of her bodily functions because of Marcos's neglect of them, her own body. Julia's imprisonment is situated precisely in the once-healthy body that is now forced, by her own son's cruel insistence, to endure hunger and thirst; physical, emotional, and sensory deprivation; and the pure filth that results from neglect and the inability to care for herself. Marcos has forced her to become a prisoner of herself, a prisoner to her body's functions and malfunctions, thus obligating her to experience some of the physical degradation that AIDS has wrought on him. With his agency regarding his own health status rapidly diminishing, he instead exerts control over Julia not only through the physical restraints, but also through the sadistic rationing of corporeal and psychological needs, deciding on a whim when and how much he will provide to fulfill her needs.

In addition to the torturous chamber in which Marcos has obligated his mother to exist, he continues to whittle away at the remaining space in the home, forcing himself into smaller and more insulated pockets in which to bide his remaining time. Part of that process consists of destroying all remnants of familial ancestry, particularly any vestiges of his late father. With these acts and omissions, Marcos alters the meaning of home, extracting from it the connection to people who represented a happier time in his life. By eradicating his father's memory, he is attempting to banish the possibility of being judged by a father he respected and loved, choosing instead to obliterate all ties to that figure and push further into the self-made void that is epitomized by the coffin he is constructing for himself.

This last physical space, obviously the most confining of all, is precisely the size of his body, allowing for no outside influence whatsoever. It is also, quite clearly, a harbinger of the fate that awaits him, as he finally acknowledges that "Estoy muy enfermo. Todo mi cuerpo está lleno de chancros y llagas y hasta un estornudo me podría matar . . . Soy víctima de una enfermedad espantosa" [I am very sick. My whole body is full of lesions and sores and even a sneeze could kill me . . . I am the victim of a scary disease] (178). The coffin is the most potent visual symbol of death and also represents the most radical departure possible from the life and environment in which Marcos previously existed. Marcos's continual construction of this final confining, isolating box is both a visual and an auditory reminder that his exile from the world will soon reach an irreversible point as he prepares to depart from life and Earth itself. As the play nears its final scene, Marcos informs his mother that he has taken the final step toward death and complete isolation, acknowledging, "Ya estoy acostado en el ataúd" [I am already lying in the coffin] (178). This penultimate act is the capstone to many deliberate steps to shun any and all offers of help, not least of which was from his own mother, despite the inhumane way he treated her.

In this sense, the extreme separation that Marcos undertakes is a physical extraction of his body from the social community, and when that body is subsequently enclosed in successive sarcophagi, it is also a psychological exile from all possible outlets of assistance. When Marcos is betrayed by his lover, he turns instead to anonymous encounters with nameless, faceless women whose only function is to provide corporeal pleasure in the most anonymous sense possible. With each successive sexual escapade, Marcos further cuts himself off from the possibility of kindling a connection with another woman. Parallel to this social withdrawal, Marcos also shuns the professional world that once held so much promise to him: the hospital and medical establishment. Instead of delving into the positive aspects of curative medicine, Marcos is repulsed by what he interprets as overwhelming evidence of the cruelty of mankind. This loathing of decay and disease provides an important clue for his subsequent departure from society when he himself falls ill with AIDS. He can tolerate neither the disintegration associated with illness nor the ominous aura surrounding it. Instead of viewing the medical establishment as an institution capable of providing hope and healing in the face of sickness, he flees the one place that perhaps could have provided him with some reprieve when his symptoms became overwhelming.

This refusal to seek help, combined with the progressively isolating tendencies that Marcos exhibits, come to a head in his interactions with Julia. He ostensibly fled medicine because he could not tolerate the evidence of the cruelty of humankind. However, he has become emblematic of that cruelty, particularly since his wrath is directed at the one person who has absolutely refused to shun him. Despite the horrors he has inflicted upon her, Julia continually makes efforts to connect with Marcos both physically and emotionally with the hopes of saving him from himself. Her attempts come across as those of a desperate woman deprived of any sort of human contact. She yearns to simply gaze at exactly the thing that Marcos is working so fastidiously to destroy—his entire body and self, as opposed to the (apparently unblemished) hands that have come to represent his entirety as he passes meager amounts of food and water through the window. Despite this torturous existence, she implores him to release her.

Her earnestness and forgiveness in light of his extreme sadistic cruelty make her situation even more difficult for the spectator to tolerate. This shocking juxtaposition of malice in the face of the offer of clemency further contributes to the repulsive effect of the work. Despite Prieto's stated intention of revealing an accurate view of AIDS to his audience, what he has instead accomplished is such a drastically fatalistic vision of the illness and a wholly abhorrent depiction of an AIDS-affected person that it makes it all but impossible to sympathize and identify with Marcos. All of his struggles and personal pain pale in comparison to what he has inflicted on his mother. There is no catharsis at the end of this work; the destruction Marcos chooses fails to resolve the dilemma he faces. Instead, the summative effect is one of cruelty, injustice, and gloom.

This tone and Julia's insistence on forgiveness despite his perverse treatment of her also become part of the apocalyptic discourse in this work. On the one hand, AIDS is depicted as a sign of the end of the world from which no one will be able to escape. Pessimism and fear reign. However, one also notes a vague reference to the religious element of the apocalypse and the belief in salvation. Julia embodies this hope when she tells Marcos that "te da asco mi amor porque me mutilaste y sigo amándote. Te asustan mi devoción y mi paciencia" [My love disgusts you because you mutilated me and I keep loving you. My devotion and patience scare you] (176). This desire to help and save her son, in the face of extreme personal duress and regardless of his self-proclaimed "pecados" [sins], his current physical condition, or his sadistic depravity, projects Julia into a God-like figure, one capable of ultimate sacrifice and forgiveness for her son, despite his sin. Significantly, Marcos has also rejected God and religion, bemoaning that "Dios nunca me escucha" [God never listens to me] (169). The one who does listen, however, is his mother, despite the fact that in doing so, she will end up paying the ultimate price for Marcos's embedded guilt and perceived sins.

Like all other avenues for help, Marcos slams the door in the face of his mother (quite literally), instead resigning himself to the belief that "Las cosas siempre nos 'suceden.' Nadie es capaz de nada" [Things always 'happen' to us. No one is capable of anything] (171), a belief that his mother vehemently attacks, urging him to see that "Somos capaces de luchar y de crear" [We are capable of fighting and creating] (170).

Undeterred, he continues on his annihilative quest, insisting that extreme isolation is his attempt to protect his mother from the world and the horrendous evils in it. His vision of salvation in the form of drastic exile has so warped him that he insists to his mother that "te até para que no sufrieras. No podrías soportar lo que ocurre por culpa de Él" [I tied you up so that you wouldn't suffer. You couldn't tolerate what is happening because of Him (AIDS)] (174). Again, Marcos is projecting his own rage and fear onto his mother, forcing her to experience the terror that he himself has internalized. According to this distorted logic, the safest way to counter the horror of AIDS and its destructive progression is to completely avoid it, sequestering the self so absolutely as to lose all connection to people, place, and time. In this way, Marcos extricates himself from society and carries out an exile not from a particular city, state, or country, but from life itself. This particular exile is fully realized when, at the end of the play and firmly locked away in his self-constructed coffin, Marcos welcomes the first outsider to have crossed the threshold to their home in ages: "La Señora Bomba" [Mrs. Bomb] (179), achieving complete annihilation of self, family, and home when he blows up the home and those in it.

Un año sin amor

While Prieto's explosive work clearly depicts the fatalistic attitudes surrounding HIV and AIDS at its inception in the early 1980s, it offers little hope for the future and no suggestions on how to live while being HIV-positive. Such fatalism is understandable given the incomplete level of understanding of the virus at that early stage and the lack of adequate medicines or treatments to combat it, but it begs further exploration, particularly as medical and social advancements in understanding have begun to change perceptions surrounding AIDS. Ever since the advent of anti-retroviral drugs in 1996, the possibility of survival with HIV has risen dramatically for those with access to these drugs, for example, AZT. The (un)availability of the drugs is crucial, particularly in underdeveloped areas of the world where poverty and the sheer volume of AIDS patients have severely limited the numbers of infected individuals who are able to benefit from this medical advancement. Still, it has become clear since AZT first appeared that "El SIDA dejó de ser una enfermedad necesariamente mortal" [AIDS stopped being a necessarily fatal illness] (R. Jacoby 10). I believe the emphasis should be on "necesariamente" because of the myriad factors that can prevent patients from obtaining the drugs, dissuade them from using them, or interfere with their effectiveness. Furthermore,

AIDS is still not a curable disease, and many people still succumb to it every year, despite these advancements. However, research and personal testimonies have shown that for many who do have the resources and fortitude to adhere to an antiretroviral regimen, it often does slow or halt the progression of the virus and can lead to a relatively "normal," healthy existence, despite the presence of the virus.

It is at this critical juncture that Pablo Pérez's diary of AIDS situates itself. Written from February 17, 1996, to the dawn of 1997, Pérez's work chronicles his personal struggles not only with the physical decay resultant from AIDS, but also with the concurrent emotional isolation in which he finds himself. At the inception of his project, "no podía imaginar el *happy ending*" [he couldn't imagine the *happy ending*] (R. Jacoby 10), but a slow transformation begins to occur near the end of the year as Pérez finally chooses to take some of the new medicines available to treat his condition. While the diary has far from a "happy ending" and is not naïve enough to suggest that everything that ailed Pablo, both physically and mentally, has been resolved, it does relate a critical transformation in both realms of Pablo's sense of self.

However, before this important alteration in outlook, much of the text is underlined with the solitary separation that Pablo endures, despite the friendships he struggles to maintain and the sexual encounters he frequently engages in. It is as if a barrier exists between Pablo and the world, subjecting him to a separation that he bemoans, but often exacerbates through the decisions he makes. Even though he still resides in his apartment, attends his classes, shows up for work, and sometimes interacts with family and friends, there is a hollowness to all of those interactions as Pablo increasingly feels alienated by his body's deterioration and is swallowed up by the loneliness and depression that accompany it. His diary is an intimate, almost daily reflection upon that contradictory state of being, and it provides the reader a glimpse into one individual's personal struggle with his own identity and how that identity is being rapidly eroded and shifted because of the progression of the disease that ravages his body. AIDS is ever-present in the narrative, particularly as it begins to influence the ways in which Pablo interacts with others, views himself, and, ultimately, forges new alliances.

The version of isolation that Pablo inhabits is one that tends toward the inner exile referenced at the beginning of this chapter, which can be composed of "autocensura" [self-censorship] and "alienación" [alienation] (Rosenkrantz 10), as well as exhibiting a "desire or need to live predominantly in their inner world" (Knapp 1). Pablo's separation is drastically different from those exhibited by Mallach's and Prieto's protagonists because

Pablo still participates to some degree in society and continues to physically reside in his native country, occupying the spaces that configure his existence in Buenos Aires, Argentina. Nevertheless, Pablo is unable to successfully negotiate the private and public spheres and still manage his illness. AIDS and the havoc it wreaks on his body take center stage, and the ensuing battle causes him to become enveloped in the physical and mental struggles with AIDS, thus preventing him from fully participating in life. As a result, he is often forced to convalesce for extended periods of time at home, thus feeling alienated and withdrawn from family and friends who remain distant from his life. Consequently, his isolation and loneliness grow, as does his anxiety about the situation. This isolation and loneliness, combined with the narrative project of documenting his battle with AIDS, heightens his awareness of the physical entrapment he experiences because of his symptoms and, as a result, causes his feeling of detachment to grow. This vicious cycle continues as different symptoms emerge and insulation grows, causing a solitary separation to emerge from a life that on the surface and without the insight provided by this diary appears more or less "normal."

Pablo's inner exile is caused by the excessive corporeal signification forced into his consciousness by the persistent ailments that assail him and that, as a result, compel him to remain in self-imposed quarantine because of either the fear of contagion or the effects of exhaustion. The insulating effect of this heightened awareness of the body is exacerbated by the narrative technique that Pérez employs: a singular focus on his corporeal realities that effectively thrusts to the forefront the continual effects that AIDS has on his daily existence, preventing him from envisioning himself as separate from his disease. This convergence of identities (Pablo-the-writer-friend-son-brother-student-teacher *plus* Pablo-the-HIV-positive person) ironically results in a reduced sense of identity and self, rather than a more complete selfhood. As a result, Pablo spends much of the year floundering beneath the burden of his oversignified body and its effect on his life, preventing him from connecting with others in any meaningful way and causing a heightened sense of solitude and isolation.

The aforementioned conundrum of Pablo's existence is an example of the extrasignification that certain bodies can acquire because of sexual orientation, gender, or, I would add, certain diseases (among other markers of identity or "otherness"). According to Ricardo Llamas, "algunas personas son más cuerpo que otras" [some people are more body than others] and oftentimes "Las categorías humanas en exceso encarnadas coinciden a menudo con sectores sociales discriminados, explotados, y oprimidos [Excessively embodied human categories often coincide with discriminated, exploited, and oppressed social sectors] (153). Using Llamas's theory as a prism through which to view the different treatment of individuals within society, we realize that different characteristics often come to carry additional significance, effectively supplanting the unique qualities of the individual, and instead overshadowing their existence with the oversignified trait.

Llamas has studied the situation of the homosexual body in particular, and he focuses his discussion on the current age of AIDS and its compounding effect on the reduction of the gay male to a "cuerpo homosexual" [homosexual body]. We have seen a similar tendency in society to reference people by their race or nationality (among other traits) not in an individual sense, but with the inherent intention of creating an oversignified body connected to a vague category ("gay," "straight," "black," "white"), effectively erasing individual characteristics. This effect is multiplied when one adds AIDS to the picture, reducing the homosexual male to not just a body, but a (often aberrantly) sexualized body. The marker "AIDS" overshadows all other elements of the body, ultimately being thrust into the forefront as the principal marker of identity. The grave consequences of this myopic vision are that "ser sobre todo cuerpo significa dejar de ser otras cosas; abandonar la posibilidad de existencia en esferas distintas de la material" [Being a body above all else means ceasing to be other things; abandoning the possibility of existing is spheres that are distinct from the material one] (154). In effect, by overemphasizing the body and reducing the entire person to this one element, one creates a split between the body and the other elements of the individual, including the mind and soul.

Llamas's argument is compelling, particularly when we extend it and examine more closely the specific situation of the HIV-positive gay male. At this point, Llamas's analysis stops short of giving a more detailed view of this fusion of two primary instigating factors often used by society to essentialize the individuals who live those identities. Pérez's account fleshes out one reality of such an individual, shifting the focus from sexual orientation and centering his reflection precisely on AIDS itself and the new meaning with which it has imbued his body. I will show how Pablo himself is guilty of overemphasizing that ill body to the point of overshadowing and nearly erasing other markers of his own identity, essentially writing a self-portrait that, if converted into images, would contain chancres, lesions, and infections alternating with the quintessential images of anonymous homosexual sex: the erect penis and the anus awaiting penetration. This is the Pablo Pérez that is drawn with the author's own pen; he has reduced himself to two alternating beings: a near-invalid succumbing to AIDS and an overly sexualized gay male cruising in search of anonymous sexual encounters to try to alleviate the loneliness of his existence. As a result of these two connecting selves, Pérez lacks any form of self-actualization, exists without meaningful human interaction, and consequently suffers from a great deal of anxiety, loneliness, and feelings of isolation. The exile he inhabits is one that is constructed by and lived within the physical body that has come to overshadow all other aspects of the protagonist's life, preventing him from maintaining meaningful connections with many aspects of the external world.

The vehicle by which the body comes to create the exile-like situation in which Pérez lives is his own writing and the process of using the body as the fountain of inspiration for his diary. The text he has produced has come as much as (if not more than) from his body as it has from his mind and soul. This complete commitment to the text, on all levels of being, is reminiscent of the process of "escribir con el cuerpo"[9] that Luisa Valenzuela expounded and encouraged in her now famous article of the same title. Although Pérez's writing does not strictly adhere to Valenzuela's edict to become fully committed to the text as a way to become socially involved, I believe that her notion of "writing with the body" offers some useful tenets for analyzing Pérez's literary project. As I see it, the process on an individual level (as opposed to the more socially engaged writing Valenzuela encourages) involves a full commitment to the act of writing and the involvement of all parts of the individual, including the oft-omitted corporeal dimension. It recognizes that the writer is a complete individual who often cannot and, according to Valenzuela, should not disconnect the distinct components of selfhood to engage in a process that was once thought to be wholly mental.

One aspect of this strategy that was not addressed fully by Valenzuela, however, is the personal effect of this type of writing, particularly the negative outcomes that could befall the writer. Valenzuela's vision is predomi-

---

9. Hélene Cixous has also expounded the notion of writing with the body in "The Laugh of the Medusa," as a way for female writers to resist and deconstruct the phallocentric symbolic order. While her theories are much more detailed than I will elaborate here, her primary focus is on "l'écriture feminine" and the connection between the female body and the texts that the female writer produces with and through her body. For the purposes of the analysis of Pérez's writing, we can certainly see hints of this intimate link between body and writing, although, and quite significantly, it is being produced by a man. The writing itself, though not done directly with his phallus, most certainly is directly related to the phallus and its sexual exploits in the age of AIDS. As such, it directly contradicts the writing proposed by Cixous; nevertheless, the notion of writing with the body, as theorized by both Cixous and Luisa Valenzuela, can provide us with a way to examine Pérez's intimate portrayal of his struggles with AIDS, since the epidemic in effect caused him to be reduced to a body, and at least temporarily, obfuscated all other elements of his being.

nantly positive, and for her, this act has allowed her to merge her mental prowess with her physical experiences, uniting them in the common goal of writing, thus fully engaging herself (and, with luck, her reader) in the texts she produces. What happens, though, when the text that the body suggests overtakes the one produced by the mind? Is this corporeal text beneficial if it lacks the full participation of the intellect or, worse, if it stifles and depresses the mental faculties in the process?

These are the issues that arise in *Un año sin amor*, where we see Pablo Pérez, the writer and protagonist, who has embarked on a search for his true self, a desire to reevaluate and redefine the self, given the transformation that AIDS has caused. On that front, Jacoby is correct in saying, "Al escribir su historia, se hace a sí mismo" [While writing his story/history, he's making himself] (11). Writing and identity are intimately linked: writing about the body insulates the lonely world Pérez inhabits, but that does not mean to suggest that writing *about* the body is always the same as writing *with* it. Here we have both—in some sections, there is an intellectual detachment as Pérez recounts the numerous symptoms and effects of the disease on his body, as if the two were separate entities. This, in my estimation, is writing about the body. However, for a much greater percentage of the text, it is the body, sometimes in conjunction with the mind and often not, that navigates the narrative, often dictating the course it will follow and making Pablo seem as if he is merely along for the ride. This, in my eyes, is a version of writing *with* the body. I would not propose that it is the idealized version of that technique that Valenzuela encourages, but rather a skewed variety of it, lacking one central element that is never mentioned by Valenzuela but is invoked by Pérez at the end of his narrative project: the soul. In the case of such an intimate project such as Pérez's, in the end, the ultimate goal appears to be the cooperation between the physical body, the entire mind, and the soul.

The references to the soul that appear in Pérez's work do not demarcate the strictly spiritual being, but rather reference the interconnected part of the person, the one that is in touch with the universe, perhaps a higher being, society, community, family, friends, lovers, and so forth. It is the part of the self that is capable of extending outside of the physical confines of the body while still tending to the needs of both the mind and the body, not in the metaphysical sense, but in a way that allows the individual to participate in the world around her or him. It is part of the mind, part of the body, and partially independent, all the while performing the vital function of linking the person to the things that give life meaning. This element appears to be missing throughout the majority of Pérez's account. We have the body (often too much of it), we have the mind (alternatively the rational, intellectual mind and that of the depressed, anxious individual feeling trapped in his body), but we do not have the soul or the spirit of the person. There is a sense throughout much of the text that he is already dead, but what is really lacking is a vibrant spirit or soul. The result is a profound emptiness and isolation exacerbated by the lopsided narrative that overly emphasizes the body while partially neglecting the mind, and wholly forgetting about the soul. This imbalance leads to the solitary separation that Pablo experiences and is the making of his own version of exile.

The act of writing is central to this text: writing about the body, writing with the body, writing despite the body, writing to quell loneliness, writing about AIDS, writing to pass time, writing simply for the sake of writing. However, at the same time as the protagonist is writing and creating an expression of the self, he is alternately erasing with his body as well. Each hour spent writing is countered by the emptiness and solitude he is trying to obliterate; each trace of the body left on paper by his pen is a way of solidifying his existence on paper while his physical self is decaying and beginning to vanish. The protagonist states this central thrust quite simply in the initial sentence of the diary: "Tengo que escribir" [I have to write] (19). He continues to explain this need and its effect by sharing that "Siento que escribiendo todo esto, tan personal, pierdo el tiempo" [I feel that by writing all of this, so personal, time goes away] (20). We see reflected in this statement the two sides of this writing project—the text being created and the days and weeks of life being swallowed up as they are translated onto paper rather than participated in and experienced directly.

The reader quickly becomes aware that Pablo is embroiled in two literary projects—this diary and the translation of the works of his good friend (and possible partner, a point hinted at, but never clarified), Hervé Guibert. This secondary project hints at Pérez's professional life as a writer, translator, and poet, but it is relegated to the background and receives only brief mention, thus illustrating how Pablo's outside world, including his livelihood, have become secondary to the daily struggle of his existence because of AIDS. In fact, he outwardly rejects the community that he once belonged to, rejecting the literary community for its pretension. He is tired of that world and takes his first step toward personal isolation by choosing to pull back from his previous involvement with that sector of the community. This important step effectively reduces the size of his world and brings the walls of isolation one step closer. In addition to the eschewing of his former colleagues and the literary sphere in which he participated, there are also very few references to any family connections or a strong support network on that front. What we see, then, is an individual who is slowly becoming more withdrawn from family and coworkers; as a result, he turns inward, toward his writing, and begins to really analyze his subtle permutations and the veritable array of symptoms he experiences. He becomes his own primary companion, and the only dialogue is the one carried out in this diary. However, because of his HIV-positive status, the body inserts itself as the primary marker of identity and dominates in this personal dialogue of self-discovery.

The body is both the motivator for the content of this diary and a hindrance that on various occasions literally impedes him from carrying out the seemingly nonphysical act of writing. From the onset of the diary, the naked, ailing body is visible, and the reader becomes privy to information that is usually reserved for a doctor–patient relationship. However, just as the diary is a stripped-down, intimate portrayal of a person's existence, so, too, is writing a form of stripping the body down to the flesh and bones. We hear about the "micosis" [mycosis] he has on his penis that needs air and thus compels him to write naked (22). He often references the "manchas" [marks] that cover his skin and the multiple trips to the countless doctors who treat him. These repetitive journeys to the hospital become the primary connection he has with others in the community. Nevertheless, despite the attention he receives from medical personnel, his maladies still exist and often get in the way of his writing.

Because of the continual progression of his symptoms and the incremental drops in his blood cell counts (indicating additional opportunistic infections), Pablo becomes preoccupied with his failing health, and for the majority of the first half of the year, he begins to believe a nagging premonition that has been haunting him: "no pasaré este año" [I won't live past this year] (41). His thoughts about this hypothetical impending death force him to consider the very real possibility that his days may be numbered. Rather than focus on death as a negative entity, he instead begins to see it as a possible "regalo precioso" [precious gift] (41). The anxiety he experiences is related not to his possible death, but rather to the lack of love he currently experiences in his life and his increasingly solitary status. Ironically, though, even when faced with this firm belief that he is living out his final months and days, he does not strive to initiate more meaningful contacts, but rather spends his time alternately between solitary confinement in his apartment, tending to his ailments or engaged in anonymous sex with partners he finds at the multiple gay theaters in the city. Both of these activities further isolate him from those who might provide solace, nurturing, or love.

What results instead is a sort of fixed temporality because the uncertainties regarding the future and his lack of reference to the past effectively fix him in the present moment. With no meaningful solution for the future because of his weakening immune system, Pablo seems to be set in time, living (and documenting) a life that is repetitive and circular rather than moving toward future points and goals. These temporal doubts become apparent in one particular entry in which Pablo considers finishing his degree to finally become a professor, but then recognizes how contradictory he is being after having all but pronounced his death sentence a few days earlier. He alternates between wanting to participate more actively in life outside of his home and feeling trapped by his body's deterioration. These two forces cancel each other and prevent him from making any real advancement on a personal or professional scale.

One of the primary personal goals that Pablo constantly reiterates throughout the work is the desire to find a true love, the lack of which serves as part of the motivation for this diary commemorating "un año *sin* amor" [a year *without* love] (emphasis mine). In fact, this facet is so central to Pablo's own vision of his literary project that at one moment, "pensé que había llegado el amor que tanto esperaba y temí por este diario" [I thought the love that I had awaited so long had arrived and I feared for this diary] (49). This thought emphasizes the fact that linked with this work is the essential condition in which Pablo finds himself: alone. His isolation is part and parcel of the functioning of the text because it both motivates the work and provides fodder for literary exploration.

This professed literary goal and the name attached to it, "diario" [diary], raise questions about the genre itself and the ways in which Pérez has manipulated it to achieve his own goals. The diary genre, according to literary critic David A. Powell, is the "least formalized of the autobiographical forms . . . has no clear-cut beginning, middle or end. There is usually no intent to publish" (182). This last characteristic is the most interesting for our purposes, because it is clear from the beginning that this diary was written by Pérez upon the insistence of his friends, with the end goal of eventual publication. Traditional diaries are inherently intimate, essentially conversing with oneself about a multitude of topics. Here, a constant sense exists that Pérez is aware of the reader, explaining references and places that one would never clarify in a diary written solely for self-use. This intent to publish calls to mind a variety of questions: Was Pérez firmly convinced at the inception of this project that he would die before its completion, thus writing a sort of memoir to be published posthumously? If not, why did he choose such an intimate form for such a public forum? What did the interplay of public and private discourse offer to Pérez on both the individual and the social level?

One possibility lies in the central preoccupation of the work: the notion of loneliness and solitude. Pérez is alone for the vast majority of the year that he chronicles, often limited from participating in his life because of the severity of his symptoms, particularly before he begins antiretroviral drug therapy. The diary becomes a place where he can explore the difficult reality he is facing, often giving him a space to unleash his distress and frustration over the physical pain, as well as the psychological and emotional isolation, he feels. This literary space grows even more important as Pablo's solitude increases, cutting him off from other types of support networks with whom he could share his concerns. However, the conscious intention to eventually publish this work, and therefore the ever-present awareness of an "other," even an anonymous imaginary reader of a manuscript that Pérez hopes to eventually publish, may on some level alleviate the loneliness that Pablo experiences. Instead of simply writing about himself to himself, he is writing about himself to an imaginary other. His thoughts connect him with future readers, and despite the separation of time and space, that bond is more than he experiences in most other realms of his life. In this way, the manipulation of the inherently intimate genre gives Pablo a way of eventually connecting with others, albeit across a significant lapse in time and space.

On a more active level, the desire to break his own solitary confinement also compels Pablo to cruise pickup places, ostensibly in search of "el amor" [love], but in reality, satisfied with sexual rendezvous in which he often does not even learn his partner's name. For Pablo, these encounters occur with increasing regularity and serve as his primary contact with the world outside of his apartment. It is important to note that during this time, he suffers greatly from his multiple opportunistic infections and often struggles during the day to complete the most mundane tasks. Nonetheless, a compulsion often drives him to the various theaters in the city in search of sex. By day, he is a disintegrating body sucked of its vital energy, struggling to sit and write in his diary. By night, however, he musters as much strength as possible to then expend it all in sexual encounters that are often sadomasochistic in nature. Recognizing this apparent contradiction, Pablo discusses it with his psychologist and shares their conclusions in his diary: "Concluimos en que el orgasmo me remite a una sensación de vida" [We concluded that an orgasm makes me feel alive] (64).

These "life-giving" erotic encounters are told with the same brashness as the symptoms that plague his body, once again asserting the body as the central image of this diary, displaying the visceral elements in an explicit manner. These details are interspersed throughout the narrative, but underlying all of these interactions is a true desire to find love and affection, rather than merely engage in sexual activities. One "cine porno" encounter is with a man named Luis, the first lover whose name we learn; we soon intuit that this more personal way of referring to his sexual partner reveals the deeper feelings that Pablo is experiencing. By individualizing this lover and thus making him stand out among many, Pablo is expressing his physical and emotional desire toward Luis and the hope he has for future encounters between the two. Furthermore, Pablo is conscious of his contagiousness, as he warns Luis: "cuidado cuando me beses porque tengo un labio cortado" [be careful when you kiss me because I have a cut lip] (72).

This awareness of the potential danger of his sexual interactions, particularly for his partners, is mentioned primarily in relation to Luis, in a tone of almost paternalistic concern and affection. On a few other occasions at various cinemas, men insist on having sex "sin forro" [without protection], and Pablo always asks them to wear a condom but relents if they refuse, figuring that "me siento responsable sólo en parte, creo que él lo es más que yo desde el momento en que se negó a usarlo cuando se lo pedí" [I feel only partly responsible, I believe he is more responsible from the moment he refused to use it when I asked him to] (143). He operates in a world where the risks of casual, unprotected sex are known by all, and he obviously feels no more responsibility to be "safe" than others, instead putting the onus on each individual to look out for his own well-being. This attitude makes his outlook toward Luis all the more remarkable, showing once again that he invested in him more emotionally than in any of his other random encounters. However, true to the title of this work, he continues to live out the year "sin amor" when Luis first does not call, and then does so only to tell him that he doesn't want a commitment.

Luis's rejection increases Pablo's state of anxiety, depression, and solitude, again causing him to confront the task at hand (writing) and to face the underlying causes for that project (the progressive decline of his health due to AIDS). This panic and fear propel him to examine his life choices, which he does through the writing that he often must force himself to do. Like someone trying to make new resolutions against his will, Pablo first flirts with giving up sex because of how much it drains his energy, but he quickly rejects that notion. Then, as his cell counts become more ominous, he flirts with giving up on everything, again showing his propensity toward total isolation. These drastic considerations underline for him that he must take some action in regard to his health in order to try to combat his disease rather than flee from it and all of its effects. Since at this point (May 6), he decides that "no pienso tomar AZT" [I don't plan to take AZT] (61), he alternates between homeopathic regimens and strict nutritional guidelines, choosing to act as his own medic despite the insistence by his doctor to consider the new "cocktail."

Near the middle of the year, Pablo reaches the apex of his isolation, where his physical pain and suffering are on par with his emotional desperation. He finds something that he cannot specifically name or identify absolutely intolerable, assuming it has to do "con la soledad o con la incertidumbre" [with loneliness or uncertainty] (84), both of which states dominate his existence at this point. He constantly finds himself rejecting even the self-imposed obligation to write, feeling overwhelmed and exhausted by his symptoms and depression. He has, quite literally, become a prisoner of his body because the physical exhaustion has reached such a point that "el cansancio nos aísla y nos obliga a la soledad" [the tiredness isolates us and resigns us to loneliness"] (87). The physical body that has been the central thrust of the textual body has reached the point that it prevents him from engaging in nearly all types of interpersonal contact and even overwhelms his personal pursuits. At this lowest point, even the ardent sexuality displayed earlier in the year has quieted some, with Pablo spending nearly all of his time alone, in his apartment, accompanied only by his thoughts and the pen and paper he uses to memorialize this point of despair. Mired as he is in such extreme depression, he finds even the diary to be a chore, no longer providing the sort of sacred space to both reflect upon daily life and project toward possible future interactions, but rather becoming one more reminder of the overwhelming physical exhaustion that prevents him from participating in nearly all aspects of life. Still, as if his textual body were crucial to the continued viability of his physical body, he continues to write.

It is obvious that the physical decline has also brought with it a profound depression, both of which prove to be paralyzing and extremely isolating. At this point, Pablo is able to reflect on his frame of mind and daily life, concluding, "Mi estado de ánimo es de lo peor. Me siento solo con mi enfermedad . . . Otra vez mi presentimiento de muerte" [My mood is the worst. I feel alone with my illness . . . Again my premonition of death] (89). Thoughts of death haunt him, and his body becomes overtly conspicuous because of the extra signification that AIDS has bestowed upon it. Even in the above quote, we note that he feels "solo con mi enfermedad," as if haunted by a specter that refuses to leave him in peace. He is constantly reminded of his altered physicality, and thus the shift in his lifestyle, interactions, and identity, something that he continually struggles to come to grips with: "No me siento muy identificado con mi nueva forma de vida y es en ese punto en donde aparece la crisis" [I don't feel very identified with my new form of life and it is there that the crisis appears] (93). He wrestles with who this new Pablo is, ultimately rejecting him and the life that has imprisoned the old Pablo, the one he still yearns for.

This extreme depression and subsequent isolation cause Pablo to fear "morirme esperando el tratamiento con inhibidores de protease" [dying while waiting for protease inhibitor treatment] (95), showing the dramatic shift in his attitude toward AZT and the drug cocktail that was becoming much more available to him during this focal year. At the beginning of the year, despite numerous infections, declining lab results, and increasing solitary living, he refused the drug, preferring instead to focus on homeopathic remedies. With the arrival of June and the drastically more severe symptoms that impede nearly all human interactions and essentially force him to live in isolated confinement convinced of his imminent demise, Pablo relents and begins a course of AZT and DDI. This decision proves to be a turning point on many fronts: physically (as he sees his libido return and his symptoms become less debilitating), mentally (as he begins to believe that he might live beyond the end of the year), and socially (as he once again forms connections with others and starts to chip away at the walls of isolation that have imprisoned him for the months leading up to this turnaround). Not everything associated with AZT is positive, however; there are still many days when he feels like a "preso de (su) cuerpo" [prisoner of his body], unsure how much longer he can endure that state (102). It also begins to magnify the effect we saw earlier in which his increasingly ill body made Pablo more and more aware of his demise and less able to disconnect himself from his physical deterioration and its subsequent imprisonment. AZT, with its strict schedule and constant need to be vigilant of symptoms,

> hace que el SIDA esté presente en todo momento, que no pueda olvidarme de mi enfermedad, me siento feo y enfermo, encerrado en mí mismo, siempre con la idea de que voy a morir pronto, casi un deseo de morir, preferiblemente sin una intervención mía, aunque empiece a aparecer más seguido la idea de un suicide.
>
> [it makes it so AIDS is present at every moment, that I can't forget about my illness, I feel ugly and sick, locked in myself, always with the idea that I'm going to die soon, almost a desire to die, preferably without my own intervention, although the idea of suicide is starting to appear more often.] (118)

Ironically, then, the very drug that is slowly making him feel physically better is also making him become more aware of the entrapment caused by the virus and makes him less able to live a life not dominated by AIDS. This conundrum becomes particularly hard to tolerate when his symptoms are so fierce that it feels as if he is not experiencing any improvement. During those moments and days, Pablo becomes desperate and frustrated, faced with a body and a medical regimen that are failing him and increasingly reminding him of his precariously numbered days. This sentiment is expressed on one particularly low day, when Pablo rants, "si tengo que morirme, morirme, pero me cansé de vivir semiahogado, en esta semivida que no me sirve de nada, que me molesta" [If I have to die, (then) die, but I'm tired of living half suffocated, in this half life that isn't worth anything, that bothers me] (119). His body and disease overshadow his entire life, causing him to question the logic of even the reduced commitments he has.

Almost unexpectedly, the text shifts, and life begins to be a possibility again. Pablo is increasingly seeing options, whereas in the past he acted according to routine because any deviation required far too much energy. Furthermore, as his body begins to recover, it is no longer seen as an enemy force subjecting its owner to a life of isolation and exhaustion. Instead, it begins to take its place as one of the many possible facets of his identity, rather than predominating as the only visible aspect. This shift is significant, because it is like the first chip in the icelike barrier that has surrounded Pablo and enclosed him in a solitary existence. Little by little, with each reconnection with the outside world, more cracks form, and he slowly reenters a life that bears some resemblance to the one he once knew.

One of the first indicators of this change in perspective is his decision to join a group that was "formada por gente con Sida" [formed by people with AIDS] (120). For the first time, AIDS is a force that unites him with others rather than separating him from them. His family enters the picture more, particularly as the holidays approach, and his friends receive more mention in the text, making him feel "tranquilo" [calm], with less desire to go to the porn theaters. That is not to say that his anonymous encounters do not continue, because they do, at times with such frenzy that protection once again is eschewed; however, for the first time in the text, Pablo begins to intellectualize these encounters, searching for the meaning behind them. He concludes that "por mi enfermedad una relación que dure en el tiempo es cada vez más difícil" [because of my illness, a relationship that lasts over time is more and more difficult] (137).

This emergent self-comprehension is indicative of the burgeoning, new identity that he is slowly forming. Part of that is reclaiming a force that once held imminent importance for him: art. He participates in a poetry reading and realizes that "es en el arte donde mi alma encuentra un poco de respiro y bienestar" [it is in art where my soul finds a little respite and well-being] (136). For the first time in the text, he is uniting body, mind, and spirit with this reference, something that was not the case earlier when the body overpowered and weakened the mind and wholly overshadowed the soul. In this return to art, Pablo once again is able to recognize the various parts of himself, and in the process he finds respite.

This new identity is best summarized by the personal ad he places, on December 22, as the twilight of the year is approaching. In it, we see a reflection of a more complex, multidimensional being than the one portrayed in the diary. Most notably, AIDS becomes part of Pablo's self-identification, rather than a hellish force preventing him from being the person he remembers. As opposed to the predominantly sexualized earlier ads, this ad addresses not only his physical/sexual needs, but his mental and spiritual desires as well. It seems as though Pablo has emerged from his solitary separation, ready to participate once again in life, albeit an altered one, preferably with a partner who can complement the multiple facets of his identity.

In addition to the shift in self-perception that Pérez chronicles throughout the year, we also notice an increasing awareness of his status as an HIV-positive individual, as was evidenced through his participation in a support group for AIDS patients and the voluntary inclusion of his status in his last personal ad. This fact becomes increasingly important when we consider that this diary was conceptualized from the beginning as a public project, one destined for eventual publication, either posthumously (as it seemed when Pablo's health faltered so drastically midyear) or after the completion of the year. By blurring the boundaries between public and private discourse, and by adding an individual perspective from someone known within the Argentine literary community, Pérez's text enters the public discourse on AIDS. By utilizing a literary space that he previously reserved for the publication of his fictional works, Pérez presents to his readers an intimate, yet self-aware, look at his struggles with AIDS. Rather than blatantly weigh in on the subject of AIDS through a more direct form such as an essay, Pérez subverts the diary in multiple ways: first, he uses it to imagine a future reader, thus alleviating some of his suffocating loneliness; and second, he offers a personal discourse underscored by a powerful social commentary both on the countless difficulties he faced as a person with advanced stages of AIDS and on the importance that the eventual creation of a community of AIDS patients had to his survival.

Arriving at this precarious acceptance of the "new Pablo" certainly was not easy, as the diary proves. Led by the trials and tribulations of his physical being, Pablo ventures in and out of many complex psychological states as he alternately fights against and passively accepts the isolation that resulted from the virus debilitating his body. Pablo's story is unique because it depicts life at a historical crossroads in the AIDS story; he experienced the "before" and "after" of antiretroviral drugs, teetering on the brink of death, withdrawing to the point of erasure from life as he knew it, only to slowly be led back to that existence as his body made feeble advances toward health.

Because it was situated at such a poignant moment in history, Pérez's diary, when published, commemorated that moment through personal reflections. In that sense, the public function of his work was not only to offer additional discourse on the topic of AIDS, but also to chronicle the impact that medical technology and advancements had on his personal struggles. By no means a cure, AZT restored enough vitality and strength to Pablo's body to enable him to rejoin his life and exit the pseudo-exile that he had inhabited. This slow transition is further bolstered by the unexpected community of AIDS patients that he joins when he becomes a member of their group. In fact, as Pablo greets the end of the year, he can be juxtaposed with the image of the solitary, naked man sequestered in his apartment that we first encountered at the beginning of the diary; instead, he is surrounded by the members of his group. At the same time, he is planning for an evening spent in the company of friends, dining, lighting fireworks, and cross-dressing, all in flamboyant celebration of the year that he never thought he would see, but welcomes with a heartfelt "feliz año nuevo" [Happy New Year] (145).

There is certainly no hint of what that new year will look like, but all indications are that with his renewed sense of community and connections with people and institutions in his life, combined with an increasingly stronger body, Pablo can, for the first time in a year, actually envision a future that contains more than the bleak existence he endured in the previous year. Although still "alone" in terms of romantic partners, the isolation and solitude that had predominated have been replaced by a community providing varying types of support, whether through the traditional support group for AIDS patients, the friends who bring him out of his shell, the sexual partners who satisfy his desires, or the family members who make small steps to reintegrate themselves into his life. Ending the diary is symbolic; instead of writing about and, at times, with a body that often betrayed him, Pablo has slowly started to live with and through that body, effectively shattering the confinement of his previous twelve months' existence and forging an enhanced vision of himself and his place in the community in the process.

CHAPTER FOUR

Forging (Comm)unity through Hybridity
Pedro Lemebel's Loco afán: crónicas de sidario

> Los enfermos se confunden con los sanos y el estigma sidático pasa por una cotidianeidad de club . . . que frivoliza el drama. Y esta forma de enfrentar la epidemia pareciera ser el mejor antídoto para la depresión y la soledad, que en última instancia es lo que termina por destruir al infectado.
>
> [The sick are mistaken for the healthy and the AIDS stigma passes through a clublike ordinariness . . . which frivolizes the drama. And this way of facing the epidemic seems to be the best antidote for depression and loneliness, which in the end is what end up destroying the infected person.]
>
> —Pedro Lemebel, *Loco afán* 69

THE PREVIOUS chapter illustrated the profound potential that AIDS and HIV have to isolate those affected by it, as the narratives by Prieto, Mallach, and Pérez dramatically illustrated. In the first of those texts, the disease triggers a self-imposed isolation, an intentional erasure of the self from the social body. In some instances, this reaction is a drastic form of self-flagellation and condemnation, as well as an attempt to flee the perceived annihilative potentials of the virus. In the second case, the departure from home to embark on a nomadic journey parallels the personal quest to redefine the self and recognize and accept its altered form. Last, we saw how the virus can completely incapacitate and physically overwhelm the people infected, effectively converting their bodies into pseudo-prisons that make them incapable of actively participating in the society around them. We saw this last scenario at play in Pérez's reflective diary of one year of his struggle with AIDS. Through it, readers are privy to his personal insights and witness both the extreme isolation he experiences and the slow emergence from that solitude as his body regains its strength thanks to modern medicine. As Pablo reenters society, the text suggests the formation of a sort of community of sufferers vis-à-vis the support group for HIV-positive individuals that Pérez has joined. His text, in adherence to his self-imposed temporal limit, ends with the year it portrays, thus failing to explore further this burgeoning notion of community that has emerged from the suffering that so plagues the protagonist throughout the majority of the year. This notion of community-building through AIDS, combined with the power that writing has in the construction of that community, will be the primary focus of this chapter.

Providing an illuminating example of this confluence of community and writing is *Loco afán: crónicas de sidario*, Pedro Lemebel's stunning collection of chronicles about the effect of AIDS on the transvestite[1] community in Santiago de Chile.[2] The collection details the fate of the homosexual, transvestite community (or "las locas" in Lemebel's terms) from the fall of Allende, through the Pinochet dictatorship, and into the transitory period of democracy that followed in the wake. During that tumultuous social and historical time in Chile's history, the protagonists faced yet another force capable of disrupting their sense of self and altering the

---

1. I am sensitive to the plurality of terminology surrounding those who cross-dress, recognizing that some critics use "drag" or "cross-dresser" over "transvestite." I have opted for "transvestite" in the general sense because Lemebel himself makes references to this term. His preferred term, however, and one that I will use throughout the majority of my study is locas, a term that I comment on later in this chapter in relation to the performance of gender that it represents. It also should be noted that while I recognize that in society transvestites may be hetero-, homo-, or bisexual, in this work, all of the transvestites (or locas) are homosexuals. Therefore, I will reference the "transvestite community," "gay community," and "locas" as interchangeable entities in this work only because Lemebel himself uses all three referents.

2. Lemebel's text is not the only work I had considered in relation to the formation of a community of AIDS patients. I initially considered Mario Bellatín's *Salón de belleza*, a novella, in which the protagonist, a transvestite, has converted his beauty salon into a sanatorium where young men dying of AIDS (referred to as "el mal") come together to die. While this narrative does contain several potential and interesting components to contrast with Lemebel's work, my goal with this chapter is to provide a counterpoint to the various stigma-laden messages contained in the texts analyzed in the previous chapters. As such, Lemebel's work is the most illustrative of this message because it completely encapsulates the destigmatized message about HIV/AIDS that many other texts I have analyzed lack. In that manner, Lemebel's work shows a new avenue for AIDS literature that envisions the AIDS-infected individual as being *part* of a self-constructed space in society rather than separated from it. Bellatín's text stops short of this liberating message in that the protagonists continue to be separated from society, albeit in a nurturing space. In contrast, Lemebel's work challenges the concept of separation and isolation and instead shows how his protagonists renegotiate their position *within* society.

notion of community: HIV/AIDS, a central topic in the lives of Lemebel's protagonists as they continue to engage in prostitution and to frequent brothels, baths, parks, and other locales of the urban landscape known for the exchange of sexual currency. Lemebel's use of language creates an extremely rich and detailed portraiture of the *locas* who inhabit his texts, alternating between the colloquial speech emanating from their lips and a philosophical discourse illustrating the author's own perspectives on the many ills befalling his homeland.

Through various metaphors and stunning visual imagery, Lemebel's work creates for the reader a remarkably thorough snapshot of his protagonists' lives, manipulating language in what has been called "un estilo que depende de una estrategia poética encubridora, que impide el decirlo todo directamente" [a style that depends on a masked poetic strategy, that prevents saying everything directly] (Atenas 132). Literary critic Ángeles Mateo del Pino has described Lemebel's works as "un discurso íntimo, a medio camino entre la poesía y la prosa" [an intimate discourse, halfway between poetry and prose] (18). I recur as well to Mateo del Pino's apt description of the sensation that Lemebel's technique produces, asserting that Lemebel uses "un registro que bien podríamos llamar filmográfico. Cada crónica es como un *sketch* que reproduce una parte de la ciudad santiaguina: . . . Un cuadro de sus habitantes . . . prostituta, el travesti, el milico" [a register that we could well call filmographic. Each chronicle is like a sketch that reproduces a part of the city of Santiago: . . . a portrait of its inhabitants . . . (the) prostitute, the transvestite, the soldier] (24). While Mateo del Pino here is referencing Lemebel's earlier chronicles, *La esquina es mi corazón*, his description could also apply to *Loco afán* and the plurality of characters represented through Lemebel's prismatic writing.

As a result, Lemebel's work has begun to garner a good deal of critical attention, particularly since the publication of *Loco afán* in 1996. Lemebel's career has been as multifaceted as his work, beginning first as Pedro Mardones, the performance artist and member of "Las Yeguas del Apocalipsis," a group of poets dedicated to video productions and performance art during the Pinochet dictatorship. With an alteration in surname in an attempt to pay homage to and connect with his maternal lineage, Pedro Lemebel-the-writer was constructed. He continued to employ a variety of techniques and genres, experimenting with poetry, short stories, pamphlets, oral dissemination of his thoughts and ideas (primarily through the radio, in which he still participates), and eventually the urban *crónica* that became his genre of choice through three collections of works.[3] He has

---

3. *Loco afán*, *La esquina es mi corazón*, and *De perlas y cicatrices* are all chronicles.

since delved into long-story/novel[4] format as well as a historical study on the history of homosexuality in Chile.[5]

This diversity of technique, as well as the plurality of voices and hybridity of genres presented within the works, is one of the central characteristics of Lemebel's work, as is his unwavering dedication to what he terms "el mariconaje guerrero," a more militant form of homosexuality that strives to uncover the multiple layers of segregation that the transvestite endures in Chilean society. In addition, he combats the aggressively negative language and imagery used against homosexuals (Jeftanovic 76) by offering an unapologetic glimpse at urban life, uncovering those characters and scenarios that do not adhere to the traditional notion of nation. What I intend to illustrate, through a detailed study of the sketches depicted in *Loco afán*, is how Lemebel's textual project seeks to combat a predominant cultural nationalism that has consistently erased homosexuals and transvestites from the national "family."

I will utilize the theories of Homi Bhabha, particularly those expounded in *Locations of Culture*, to show how Lemebel's text takes advantage of the liminal space produced between the pedagogical and performative aspects of national identity to insert itself as an alternative cultural history. By utilizing this space, Lemebel continually employs the notion of hybridity to achieve his project and write the transvestite community into the literary history of Chile. There are multiple manifestations of this hybridity, but I will focus on six specific examples, each illustrated in Lemebel's work, although not necessarily in this order. First, the genre of the text itself, the *crónica*, is an amalgam of many different genres, making it the ideal structure to carry out Lemebel's narrative project. Second, we can examine the notion of gender, a sexual hybridity that is depicted by the transvestites who protagonize the works.[6] Third, multiple urban spaces are represented in the text, providing no centralizing location, but rather shrouded locales and undisclosed spaces that the characters traverse in their daily encounters. Fourth, historical time is multiple, with flashbacks to pre-dictatorship and references to the indeterminate current reality of the "transition," an unstable political and social climate. Fifth, there is a national–transnational hybridity in the cultural influences examined in

---

4. I refer to "Tengo miedo torero," which Lemebel called "un cuento largo" [a long story] or "novela breve" [short novel] (Jeftanovic 78).

5. The primary source of this biographical information is Jeftanovic's interview with Lemebel, published in 2000.

6. It is interesting to note that in Spanish, both "genre" and "gender" are expressed by the root word "género," with "género sexual" used to demarcate sexual gender. In this sense, the first two hybridities are defying attempts at categorization, both textually and sexually.

the text and in the interplay between external–internal cultural factors. Finally, the influence of AIDS creates hybrid bodies—blurring the boundaries between illness and health, youth and old age, life and death. In this sense, its presence becomes a constitutive force of the community that is constructed both because of and in spite of the virus. In the end, by uncovering national subjects that have been wholly erased or intentionally overlooked in the predominant cultural nationalism, particularly that of the dictatorship, Lemebel's text functions as a counternarrative that challenges dominant images of Chile, giving voice to and creating imagery of individuals who are often left outside of traditional communities and who thus forge a unique community of those affected by AIDS and dedicated to Lemebel's version of "mariconaje guerrero."

I am approaching the formation of community from the perspective of theories of nation-building, particularly postmodern versions such as Bhabha's. Such postmodern theories take into account the unique identities of developing countries and the diverse citizens within them, and they reject some of the totalizing views projected in early theories of nation-building, such as that of Benedict Anderson in *Imagined Communities*. I concur with McClennen's conclusion that "the inception of nationalism was central to the formation of modern nations because it described the inalienable ties between the subject and the state. Nevertheless, while nationalism projected a unified national body as part of its ideological persuasion, such unification rarely, if ever, existed" (53). Despite this apparent disconnect between theory and reality, I believe there still are usable aspects of Anderson's theory—in particular, the notion of an imagined link between fellow members that allows for the construction of a coalition or community between disparate individuals who may never meet one another, but who prescribe to the same concept of nation. However, Anderson's focus is on the emergence of nations during the eighteenth century as they fought for independence and tried to surface from under the cloak of religious dominance and governance. Essentially, nationhood was linked to modernity and connected to capitalism, to the capacity to communicate through print, and to the demise of linguistic diversity and thus the emergence of language communities.

While these elements certainly provide a scope through which to view the creation of nation, they lack the ability to adequately address the concept of community for those who fall outside of the traditional definition of the nation's members and who therefore exist in the margins. Their concerns often have less to do with the interrelation between nations than with the connection between others in their cultural community and the coexistence of that group within the larger context of nation. Essentially, with the relative stability of sovereign nations in Latin American contexts, the notion of nation-*building* is no longer as relevant as the notion of *construction* or *production* of national identity or the national subject, particularly in the contexts of the dictatorships of the 1970s as well as the transitions to democracy that followed (Kaminsky 25).

Kaminsky reminds us of the multiplicity of interpretations of nation, interpretations that depend on the group doing the defining. She also reflects that during the Southern Cone dictatorships of the 1970s, "the state took as its task the absolute and complete assimilation of the nation to its definition of itself, emphasizing the subjection of the individual to the state in the term 'national subject'" (25). McClennen adds that authoritarian nationalism projected a totalizing view of its citizens, with dictatorships opting to "appropriate nationalism to repress and contain national identity" (59). This conceptualization is pertinent to our discussion, given the historical context of Lemebel's work, which spans the transitions both from socialism to authoritarianism and from authoritarianism to democracy, essentially a period from 1972 to the early 1990s. During the vast majority of that period, Lemebel's protagonists, like the citizens of Chile, were subjected to a controlling nationalism that discursively "linked the family with the nation, the dictator with father and the people with children" (55). Given this situation, it is necessary to ask: How was this nationalism consciously exclusionary? What happens to those who do not fit the traditional roles projected by the "nation"? How do they participate in the construction of national identity when they are not recognized as members of that fabricated space? How can they insert themselves into both the literal and figurative communities within their nations?

The answers, I believe, lie in Homi Bhabha's theories on liminality and hybridity and their relation to nation-building. In his provocative work *The Location of Culture*, Bhabha contends that

> It is in the emergence of the interstices—the overlap and displacement of domains of difference—that the intersubjective and collective experiences of *nationness*, community interest, or cultural value are negotiated. . . . Terms of cultural engagement, whether antagonistic or affiliative, are produced performatively. The representation of difference must not be hastily read as the reflection of *pre-given* ethnic or cultural traits set in the fixed tablet of tradition. The social articulation of difference, from the minority perspective, is a complex, on-going negotiation that seeks to authorize cultural hybridities that emerge in moments of historical transformation. (2)

These "interstices" have also been referred to as liminal spaces or hybridities, in which there is a constant sense of movement, overlap, convergence, and negotiation. According to McClennen, it is through this aperture and from within this ambivalent state that the colonized are able "to challenge the colonizer through the construction of 'counter-narratives'" (67). While the protagonists of Lemebel's work are not true colonized subjects, I believe that the dynamics articulated by Bhabha and McClennen of colonized–colonizer are parallel to those of the margin–hegemony seen in Lemebel. Furthermore, Lemebel himself envisions AIDS and the subsequent marginalization it causes as a new form of colonization (see epigraph to *Loco afán*). The commonalities between social marginalization and colonization derive from the power structure at play and the social positioning that is a result of that differential. In both, an inherently unequal balance of power exists in which the hegemony (and the colonizer) wields control in an attempt to subjugate and marginalize those in the subordinate position. What Bhabha's theory provides is a way to see how the individuals in the subjugated position, whether they are colonized subjects or those demonized and shunned by the dominant society, are able to appropriate their position as a way to create a space for themselves within society. What we see in Lemebel is the production and manipulation of multiple hybridities, all with the end goal of counteracting the hegemony and forging a cultural identity out of the triply marginalized homosexual, transvestite, and HIV-positive protagonists who inhabit the text. Instead of hiding or erasing this ambivalent space, Lemebel shines light on it through his text, illuminating the characters who populate it and giving voice to their histories. He embraces and celebrates the interstitial margin, accentuating the multiple hybridities that are played out within it.

Perhaps another way to envision the reality of Lemebel's protagonists and the way in which Lemebel codifies it in his work is through Emily Hicks's theories from *Border Writing: The Multidimensional Text*. According to Hicks, her critical project is concerned with addressing thinking about culture without the boundaries imposed by nation. At the core of border writing is the border metaphor, which relies on cultural borders more than physical ones. I utilize this theory here as one way to approach Lemebel's work in constructing a cultural community of individuals residing on, and often beyond, the cultural borders of Chilean society. It provides one way of conceptualizing the marginal existence of the *locas* in these texts, with the idea of margins being just another way of referring to the cultural borders which are implicitly defined by society and beyond which Lemebel's *locas* live, work, and survive. At this cultural border, edge, periphery, or margin, depending on the perspective of who is imposing the name, culture and identity are not fixed entities, but rather remain in flux, in constant negotiation via dialogue both within the community and with mainstream society. Lemebel's text is a prime example of border writing: it is multidimensional in its execution, allowing the reader to view "the rest" of Chile through the prism that is the transvestite culture he depicts, and focusing in on that culture against the backdrop of other markers of Chilean society.

Furthermore, his subjects themselves represent decentered, nationless subjects: having been relegated to (and beyond) the cultural margins by a society that shuns them, the *locas* struggle to recreate a sense of community or nation under their own terms. Lemebel himself recognizes the multiple borders that separate his protagonists from "mainstream" cultural agents and even those who navigate borders slightly closer to the center. He affirms that

> hay minorías dentro de las minorías, lugares que son triplemente segregados como lo es el travestismo. No el travestismo del show . . . sino que el travestismo prostibular. El que se juega en la calle . . . ese es segregado dentro del mundo gay, o también son segregados los homosexuales más evidentes en este mundo masculino.
>
> [there are minorities within minorities, places that are triply segregated like transvestitism is. Not the transvestism in shows . . . but rather the transvestism of brothels. That which is played out on the street . . . that is segregated within the gay community, or also the most obvious homosexuals are segregated in this masculine world.] (Jeftanovic 76)

As we can see, there are multiple borders and layers of marginalization; it is this plurality and hybridity that Lemebel so deftly explores in his work and that ultimately provides a fissure through which a discourse that challenges the hegemony can emerge, or, as literary critic Dino Plaza Atenas puts it, "de lo que se trata es de la posibilidad de constituirse como un sujeto que acepte la 'diferencia' como un otro legítimo" [what we are dealing with is the possibility of constructing oneself as a subject who accepts "difference" as a legitimate other] (123).

Textual Hybridity
THE *CRÓNICA*

The first such hybrid space is the text itself, or, more precisely, the heterogeneous genre that Lemebel utilizes: the *crónica*. Lemebel has chosen what he himself terms a "subgénero o intergénero" [subgenre or inter-genre] because it offers an initial avenue by which to explore such genres. Atenas believes that, like all literary and artistic projects undertaken by Lemebel, it is a very intentional selection that allows Lemebel to break literary barriers. In fact, Lemebel himself has admitted that he chose this genre "porque tiene que ver con algo de biografía, con algo de narrativa, con una poética como coraza escritural frente a los poderes de la literature" [because it has something to do with biography, with a bit of narrative, with a poetic art that is like a written shield in the face of the powers of literature] (Lemebel[7] in Atenas 123). This textual plurality allows Lemebel the freedom to navigate both textual and cultural borders, delving into his topic from the angles that give him the tools to capture the stories he intends to share. This calls to mind the hologram metaphor that Hicks uses in describing border writing, noting that a hologram has the capacity to create an image from more than one perspective at the same time. The same is true of Lemebel's text. He is not limited by one strict genre, but instead, can operate within the fluidity that this hybrid genre affords him.

While it is clear that the *crónica*, as Lemebel envisions it, serves his particular goals as a writer and storyteller, I would also like to examine both the historical uses of the form and the way in which Lemebel restructures it to accommodate his contemporary literary and cultural project. Some of the more traditional *crónicas* were historical accounts of the Discovery and Conquest. In the contemporary landscape, the most notable chroniclers are Carlos Monsiváis (México), Edgardo Rodríguez Julia (Puerto Rico), and Pedro Lemebel (Mateo del Pino 18–19), all of whom utilized the genre to create a more heterogeneous account of their respective societies. What becomes clear is that Lemebel's interpretation of the form deviates significantly from traditional texts that essentially serve to record and witness important historical, political, or cultural events. In fact, according to Lucía Guerra Cunningham, Lemebel's crónicas completely subvert the traditional genre, in a way that

> contradice las formas tradicionales, tanto con respecto a lo fijado en la escritura como al principio que las organiza. Ubicándose en la ladera opuesta de las crónicas de la Conquista, lo heroico y memorable es aquí desplazado por lo cotidiano en los espacios marginales de la ciudad.
>
> [contradicts the traditional forms, both with respect to that which is fixed in writing as well as the principles that organize it. By placing himself

---

7. From an interview in "La Época: Suplemento Ideas," *Domingo*, el 21 de septiembre, 1997.

on the opposite side of the chronicles of the Conquest, the heroic and memorable here are displaced by the every-day things in the marginal spaces of the city.] (83)

Essentially, Lemebel has taken a historical form typically reserved for commemorating the lives and deeds of significant people and has used it to delve into an up-close and very personal look at "una pleyade de antihéroes, personajes malditos que han sido expulsados del paraíso-espacio público, entes desposeídos que habitan en los márgenes, en los bordes, en la periferia" [a plethora of antiheroes, wretched characters that have been expelled from the paradise-public space, dispossessed beings that inhabit the margins, the borders, the periphery] (Mateo del Pino 22). In short, Lemebel's hybrid genre and border writing allow him to capture those who inhabit parallel spaces, or those defined precisely by the same multidimensionality and fluidity as the genre used to depict them. By matching text with subject, Lemebel creates a space in which to write the diverse individuals that make up the liminal environs to which they have been relegated.

Additionally, Lemebel takes advantage of this traditionally historical form to offer a textual record and serve as a witness to a very significant historical and cultural event in Chile, but one that, according to cultural critic Adela H. Wilson,[8] "La sociedad chilena pensó que no era un tema que debería abordar con fuerza y, como casi siempre, por debajo asomaba la verdad de una realidad escamoteada y oculta. La negación de la enfermedad que mató y sigue matando a cientos de personas" [The Chilean society thought that it wasn't a topic that should be tackled with strength, and like almost always, from underneath, the truth of a hidden and secret reality appeared. The denial of an illness that killed and continues to kill hundreds of people] (143). That topic is AIDS, particularly as it affects those who are already seen as peripheral citizens, such as homosexuals and transvestites. The *crónica,* as a document that serves as a textual record of a historical moment, affords Lemebel an avenue to record the effect that the epidemic has had on the transvestite community in Chile and to uncover a topic that has been so shrouded in taboos and silencing, not only in Chile, but throughout Latin America (and many other parts of the world). Wilson affirms that "El SIDA es . . . la enfermedad más cargada de connotaciones morales negativas y rechazo social de que se tenga noti-

8. This name is a pseudonym under which a gay Chilean woman published a detailed and unapologetic study on homosexuality and AIDS in Chile. Her use of a pseudonym is significant because it both illustrates her fear of reprisal and exemplifies the degree to which the topic of homosexuality and AIDS has been silenced in Chile.

cias en la historia de la humanidad" [AIDS is . . . the illness that is most charged with negative moral connotations and social rejection that we've known about in the history of humanity] (145). This additional moral burden further relegates an already sensitive topic to the margins, precisely where Lemebel picks it up and unabashedly reveals it for all to see. His text, then, is a timely record of a specific social moment, one that has far-reaching consequences for those touched by the virus. Not only is it a historical record of the effects of AIDS, but, through the plurality of voices and the multitude of vignettes, it offers a testimony to a specific, traumatic moment in time, one that Lemebel himself has likened to another form of colonization: "La plaga nos llegó como nueva forma de colonización por el contagio" [The plague arrived to us like a new form of colonization through contagion] (see epigraph to *Loco afán*). Like chroniclers before him, Lemebel witnesses that colonization and uses his text to give voice to those who are the targets; in doing so, he advocates for his community and offers them a path of resistance not only against the morbid reality of AIDS, but also against the society that ignores the plight they face.

Diachronic Time
THEN AND NOW

Historical time is very central to this work, serving as a frame for both the individual texts and the work as a whole. In this sense, Lemebel adheres to the notion of *crónica* as a document that provides a record and a testimony of a specific historical period. For Lemebel, that period covers the span of 1972–95, and because of the specificity of his text to Chile and the focus on the AIDS epidemic, it represents a particularly tumultuous time period not only nationally, but internationally as well. In Chile, 1972 represented the second year of Allende's socialist government, one that presented the ideal of a unified society providing for more equality among all individuals. After Allende's assassination and Pinochet's coup in 1973, Chile took a drastic swing away from the ideals promoted by Allende. Instead, "the doors opened for international business investment and the cultural climate stagnated under extreme repression and censorship" (McClennen 53).

Pinochet became "the self-proclaimed 'Father of the Nation'"(ibid.), and, in doing so, he eradicated the possibility of an egalitarian societal structure, instead promoting a strictly patriarchal paradigm that anchored a strong male figure at the top, with power trickling down to those below (indeed, if ever even reaching them). Under this structure, the father figure not only controls but configures his version of family, something that Pinochet executed through the brutal disappearance and elimination of thousands of citizens who did not fit his vision of nation or family. As a result, those who failed to meet the criteria of acceptable national citizen were cast out of the national community both literally and figuratively. They either fled Chile as exiles or moved into the margins and inhabited the shadows outside the space occupied by the hegemony. For Lemebel's protagonists, this was their reality from 1973 to 1989, while Pinochet authoritatively controlled his country and his "children."

The text is also concerned with the postdictatorial period when the nation slowly began to transition back to democracy. This period from 1989 to 1995 (when the work was published) makes up the majority of the "present" period in the text and is colored with both the vestiges of the dictatorship and the bittersweet memories of the Unidad Popular. It is this period that represents the hybrid historical time from which Lemebel's text emerges. It straddles two distinct pasts, a tenuous present, and a very unclear future. With no clear definition of nation or community at this point, and with the abandonment of the strict patriarchal hierarchy that preceded the period, Lemebel has the opportunity to textually insert himself and the gay community into the emerging national identity through the aperture provided by this ambivalent historical period. In essence, he can contribute to the construction of a new nation, one that perhaps provides the possibility of societal participation for him and his compatriots.

Lemebel envisions the gay community as one that, despite its position at the periphery of society, is undeniably interconnected and affected by the larger political and social forces at work. This is not to suggest that the governments, particularly the dictatorship, were explicitly concerned about the possible negative impact that policy decisions would have on the gay community. Rather, it is intended to show that, despite the perceived distance between mainstream Chile and the gay community, the distance did not provide insulation against the harsh social climate of the dictatorship. Despite efforts to erase the transvestite community from the national project, the community not only remained, but continued to be influenced by the multiple changes occurring in Chilean society. Lemebel is conscious of this fact, and his text explores the pre-dictatorship era, the Pinochet years, and the transitional period that represents the "present" in the text. All impacted the gay community and were factors in the degree to which they participated in and envisioned themselves as part of the national project.

The first text, "La noche de los visones," is the most demonstrative of this consciousness of political time. It recalls a black-and-white photograph depicting the last party of the Unidad Popular, providing a very cohesive, almost utopic, snapshot of the transvestite community, assembled in a public space and mingling openly with the proletariat. The use of the word "community" is intentional here because Lemebel describes a scene in which *locas* from all different classes and areas of the city are present, together, celebrating the end of 1972. The celebratory scene highlights the cohesion that was possible among the community during Allende's government, which is connected to the color white (in the photo and as a symbol of purity). Lemebel considers the photo itself to be the "último vestigio de aquella época de utopías sociales [the last vestige of that era of social utopias] (21). However, the night also serves as a harbinger for the drastic change just over the horizon, with the color black providing an omen about what 1973 would bring. This sense of foreboding made it feel "como si viniera una guerra [as if a war were coming] (13). Shortly thereafter, Pinochet's brutal dictatorship took over and effectively ended the public celebrations and displays of unity depicted in this photo.

This shift is significant because it effectively erased the gay community, and more specifically the transvestite subcommunity, from the public sphere, pushing it into the shadows and the margins, preventing its members from being a visible force in Pinochet's Chile. Without this public presence, the sense of community diminished somewhat as the distinct factions searched for less-ostentatious places to continue to live their lives. As a result, there were fewer central spaces and no sanctioned public spaces to come together. It is that lost sense of community that Lemebel's text strives to recreate by providing a centralized textual space to unite and recount the episodes that have left their mark over the years. Unfortunately, one of those episodes is the emergence of AIDS and the overwhelming impact it had on many of the protagonists depicted in this work. In essence, it was one of the factors involved in the creation of a new sense of community, one devastated by, but determined to overcome, the relentless progression of the virus.

Because of AIDS, these protagonists unwittingly became linked once again, not only by their lifestyles and marginalized status, but now by their battles with a potentially fatal virus. Bhabha reminds us that "political empowerment . . . come(s) from posing questions of solidarity and community from the interstitial perspective" (3). The loss of public space forces these protagonists into a liminal space. Rather than disappear, they utilize that perspective to combat a common enemy, AIDS, and through this text to make their voices heard in society.

The Emergence of AIDS in the Chilean Context

The notion of historical time is additionally echoed in the portrayal of the AIDS epidemic. In 1972, the specific moment of the first text in *Loco afán*, AIDS, of course, was generally unknown; it did not enter the worldwide scene until 1981. In the Chilean context, the first case was reported in 1984.[9] However, the earlier date of emergence proves to be more significant for the protagonists in these texts because of their international connections and the fact that the majority of them who fell ill contracted the virus abroad. The pre-AIDS era that is depicted in this work coincides initially with the Allende years, which are remembered as utopic. Repression, illness, and a divided community existed on the horizon, but for those who lived those years, there was, according to Lemebel's description, a joyous, celebratory atmosphere that united gays and transvestites from diverse backgrounds into a cohesive community. They lived in a time "donde el territorio nativo aún no recibía el contagio de la plaga, como recolonización a través de los fluidos corporales" [where the native territory had yet to receive the contagion of the plague, like recolonization through bodily fluids] (22). In essence, the social liberties that were celebrated under Allende were mirrored in the sexual liberties that many of these individuals enjoyed. That sense of civic equality and freedom was eroded by Pinochet's repressive dictatorship, with sexual freedom diminishing with the arrival of yet another oppressive force: AIDS.

In the first *crónica*, the aforementioned "La noche de los visones," Lemebel presents a diachronic vision of the Chilean political and social climates as well as the epidemiological shift due to the emergence of HIV. The event that is remembered is firmly grounded in the "before," but despite the fact that the physical presence of HIV/AIDS had not yet been recognized in 1972, HIV/AIDS hang like specters over the photo. Subtly, Lemebel refocuses his textual gaze, allowing the sharp memories of the Allende years to fade to the background as the more immediate past comes into focus, providing a glimpse of what became of those pictured in that early photo. What follows is an enumeration of the central figures who were infected by the virus and eventually succumbed to it, depicting not only a loss of the freedoms and liberties that were abundant in the time period of the photo, but also a loss of innocence. True to the *crónica* genre and its multiple purposes, these references serve as a type of testimony about the impact of the virus on the community, humanizing it and giving voice to individuals who would otherwise end up as mere statistics, if that.

9. http://www.aegis.com/news/ips/2004/IP041009.html.

The first member of those in the photo to bring the virus back to the community was Pilola Alessandri, who, through prostitution, as Lemebel reveals with a great deal of irony, "se compró la epidemia en Nueva York, fue la primera . . . , la más auténtica " [she bought herself the epidemic in New York, she was the first . . . , the most authentic] (16). Also infected abroad was la Palma, who contracted the virus in Brazil. Shortly thereafter, Chumilou became infected, because "eran tantos billetes, tanta plata, tantos dólares que pagaba ese gringo" [there were so many bills, so much money, so many dollars that that gringo paid] and despite the fact that she was out of condoms on that particular night, she believed that her luck could not possibly be so bad that she would contract the virus on that one night (18–19). Not only do these vignettes manage to humanize the people behind the statistics; they also serve as an intimate portrayal of the epidemiological history, depicting not only *how* the virus was transmitted in these particular instances, but *why*. Particularly in the case of Chumilou, the reader is privy to her thought process before she makes the decision that eventually led to her contraction of HIV. Here we can see a mixing of textual strategies: diverging from the strict *crónica*, Lemebel incorporates fictional narrative strategies as well as psychological viewpoints that allow him to provide a plurality of perspectives. Again, this sort of hybridity calls to mind Hicks's metaphor of the hologram. Here, each pane reveals a different perspective regarding AIDS; taken together, they present a more complete picture of the AIDS epidemic and the complexities that are inherent to it.

This presentation becomes yet another one of the functions of Lemebel's *crónicas*. Despite the fact that AIDS was envisioned as another form of "colonización" [colonization], and certainly not a welcome immigrant to the gay community, Lemebel recognizes the importance of studying, revealing, and presenting this alternate history of AIDS in Chile, one that is unlikely to be heard in other arenas. The work becomes not only a textual history and testimony of the transvestite community, but also a written account of the epidemic. It serves a social function through the blend of accurate historical information combined with real-life personal testimony regarding the AIDS epidemic. However, it also retains some elements of fiction, drawing upon multiple narrative strategies as well as literary embellishments that make it difficult at times to accurately distinguish between what is fact and what is fiction. Perhaps for that reason Lemebel chose a genre that tends to lend more credence to its content by virtue of its traditional connection with historical events. Like the rest of this work, the fuzziness is intentional, allowing Lemebel to continue to straddle multiple arenas at one time. In fact, Lemebel admits that "cruzo temas como el Sida y la homosexualidad, pero el Sida desde los cuerpos vivos, no desde la medicina y el virus" [I cross themes like AIDS and homosexuality, but AIDS from (the perspective of) live bodies, not from medicine and the virus] (Jeftanovic 78).

This affirmation is central to understanding the way AIDS is treated in this work. Although it was most certainly not a positive change for the community, Lemebel's work strives to present *life* with AIDS, as well as the way that the community, displaced and divided by the dictatorship, slowly began to reunite because of AIDS and the commonality that it created among disparate individuals. Even if we look back at the depictions of Pilolí's, Chumilu's and la Palma's methods of contracting the virus, the tone alternates between sarcastic and humorous, celebratory and defiant. Unlike other authors I have been discussing in this study, Lemebel does not tend to recur to any of the predominant negative metaphors about AIDS that are used to euphemistically reference the disease while refusing to name it. Instead, AIDS is named so many times in this text that it loses its shock value. It exists, period. It has affected this community in countless ways.

Metaphors are used, but they become one of the ways in which Lemebel manipulates language and plays with his topics to tease out unique perspectives. He uses countless direct references to AIDS as well as clever puns that often add humor to the text. For example, he writes a sarcastic letter to Elizabeth Taylor, asking her to donate her emeralds to him so that he can use them to buy AZT. He closes the letter by assuring her that "Te estaré eternamente agrade-sida" [I will be forever grateful to you] (56). "Agrade-sida" is a play on "agradecida = grateful," illustrating one of many instances where Lemebel consciously uses references to AIDS not only to call attention to the situation of his protagonists, but to discharge some of the symbolic weight that the words carry. Lemebel plays with the word "SIDA/AIDS" and the imagery surrounding it in so many different ways that it begins to become impotent, thus permitting the individuals behind the virus to reemerge and continue living their lives and to commune with others, whether ill or healthy. As a result, Lemebel's focus is instead on capturing the way in which AIDS is lived by these protagonists and the effects it has on the group as a whole, particularly in relation to their position on the periphery.

HIV and AIDS contribute to the notion of liminality as well, in that they create an existence for those infected that often is a state of limbo. Particularly in the beginning of the trajectory of the personal experience with the virus, the individual can continue to appear and feel healthy, either unaware of the illness or not feeling the need to attend to it. Yet, as more and more friends, lovers, and acquaintances perish as a result of the illness, death beckons those infected, thus influencing the way life is approached and lived. Those infected stand on the fringe of life and death, navigating the interstitial space with resistance, friendship, love, and community. Most importantly, the topic does not remain shrouded in silence, either because of the openness among friends and colleagues or because "en el ghetto homosexual siempre se sabe quién es VIH positive, los rumores corren rápido" [in the homosexual ghetto, it is always known who is HIV-positive, the rumors spread quickly] (69). As a result, everyone shares in the reality of the epidemic, either through firsthand experience or through the companionship created among the *locas*. Because the virus has become so omnipresent in the community portrayed in Lemebel's work, he strives to capture the responses to it, expressing them in the plurality of voices that emitted them, thus uncovering rather that shrouding the reality, all the while celebrating the lives of those portrayed rather than prematurely writing their deaths.

What he reveals is that those infected recognize death as an imminent threat, but shift their focus instead to the other side of the gap that they straddle: life. We hear this echoed in the opinions captured by Lemebel: "El mismo SIDA es una razón para vivir. Yo tengo SIDA y eso es una razón para amar la vida. La gente sana no tiene por qué amar la vida, y cada minuto se les escapa" [AIDS itself is a reason to live. I have AIDS and that is a reason to love life. Healthy people don't have a reason to love life, and each minute escapes them] (71). One extreme example of this insistence on life over death is the ignorance portrayed by one of the protagonists, la Loba, when she discovers she is HIV-positive. Despite the news, she continues to believe herself to be healthy. This denial apparently serves her well, causing her roommates to wonder whether she had a pact with the devil because, despite her positive status, she lasted what seemed to be an impossibly long time without any medicine, projecting a healthy image that masked her physical deterioration. In la Loba's case, denial and refusal to truly contemplate death have allowed her to live her remaining life more fully, even tricking those around her into believing she was healthy even when they knew that she was in reality gravely ill.

Still others viewed AIDS as an advantage in a society that otherwise affords little or no support: "me hace especial, seductoramente especial. Además tengo todas las garantías . . . como portador, tengo médico, sicólogo, dentista, gratis" [It makes me special, seductively special. Moreover, I have security . . . as a carrier, I have free medical, psychological, and dental care] (71). Furthermore, the promise of a premature death is seen by some as an additional benefit because "nunca seré vieja, como las estrellas. Me recordarán siempre joven" [I'll never be old, like the (movie) stars. They'll always remember me young] (72). For the *locas* in this text concerned with artifice and performance, as well as the conscious manipulation of outward appearances, the promise of eternal youth is particularly alluring. It allows them to live an eternal present, adhering to the principles of *carpe diem*, rather than fearing the inevitable decline and loss that accompany aging.

What we see from these perspectives is a deliberate choice: when faced with the bifurcating roads that represent the options to one with AIDS, these protagonists chose life, and they chose to live it in the most ostentatious way, inviting all of their friends to join them in celebrating life as if it were a party. In fact, critic Margarita Sánchez has studied this performative, celebratory aspect of AIDS and concludes that "los síntomas de la enfermedad se convierten en vestuario, el cuerpo pálido y enfermo un monumento estético, la medicina en bebida embriagadora" [the symptoms of the illness become a wardrobe, the pale and sick body an aesthetic monument, medicine an intoxicating drink] (25). An important tenet that I would add is the fact that the makeup, outfits, and other external performative accoutrements are all intended for an audience, thus indicating the fact that these protagonists do not function in solitude. Their created selves not only reflect the individuals they strive to present publicly, but are their tools for seducing clients and are their common interests within their community. What we find is that all of the facets that would traditionally alienate and marginalize these protagonists from society (AIDS, homosexuality, transvestism, prostitution, and overt sexuality) are precisely what joins them and foments the creation of community.

In certain instances, the disease also becomes an instrument of resistance to be used by the gay community, as Lemebel portrays in the vignette "La Regine de aluminios el mono," in which soldiers regularly visit Regine, a prostitute, and use sex as an amnesiac for all of the atrocities they have committed, for which they overtly show no remorse. Her space infiltrated by representatives of the "enemy," Regine utilizes the scant tools at her disposal to subtly control and manipulate those who live under the illusion of absolute domination. She uses sex to moderate their bravado, all the while conscious of her secret weapon, AIDS. This secret device, AIDS, was freely transmitted to all but one soldier, Sergio, who frequented her; the lone soldier was the only one to show any sort of remorse or sense of conscience over the torture in which he participated. Regine and Sergio develop a platonic relationship that the other soldiers never understand and frequently criticize. Regine, however, is comforted by the thought that "mucho después que pasó la dictadura, el teniente y la tropa iban a entender el amor platónico del Serio y la Regine. Cuando los calambres y sudores fríos de la colitis les dieron el visto positivo de la epidemia" [long after the dictatorship passed, the lieutenant and troops would understand the platonic love between Sergio and la Regine. When the cramps and cold sweats of colitis gave them a clear view of the epidemic] (30). Despite her compromised position serving representatives of a government that brutally repressed her and her companions, Regine finds and uses the one weapon she possesses, her fatal disease, to silently fight back against the repressors. Ironically, it is her embodiment as a female that gives her the ability to use her sexuality to her advantage; she uses this constructed identity to attract and seduce the soldiers, and ultimately transmit HIV to them.

The *Locas*
PLURALITY OF GENDER

Lemebel's text has as its central thrust gender-crossing and transvestism, which are defined by plurality and ambivalence. The outward projection is female, a constructed self achieved through artifice, makeup, and, at times, medicine. Beneath it all are hidden male markers of identity, utilized during sex and revealed discriminately. Judith Butler, in *Gender Trouble*, through an analysis of drag, asserts that "we are actually in the presence of three contingent dimensions of significant corporeality: anatomical sex, gender identity, and gender performance" (137). In the context of Lemebel's protagonists, we can examine each of these three realms. All of the protagonists are anatomical males, but little to no emphasis is placed on this biological fact. Instead, all project a feminine gender identity, referring to themselves and each other as women. There is no instance in the text when they consider themselves men dressing as women; instead, they interact and communicate based on the premise that all identify with the female gender rather than the male gender. Furthermore, in the public sphere, this female gender is *performed* by the protagonists as they carefully strive to project a female visage to the world.

Lemebel's text, then, focuses on gender identity and performance rather than anatomical gender. This focus is further supported by the manner in which Lemebel references the protagonists, consistently choosing female-gendered pronouns and suffixes to demarcate the gender identity of his protagonists. Self-identification as a female while outfitted as such requires the use of female grammatical referents. Such referents become more apparent in Spanish, in which articles and adjectives additionally announce the gender of the subject. Lemebel announces the projected gender of the protagonists through his choice of words and suffixes. I have also upheld this convention throughout my analysis by referring to the protagonists as "she" as a manner to codify their gender identity and the performed gender rather than the anatomical gender. Although a simple change in pronoun cannot change the anatomical gender of the referent, it does call into question the constructed nature of gender itself.

Judith Butler expounds upon this concept by explaining that performativity

> must be understood not as a singular or deliberate "act" but, rather, as the reiterative and citational practice by which discourse produces the effects that it names . . . [and that] . . . the regulatory norms of "sex" work in a performative fashion to constitute the materiality of bodies and, more specifically, to materialize the body's sex. (*Bodies That Matter* 2)

Literary critic Ben Sifuentes-Jáuregui further elaborates on this notion in his study titled *Transvestism, Masculiniity, and Latin American Literature*, asserting that "transvestism is a performance of gender" (2). Utilizing both Butler's and Sifuentes-Jáuregui's theories, we can see how Lemebel's protagonists reveal the very constructedness of gender through the performance of female gender in the private and public spheres vis-à-vis transvestism. Butler describes this potentially subversive potential of drag by noting that "drag is subversive to the extent that it reflects on the imitative structure by which hegemonic gender is itself produced and disputes heterosexuality's claim on naturalness and originality" (*Bodies That Matter* 125). I agree with Lucía Guerra Cunningham's assertion that "La loca, en la ambigüedad subversiva de Él/Ella, es el desecho de la cultura y el patrimonio nacional . . . desafiando roles genéricos y esfumando fronteras" [The "loca," in the subversive ambiguity of he/she, is the reject of national culture and patrimony . . . challenging gender roles and blurring borders] (87). By projecting a feminine gender identity despite their understood but ignored masculine anatomical identities, these protagonists present a challenge to the hegemonic tendency to identify individuals through the categories into which they can be inserted. Instead, the protagonists function as the consummate border crossers, capable of inhabiting the worlds of both genders, comfortable with a plurality of identity and resistant to an overly reductionist sense of self.

Even the name chosen by Lemebel, *locas*, to refer to these individuals resists categorization. This choice of terms merits some further discussion. Quite a diverse range of terminology throughout literature and criticism is used to refer to varying tendencies toward cross-dressing by both heterosexuals and homosexuals. Butler discusses drag and the implications it has for gender performance. She reiterates, however, that many individuals who participate in drag are heterosexuals, thus disconnecting drag from an inherent relationship with homosexuality. Sifuentes-Jáuregui's study utilizes the term "transvestite," again never connecting it specifically to hetero- or homosexuals. Lemebel opts for the term *loca* to distinguish his protagonists from the more general category "gay," while at the same time illustrating the interconnectedness of the two identities. The *loca*, as Lemebel posits it, is not only the constructed female identity of his homosexual male protagonists, but a way for them to connect with their emotional, maternal side. This importance of the mother and femininity to the construction of identity calls to mind another *loca* in the Southern Cone context: Las Madres de la Plaza de Mayo, who were often disparagingly referred to as *locas* by the Argentine government in an attempt to discredit them and counteract the power they had acquired through unified, public protest. While that term aimed to destruct a legitimate, increasingly powerful figure in Argentine dictatorial society, Lemebel uses the term in nearly the opposite way. It is celebratory rather than derogatory, and it has as its goal the construction of a category for previously illegitimate, displaced citizens.

In fact, Lemebel has consciously crafted this figure and reflected the multiple reality of this being in his literature to resist the totalizing vision that was projected for Chilean society, particularly under Pinochet. Pinochet sadistically tried to meld Chilean citizens into a homogenized citizenry that represented the patriarchal, family-centered ideal that he projected. Obsessively driven by this objective, he subsequently cast out all those who did not fit his model, attempting to physically erase the so-called errant individuals in the search for his illusive model of societal perfection. Lemebel intentionally works to expose this strategy and criticize it through the exaltation and unapologetic celebration of a multiply marginalized being. In fact, literary critic Sandra Garabano affirms that "le interesa la figura del travesti por la fuerza desestabilizadora que la misma encierra" [he is interested in the figure of the transvestite for the destabilizing force that it entails] (48) and that Lemebel feels that this figure "es una construcción cultural y existencia poderosa, un regalo visual en este paisaje homogéneo y torturante" [is a cultural construction and powerful existence, a visual gift in this homogeneous and torturous landscape] (48).[10] Garabano continues that "Lemebel ha transformado

10. This original reference appeared in an interview that Claudia Donoso conducted with

la figura del travesti en ícono de resistencia frente a la uniformidad del consenso político chileno" [Lemebel has transformed the figure of the transvestite into an icon of resistance in the face of the uniformity of the Chilean political consensus] (48). The body of the transvestite "lograría revisar ciertas categorías tradicionales que definen lo femenino y lo masculino. La loca siempre está en proceso de construirse y como metáfora, se encuentra siempre en proceso de resignificación" [would manage to change certain traditional categories that define what is feminine and masculine. The loca is always in the process of constructing the self and as a metaphor, always finds himself/herself in a process of re-signification] (50).

This central figure not only represents hybridity, but *is* hybridity, presenting him- herself as both genders, navigating an epidemic that puts questions of life and death on the table, inhabiting a society in which "es un ser negado por la sociedad. Nadie quiere saber de él, pero todo el mundo aprecia la figura femenina que el mismo ha creado para la pantalla" [he is a being that is denied by society. No one wants to know about him, but everyone appreciates the female figure he has created for the screen] (Atenas 130). As such, she or he is elusive, resisting categorization and definition and failing to fit into any predefined societal space. As a result, this prismatic individual has the option of creating a desired version of self and projecting that identity back toward a society that at once rejects and embraces the image that is created. This facet becomes central to Lemebel's literary project: by focusing on an individual so imminently attached to the border and margin, yet so incapable of being pigeonholed into any one specific category, he is challenging the hegemonic discourse that assumes a homogenous society and refuses to recognize individuals such as these protagonists as members. Instead, Lemebel's text is an aperture through which members can be written into Chilean society, following their own rules rather than those imposed by the patriarchy. Instead, the *locas* have placed greater emphasis on creating a community centered on the importance of the female figure, starting with those whom they themselves project.

This connection with femininity begins with Lemebel himself, who sees females as his allies and constitutive of the majority of his interlocutors (Jeftanovic 76). His logic is circular, however, because the female entity is the link between all elements of humanity, and this vision breaks with the traditional paradigm of the patriarchy that sees a hierarchical distribution of power, centered on and controlled by the male figure.

Lemebel in *Paula*, July 2000, 84.

Instead, by invoking femininity in his particular expression of homosexuality, Lemebel is able to use homosexuality and transvestism as a counterdiscourse to patriarchy and hegemony.

Lemebel's texts are not simply about what the characters do; they are also about what they mean to society and how their actions can be read in relation to what surrounds them. Lemebel asserts that "me interesa la homosexualidad como una construcción cultural, como una forma de permitirse la duda, la pregunta; quebrar el falogocentrismo que uno tiene instalado en la cabeza" [I'm interested in homosexuality as a cultural construction, as a way to permit the self to doubt, question; to break the phallogocentrism that one has in their head] (Jeftanovic 76). Accordingly, "la loca no es real, es más bien una metáfora sobre la homosexualidad y la feminidad" [la loca isn't real, it's more a metaphor about homosexuality and femininity] (Jeftanovic 77). This textual figure as a cultural border crosser permits a free exploration of gender conflation, sexual fluidity, and social dynamism. She/he resists strict definition and represents the juxtaposition of previously separated contexts or ideals. By presenting such a figure as the central protagonist of these works, Lemebel is openly questioning the rigid delineation of sexuality and gender that Pinochet and others attempted to indoctrinate into society. He offers an alternative to multiple binaries, providing evidence of the possibility of crossing previously unbreachable borders. Multiplicity is permitted, accepted, and celebrated in this textual world. Moreover, healthy and ill bodies merge in a celebration of life while in the presence of death. Sexuality resists strict rules that seek to police its expression; instead, these protagonists comport themselves in a way that defies and subverts society's rules about sexual conduct.

Perhaps most importantly, there is a firm credence in the ability and the right to invent oneself, whether through external, corporeal preparation and presentation or through linguistic manipulation carried out in the process of renaming. The former is intimately connected to the figure of the *loca,* particularly the public persona whose acts and performances are crafted with an audience in mind. Many of these protagonists construct an identity based on international female icons, particularly from Hollywood. This image appropriation illustrates an international and intercultural awareness that serves as evidence of Chile's gradual transition toward globalization, particularly post-dictatorship. As the nation becomes a player on a global scale, its inhabitants become international consumers, particularly susceptible to the images projected by Hollywood. The uniqueness evidenced by Lemebel's protagonists, however, lies in the fact that female images are being appropriated rather than the "imágenes posmodernas de Rambo y Schwarzenegger" [postmodern images of Rambo and Schwarzenegger] (Cunningham 87). Madonna finds her Chilean form in one of the *locas* who obsessively copies her image. Elizabeth Taylor is the recipient of a sarcastic letter from another *loca*. Such intercultural dialogues and the desire to mimic these iconic female figures is a way of creating a female-centered global awareness, one that finds its expression in the community of *locas* who reject the male-anchored images pervasive in Chilean popular culture.

In addition to the appropriation of female images for the reinvention of self that many of these protagonists undergo, they also rename themselves in what Sánchez has called "su modo de resignificar la ceremonia del bautismo" [their way of re-signifying the baptismal ceremony] (32). In this traditional Catholic ceremony, the child is anointed by a male Church figure into the religious doctrine and receives an additional name as a symbol of that initiation. The priest or "father" presides over this ceremony, officially recognizing the name that was selected and imposed by the familial father. Conversely, "Al (des)bautizarse y anular la inscripción paterna, el travesti elige un nombre que lo hace parte de otra comunidad. El uso del apelativo femenino en este caso, rompe el pacto social familiar y genera un pacto con la comunidad travesti" [Upon (un)baptizing oneself and annulling the paternal inscription, the transvestite chooses a name that makes him part of another community. The use of a feminine name in this case breaks the familial social pact and creates a pact with the transvestite community] (33–34).

This process was also undertaken by Lemebel himself. While a member of "Las Yeguas del Apocalipsis," Lemebel was known by his paternally imposed name, Pedro Mardones. Around 1986–87, he began to reject his paternal moniker (Blanco and Gelpí 93) and subsequently decided to reject that name in favor of his mother's last name, Lemebel. He envisions this gesture as a manner of forming an alliance with "lo femenino" [the feminine], thus re-inscribing himself into a gynocentric linguistic history. By opting for a name not only connected to his maternal lineage, but also commemorative of a woman he describes as a "huacha," he is choosing to align himself with a subordinate citizen. Two ways of interpreting this appellative are its connection to labor, in this case, "washer," and its connotation of a person with no family lineage, in other words, an "orphan."[11] His mother, as a woman working in menial physical labor after fleeing from her family home, would have been seen by a traditional family as

---

11. The first definition comes from HarperCollins Spanish-English dictionary, while the second, less literal, connotation is a reference uncovered in other Chilean texts by Ksenija Bilbija (personal correspondence, 2004).

an outcast for leaving home at a young age, thus converting her into a family-less individual or orphan. However, in the eyes of Lemebel, she is yet another member of the margin and, as such, becomes representative of what Lemebel himself strives for and expresses in his texts: a celebration of the inhabitation of the liminal social space while creating alliances with others who operate outside of social norms. Lemebel sees his appropriation of the maternal name as a way to "reconocer a mi madre huacha desde la ilegalidad homosexual y travesti" [recognize my washer/orphan mother from the illegality of homosexuality and transvestism" (Blanco and Gelpí 94), thus connecting three distinct types of marginalities: femininity, homosexuality, and transvestism, all of which find their expression in this text.

In much the same way that Lemebel himself rejected the paternally inscribed moniker, each of his protagonists also participates in renaming herself to encapsulate the being she becomes as a transvestite. While striving to choose her personally selected names, each undergoes a detailed, complex process. Lemebel highlights the most popular ways people arrive at their new names. Some simply choose the feminine form of their male names, primarily by adding an "a" to the end. Others rename themselves as family matriarchs ("mamita," "tía," etc.), thus embracing a female-centered community. Still others (particularly the more innocent ones, in Lemebel's estimation) appropriate names from folklore, creating "Chelas" and "Rosas" based on popular female figures, effectively inserting themselves into popular cultural tradition. For the most sophisticated, Chilean imagery is not enough; instead they turn their gazes outward and rename themselves in honor of the great women of Hollywood, thus imitating and recreating "la Monroe, la Dietrich, etc." (59). Regardless of what name is chosen, this process is of utmost importance for these individuals striving to create a new community composed of those rejected by the hegemony. Naming is like starting anew, except this time the *locas* assume creative and linguistic control over their lives, projecting unto others the exact image they choose to craft. There is a very deliberate air to this systematic deconstruction of the markers of patriarchy that were initially imposed and that, through naming, makeup, clothing, and performance, are carefully reconstructed through an exaltation of femininity.

This process becomes even more important for those suffering from AIDS, a disease that threatens, through its fatality, to erase the identity markers that have been created. Furthermore, given the gravity that being a carrier brings, many see the process of naming as a way to find levity in a serious situation. Lemebel suggests such pun-filled names as "La María Sarcoma," "La Mosca Sida," "La Ven-seremos," and "La Sui-Sida" (60). Furthermore, by naming the self and rejecting the signs imposed by others, these protagonists allow themselves a fluidity of identity that permits them to navigate multiple spaces, projecting a modified self crafted for each situation or space. This notion of social space and place becomes yet another example of the plurality that these protagonists encounter on a daily basis.

Private and Public Space
LIMITED OPTIONS

Ever since the fall of the Unidad Popular and that utopic night frozen in time in the commemorated snapshot, the public space that was once open to all citizens, in accordance with the ideals of socialism, abruptly became controlled by the regime. As a result, the city attempted to regulate those who were considered part of the national project (Atenas 129). The regulation became rather overt under Pinochet, with the government physically removing, torturing, and killing those considered "subversive" or detrimental to the construction of nation. The *locas* inadvertently became part of this outcast group, relegated to the physical and social margins of society, no longer freely able to navigate the myriad public spaces in the more restricted dictatorial Chile.

As a result, the *locas* found the need to carve out whatever space they could salvage from the forbidden territory of authoritarian Chile. Sánchez summarizes this displacement and the strategies used to overcome it as she explains:

> La desaparición del espacio abierto dio lugar a la creación de otros lugares que, además de representar una alternativa de subsistencia, fueron locus de desafío contra el poder absoluto a través de actos prohibidos. La celebración travesti continuó en las esquinas oscuras, las discotecas subterráneas, los burdeles sin nombre.
>
> [The disappearance of open space gave way to the creation of other places that, in addition to representing an alternative for survival, were loci of defiance against the absolute power vis-à-vis prohibited acts. The transvestite celebration continued in dark corners, subterranean discotheques, nameless brothels.] (50)

In essence, the remaining public spaces available to the protagonists are those that have been set aside to accommodate those on the periphery or, more frequently, those that have been appropriated and created despite the increasing repression from the hegemony. The underlying consequence of this ever-shrinking public sphere is a growing sense of cohesion and community among those forced to seek refuge in places that are effectively invisible to the dominant culture—in other words, in places that mimic the sociocultural position of these protagonists and that are predominantly liminal entities with undefined boundaries.

One of the most visible public locations still occupied and frequented by these protagonists is "el disco gay." It is a place that belongs to the gay community, a venue in which these individuals who do not "fit" in other areas of society are at home and can be whoever they want to be and can act as they wish. It also functions as a place to connect and unite with old acquaintances or to find a potential partner, particularly for casual sex. People go to see and be seen. Lemebel is quick to point out the similarities between these gay discos and those catering to heterosexuals throughout the city, thus establishing a commonality between two disparate groups. He also recognizes the distinctions between the two, humorously pointing out that "si no fuera por el 'ay' que encabeza y decapita cada frase, podrían verse sumados a la masa social de cualquier discotheque" [if it weren't for the "ay" that starts and ends every sentence, they could see themselves added to the social masses of any discotheque] (52–53). This example shows that despite similar behaviors and goals, particularly when in a pickup bar, few ever look past small details such as this verbal tic to forge any connections. As a result, the gay community continues to be marginalized and to strive to make connections within, rather than without, their social group.

One of the most profound impacts of the loss of public space was the lack of a central location to organize, protest, and engage in critical discourse, particularly aimed against the government. With their freedom infringed, their speech severely censored, and their place in society effectively erased, the gay community had little springboard from which to foment activism. Consequently, the few public spaces available to them, such as the disco, became even more important. They were the only public spaces in which to exchange ideas and share strategies of resistance and, more importantly, survival. Otherwise, the *locas* were forced to turn inward and unite in private, thus forging connections with others on a smaller and more intimate scale.

One such locale was the whorehouse, a unique space in which interior and exterior worlds collided and differences were nullified by the common currency of sex. Here, the *locas* intermingled with the victimizers, literally sleeping with the enemy. However, it was their turf, and they had control. Lemebel depicts men who consider themselves heterosexuals succumbing to the seduction of the *locas* and disregarding the obvious males behind the female façades, uniting via sex with individuals they would likely avoid or scorn in public. In the whorehouse, the transvestites have the power and use it to control and manipulate their clients. In that unregulated space, sex and money are more important than social and political differences.

Moving to yet a more private space, we can also delve into the apartments shared among friends and the gift from Chumilou after she died, a gift whereby she bequeathed to her friends "la mansión de cincuenta habitaciones que me regaló el Sheik. Para que hagan una casa de reposo para las más viejas" [the fifty-room mansion that the Sheik gave me. So that you can make a rest home for the oldest ones] (19). This gift of a private, communal space provides a way to care for one another in their neediest moments—when ill or facing death, a scenario many encounter because of the prevalence of AIDS in the community. The choice to rely on one another rather than external sources of assistance and care during these critical times belies the distrust felt toward the dominant society and, conversely, the trust bestowed upon friends and those who share common bonds. In the vignette "El ultimo beso de Loba Lamar," Lemebel explores the intimate relationship between roommates occurring within the privacy of a shared apartment, relatively insulated from the outside world. Loba's final days fighting AIDS illustrate the importance of the community to the individual in need and the use of the private space to compensate for each other's weaknesses without repressive or judgmental input from members of the hegemony.

Despite Loba's rapid decline, she shuns official sources of help, seeing them as simply another space designed to segregate and stigmatize rather than unify and help. Consequently, she turns to her roommates and friends, who find themselves doing what they can to meet her needs. Because of the segregation and marginalization of this community, friends perform multiple roles in such dire situations, at times subordinating their own needs and desires to serve those in need, particularly recognizing that nowhere else would their friend or loved one receive the type of loving treatment that they could provide. Loba's situation hyperbolically shows the extreme sacrifice that friends make for one another, feeling duty-bound to perform even the most menial tasks. Those who tend to Loba show a remarkable willingness to satisfy her needs, even venturing out in the middle of winter to find fresh peaches and withstanding her dramatic tantrums and unrealistic expectations.

In addition to tending to her physical needs, such as bathing, feeding, and alleviating her pain, the friends serve as counselors, dealing with the delusional thoughts that befall her in her final days, particularly her belief that she is pregnant. Rather than confront her on this disillusion and create chaos and conflict in the final days of her life, the *locas* instead dedicate themselves to the fruitless task of knitting hats and booties for the "baby" and singing lullabies for the gestating "fetus." They also refuse to shatter her new-found illusion of self, covering all of the mirrors in the house to prevent her from seeing her altered form. They recognize that she has already dissociated from her dying self, and therefore they focus all of their energies on making her comfortable and providing companionship as she quickly approaches the end of her life.

On the night of her death, the *locas* are still there, resolute, refusing to leave her side despite the obvious strain that her hospice care has put on them. They accompany her through her agony: "Todas allí . . . esperando el minuto, el segundo que partiera la loca" [All of them there . . . waiting for the minute, the second that the loca passed] (45). This reference to "todas allí" illustrates how AIDS and the premature deaths that it has wrought on this particular group of individuals has had an unexpectedly positive effect of bringing the members even closer together, solidifying their love and support for one another and helping them construct a true sense of community in which they think of each individual as a part of the whole. They provide for one another what society cannot and often will not. They sacrifice their own selves to make sure that the days and weeks approaching death are not only bearable, but, if possible, even enjoyable. Despite their complaints to one another about the toll it takes on them, they never reveal to the departing member their feelings, protecting her from any and all negativity. Their loss is very real and deeply felt, regardless of the frustration expressed toward the merciless demands of the dying person. When Loba dies, they all protest her departure and try in vain to "bring her back" by begging her, rubbing her hands and feet, and showering her with hugs. When these acts are obviously unsuccessful, they go back to work, for the task of preparing her body also befalls them, making them not only pseudo-nurses, -nannies, -doctors, -priests, and -psychologists, but also funeral directors and morticians. Their ritual of preparation resembles that used to create the female image in life. Each aspect is of utmost importance, all with the express intent of projecting the appearance of a healthy being, despite the illness that has befallen her. Their meticulous preparation gets rather excessive when they decide they do not like the way her jaw has set in rigor and decide to try resetting it. In the end, they achieve the desired look, content that the body they have prepared is exactly how Loba would have wanted to look for her next public appearance: her funeral.

The funeral, an event that has become increasingly frequent in the lives of these protagonists because of AIDS, represents an intimate yet public event that has been redefined and re-inscribed by the *locas* to subvert the macabre and depressing aura typically surrounding it. Despite the official discourse that tends to ignore and underreport the number of people falling victim to AIDS in an effort to cover "una realidad escamoteada y oculta" [a secret, hidden reality] (Wilson 143), these protagonists refuse to pass from this life silently. Their most defiant moment is the funeral—an event that celebrates life in an extravagant, gala-like affair. Even before death occurs, the protagonists relate to one another in exactly the way they envision this culminating event. Chumilou, who died the same day that democracy arrived in Chile, demanded a grand event that united all members of the community. She was quick to point out that her body should be prepared so that "ni rastros de la enfermedad" [not any traces of the illness] (20) remained, thus projecting an image of health, beauty, and serenity despite the obvious agony she has undergone. The protagonists must rely on one another to meticulously attend to each detail of beauty and presentation in the same manner they would have done if they were alive. This perpetuation of the female image, one unmarred by illness and untouched by age, is vitally important to the constructed identity of these individuals. The funeral is the last public space in which to project that identity, and, as such, it is not viewed as a depressing event but instead "los funerales de una loca contagiada por el SIDA, se han transformado en un evento social" [the funerals of a loca who contracted AIDS have been transformed into a social event] (75).

This "event" status was particularly true in the 1990s, when some of the negative stigma attached to the early days of the epidemic had passed. Appearance is paramount, not only for the deceased, but also for the attendees, who see it as a place to "debut" their latest looks. This notion catapults the event to a nearly Hollywood-esque status, painting the dead as the star and the mourners as her loving, adoring fans. No one in the community would dream of missing such a vital chance to show off the latest fashions and thumb their noses at death in this ultimate defiant act. The *locas* choreograph everything as if it were a true performance, knowing that it will be judged afterward by all attendees.

They convert the act of mourning into a perpetuation of all of the image-constructing elements that the departed person would have loved or coveted herself. In the process, they re-semanticize death itself, converting it into a moment of resistance and defiance toward the imposed social codes of comportment. It also becomes a marker of community and a chance to strengthen the bonds that are already shared. They are initially connected by their marginalized status as homosexuals who have chosen to construct a female identity through transvestism, but AIDS and the rites of death are events that the majority also share, aware that with each funeral, they could very well be the "next" to be visited by death and repeating the creed: "hoy por ti, mañana por mí" [today it's you, tomorrow it will be me] (76). Their intimate knowledge of death, disease, and marginalization, as well as their common philosophy of celebratory, performative resistance, bonds these protagonists in their struggles against social and biological repression.

Community
LOCAL AND GLOBAL

Much as there is an awareness of shared bonds between the members of the community depicted in his text, Lemebel also exhibits a consciousness of global connections between these protagonists and others around the world suffering from similar plights. An awareness exists of the need to insert this local community into the national and international discourse through the only aperture possible at the time: the blurry, undefined space of the border, both literal and figurative. As border dwellers, these individuals, according to Atenas, appropriate the only "terreno que le(s) parece posible para existir y éste es el espacio del Otro" [terrain where it seems possible for them to exist and this is the space of the Other] (134). They are exceedingly aware of their differences from mainstream society and the hegemony's attempts to use these differences as justification for repressing and casting them out of the definition of nation. However, as we have seen throughout, they take advantage of this liminal space and marginalized status, choosing to celebrate and exalt it rather than simply succumbing to the pressures of the patriarchy. Bhabha captures this tendency, noting that "the boundary becomes the place from which *something begins its presencing*" (4). In other words, these individuals, relegated to the boundary of a society that would like to erase their existence, instead have created their own definition of community and in a sense have constructed their own nation within the borders of Chile, but operate according to their own ideals and standards. The epoch captured in this text represents a nation and individuals in a time of extreme transition on social, political, cultural, and epidemiological levels. According to Garabano, during this time period, "El mapa de la nación cambia, las fricciones entre el centro y la periferia se rearticulan alrededor de un nuevo proyecto político en el cual el corpus de la cultura gay . . . ayuda a crear una subjetividad conectada a los movimientos internacionales de liberación sexual" [The map of the nation is changing, the frictions between the center and the periphery are being rearticulated around a new political project in which the body of gay culture . . . helps to create a subjectivity connected to international sexual liberation movements] (53).

This growing global consciousness and interconnectivity are evident in Lemebel's work, particularly as it relates not only to the status as "other" in a repressive and dominating culture, but also in reference to the AIDS epidemic that has affected people on a global scale. Rejecting much of the common cultural currency of modern-day Chile, particularly because it refuses to recognize these *locas* as part of the nation, they instead adopt a more transnational attitude, one that, according to McClennen, opposes a strict cultural nationalism in that it projects a cultural identity that is devoid of any "myth of origins" (54). She goes on to posit that transnationalism is often representative of the exile because she/he is someone "who has lost national ties" (48). However, she also concurs with cultural critic Rosalba Campra that the Latin American national essence "is a cultural hybrid" (Campra quoted in McClennen 46), one composed of many different influences. Therefore, even those who still reside within the physical borders of a nation experience varying degrees of hybridity. What we can see in Lemebel's protagonists is a multiplication of hybridities on many different levels. They refuse to be bound by specific national constraints or any imposed markers of self. As a result, in their creation of personal and communal identity, they continue to cross borders, forming alliances with national and international subjects and thus projecting a diverse community that is influenced by and dialogues with both the Chilean dominant culture and multiple global movements, particularly in the realm of HIV/AIDS.

AIDS is an international health and social issue, and, as such, it links the *locas* to millions of others infected worldwide. Lemebel depicts his profusion of information and images both as a common theme understood by individuals from divergent backgrounds and also as a theme that "da para instalar un super mall, donde las producciones sidáticas se venden como pan caliente" [is enough to erect a super mall, where AIDS-related productions sell like hotcakes] (67). The exploitation and commercialization of the topic become a focus of Lemebel's wrath, filling an entire chronicle in which he laments the excessive promulgation of imagery and information, fearing that overkill will lead people to ignore the important messages being transmitted. On the other hand, he spends time highlighting such projects devoted to the memory of those who have died from AIDS, such as the international AIDS quilt and a local project in which families of AIDS victims created tapestries as a physical memory of their family members. The parallel projects, one global and one local, illustrate the common theme of remembrance, one experienced by all affected by AIDS. On this level, an intercultural understanding is produced via the negative experiences of the epidemic.

Even though the *locas* are united in actions and feelings, in the end there is recognition of the need for a local coalition to effect change in one's own community. Lemebel appears to advocate a more local approach to AIDS education and prevention, promoting "pequeños esfuerzos, cadenas de solidaridad y colectas chaucha a chaucha que algunos grupos de homosexuales organizan para palear el flagelo" [small efforts, chains of solidarity and collections penny by penny that some groups of homosexuals organize to beat back the scourge] (68). Against the backdrop of an international struggle, and aided by information and experiences garnered from individuals both in Chile and across the world, these activists work to change their particular part of the world, focusing their efforts on their own communities, thus making small steps of progress. As a result, they become more interconnected locally as they unite in their fight against this disease.

Although *Loco afán* advocates for more local activism on the part of autochthonous groups, it stops short of showing this philosophy in action, instead focusing on the process of forming a cohesive consciousness by way of intracommunity cooperation and assistance. The type of community that these protagonists have not only imagined but created aligns itself more with Bhabha's theories than with Anderson's original concept of imagined communities. Perhaps Bhabha summarizes it best when he notes that

> The currency of critical comparativism, or aesthetic judgement, is no longer the sovereignty of the national culture conceived as Benedict Anderson proposes as an "imagined community" rooted in a "homogenous empty time" of modernity and progress. The great connective narratives of capitalism and class drive the engines of social reproduction, but do not, in themselves, provide a foundational frame for those modes of cultural identification and political affect that form around issues of sexuality, race, feminism, the lifeworld of refugees or migrants, or the deathly social destiny of AIDS. (5)

Lemebel's work, in my estimation, exemplifies what Bhabha theorizes: it depicts a group of individuals marginalized by issues of sexuality and AIDS and illustrates how the individuals have utilized the liminal spaces they inhabit to inscribe themselves into the social narrative. Lemebel's protagonists have joined with one another to face a brutally tumultuous political epoch, followed by a devastating pandemic that hit this community particularly hard. Refusing to allow these individuals to be completely erased from a society that preferred to relegate them to (and beyond) the periphery, Lemebel appropriates this liminal space vis-à-vis the *crónica* to construct their own version of nation, one defined by multiplicity of gender, time, and space and united by difference, transvestitism, and AIDS. Instead of conforming to the version of nation imposed by the hegemony, these protagonists forge their own collective space out of the precise "differences" that were cause for their persecution by the dominant culture. Within that nascent community, interconnectivity provides the support necessary to continue resisting the numerous repressive forces at work in the Chilean society, forces that continue to be obstacles to countless individuals lacking the collective strength of community.

CONCLUDING THOUGHTS

Future Markers of Identity
An Ever-Shifting Landscape

Throughout the thirty-year history of the AIDS epidemic, there have been many significant advances in the areas of both prevention and medical care, drastically slowing the progression of the disease in infected individuals and cutting the rate of infection. Despite these medical advances, the physical reality of having AIDS is often compounded by the social construction of the disease and the multiple meanings attached to it in a particular society. Einhat Avrahami, in an enlightening study on illness autobiographies, asserts, "Clearly associated with not only the devalued category of the body but also with the subcategory of the ailing body, sick and disabled people are marked as Others" (41). Avrahami's assertion is particularly relevant in the case of narratives about HIV/AIDS because of the compounded issues of physical and psychological decline combined with the oft-stigmatized views of the disease and the perceived behaviors of those who contract it. As we have seen throughout this study, the authors discussed often have keen awareness of this subaltern status: it has become a formative part of each of their texts. The protagonists, while divergent in many ways, all contend with the serious notion of how to confront a drastically altered sense of self in the face of a potentially fatal illness, and they struggle to find a place in societies that often attempt to marginalize and ostracize those afflicted with HIV and AIDS.

Throughout the course of my study, I have focused on these multiple markers of identity and the ways in which these protagonists conceptualized and navigated their status as others at distinct moments in the history of the epidemic in Spanish America. Despite this vastly diverse depiction of AIDS in the lives of drastically different protagonists from authors from divergent areas of Spanish America, certain common themes and trends emerge in these works that merit further discussion. The first is the notion of agency and how each protagonist, vis-à-vis his or her particular struggle, attempts to come to terms with the fact that his or her body has been subjugated on a cellular level by a pervasive virus that often causes drastic physical and psychological changes which impact all areas of their lives. In the face of this waning control on a biological level, many of the protagonists turn their focus toward other avenues to exert agency over their own lives or, in some cases, the lives of those around them.

The concept of agency intersects and often overlaps with the other two notions that reappear in these works: the act of writing as one manner to construct and exert a reconceptualized identity and the importance of space to understanding one's new reality, particularly in relation to the hegemony that often seeks to exclude or erase HIV-positive individuals from the social body. In that sense, the appropriation of individual and communal space on the part of these protagonists, as well as their appearance in texts that delve into these complex, oft-ignored issues, is one of the fundamental steps necessary for the re-inscription of HIV-positive individuals not only in literature, but in the broader social ambit. Each of these texts examines to some degree the notion of agency, often in conjunction with the mechanism of writing, as an attempt to exert control over their protagonists' new situations as well as carve out space for their altered beings.

In the texts examined in chapter 1, agency is the primary preoccupation, whereby each protagonist manipulates the body, recognizing the potential to use his or her body as the weapons they have become due to HIV infection. All three choose to exert that potential, opting to eschew any moral responsibility for their conditions and instead directing their rage toward other, seemingly "healthy" bodies. Despite exhibiting agency, the way in which it manifests itself in these texts is disturbing because it involves the overtaking of another person's body in the name of dominancy and authority on the part of the protagonists. In other words, in the process of taking control over their own body and life, these protagonists encroach on others and usurp their societal space through sadistic manipulation and determined destruction of the other. While Eloy Martínez's protagonist acts out this cycle on one unwitting victim, Solari's and Griffero's characters turn it into a pattern, carving an increasingly larger niche for themselves out of the void left from the destruction of others.

The authors structured this dynamic within the realm of revenge narratives that focus much of the narrative attention on the protagonists' perceptions of self and thoughts about their actions rather than on the victims. However, the implications of those actions on a societal level raise serious questions about this type of representation. This depiction of HIV-positive individual as violent, destructive aggressor plays into societal paranoia about the disease and contributes to negative stereotypes about AIDS because it promotes, and perpetuates, the notion that HIV-positive people are inherently dangerous to those around them. This stance is further supported by the recurrence to damaging plague, militaristic, and apocalyptic metaphors that continually reinforce pervasively negative and judgmental attitudes about AIDS.

What results is a distinct sort of identity-construction process quite different from what is examined in other chapters. Because so much of the focus is on one component of the new bodily reality brought about by AIDS, namely, the possibility to wreak havoc and harm on others, the gaze remains focused outward. Very little self-reflection occurs, thus truncating the possibility of truly reconceptualizing the individual identity. Instead, the protagonists exert their energies by intentionally destroying others to create the illusion of power over their new corporeal identities. Despite the illusion of control created by these destructive actions, none of the protagonists actually takes over the narrative power, thus illustrating the incomplete process of constructing a new identity based on a "dominating body" that destroys others for its own benefit. What we see in later chapters is that when agency, writing, and space all converge, the protagonists appear more at ease with their new identities, suggesting that the act of writing and creating a textual space to explore the conceptualization of self is essential to the full actualization of agency.

In chapter 2 the concept of control manifests itself quite differently. In both Ramos Otero's and Blanqué's works, the protagonists come to accept their compromised physical states and choose to confront their impending deaths by guiding the way in which their lives are to be remembered. Armed with the tools of poetry and fairy tale to construct their own biographies, both protagonists have the freedom to portray their sexuality as they choose. Ramos Otero's poetic voice confronts his past and future through the construction of an "hombre de papel" that utilizes the poetic conventions of both traditional love poems and elegy to exalt his sexual self while coming to terms with his impending death. Writing provides a space to explore these conflicting realities, ultimately bestowing upon the poetic voice the power to portray his life through his own pen, and to confront AIDS through memories and words.

In Blanqué's case, although her protagonist does not have the ultimate control granted in Ramos Otero's work, the story is constructed as a retelling of the protagonist's own words about her life, sexual exploration, and impending death. For Ten-Ying, agency manifests itself first in her defiant decision to leave home despite her family's wishes, and, further, through her insistence on romanticizing her life as a prostitute, celebrating an otherness that society would typically condemn. The story she conveys depicts a fairy-tale-like existence as she travels the world after intentionally fleeing her father's control, much as Rapunzel did in the classic fairy tale. Ten-Ying portrays a life in which she appropriates spaces dominated by males, offering her sexualized body as currency to obtain adventure, excitement, and freedom. Even when her body succumbs to AIDS' advances, her mind relives her experiences with satisfaction and pride, allowing her to confront death without any expressed fear.

Both Ramos Otero's and Blanqué's protagonists choose to direct their gazes backwards, toward memories of lives filled with sexual adventure and defiant freedom, envisioning their bodies as portals of pleasure rather than vectors of disease. In the process, they renounce castigatory views of sexuality and their conditions, effectively celebrating their subaltern status in a way that allows them to commemorate life to the fullest, despite AIDS. Throughout that process, narrative allows them to exert control over the construction of their memories and, ultimately, their lives.

In chapter 3, the protagonists depicted by Prieto, Mallach, and Pérez are all acutely aware of their status as others in society as a result of their HIV status; as such, they all grapple with the compounding effects of the social taboos against HIV and AIDS, made more difficult to contend with because of their physical deterioration and concurrent unwillingness to accept their burgeoning identities as HIV-positive individuals. They all perpetuate this notion of subalternity by choosing to erase themselves from the social space through extreme isolation and self-imposed exile. The most perverse example of this attempt to re-assert control over one's life and redefine one's personal space is seen in Prieto's work, which is significant because it reflects some of the perceptions circulating at the inception of the epidemic in 1981.

His sadistic protagonist, Marcos, has internalized all of the negative connotations surrounding the virus, including the notion that AIDS = death, and he views his own infection as a harbinger of a personal and familial apocalypse. He sees no way to live with the disease and exerts his agency by taking control over his mother's life. We saw his control exert itself through a drastic reduction in space, to the point where the family home is cloistered and the mother is physically restrained in her own bed.

Marcos reduces his own ambient to a coffin that he is constructing as he prepares for his own demise. In addition to the manipulated physical surroundings, Marcos becomes obsessive in his need to control. Convinced that the arrival of AIDS is a sign of the destruction of mankind, Marcos cuts his mother off from all external contacts and sadistically controls her body. Being unable to stop the destruction going on in his own body, he turns his focus to his mother. However, instead of transferring any desire to become well onto his treatment of her, he instead regulates her daily bodily functions, often neglectfully. The ultimate assertion of agency comes in the end, when Marcos chooses to take not only his own life, but that of his mother, again in adherence to his deluded belief that AIDS would destroy humanity.

Negative social connotations regarding AIDS also infiltrated Mallach's work, in which his protagonist, Rodrigo, chooses to flee his life rather than learn how to continue to live it while succumbing to the physical deterioration that accompanies AIDS. His agency presents itself in the intentional extrication of self from his surroundings, as he chooses to travel through unknown locales, avoiding contact and communion with most others. For Rodrigo, this shifted space was necessary to be able to begin the process of reconceptualizing his identity, having freed himself from all of the traditional markers associated with the physical spaces and social connections he left behind. Initially, distance serves as a way to try to erase and forget his identity, particularly the diseased portion of it. However, through some interactions with others, as well as an eye-opening experience in the solitude of the Amazon, Rodrigo, in the end, uses this self-created distance from his previously known existence to confront and slowly come to terms with his new identity. It is only upon accepting his new self that he is able to re-enter the world he fled, altered not only physically by the disease, but also by the journey of self-discovery he undertakes.

The last text of chapter 3 illustrates the degree to which extreme physical weakness and deterioration can lead to a reduction in social space and interaction. Such is the case for much of Pérez's diary, in which he recounts his daily issues with HIV and his concurrent psychological depression and conviction that death will come within the year. For most of that period, Pablo's body is so weak that it usurps much of his agency, rendering him unable to function in most aspects of his life. Despite this physical lack of control, Pablo's diary and the very act of writing are the primary manifestations of agency he can render, providing him the forum in which to grapple with his altered sense of self and the increasingly reduced social space within which he functions. Short of being liberating, the diary becomes the only destination he has the strength to visit on an almost daily basis, at times providing solace for the claustrophobic physicality and social and personal isolation that dominate his life. This text is significant because it marks an important moment in the history of the epidemic—the introduction of AZT and other antiretrovirals into the medical arsenal to fight the disease. This diary depicts that drastic shift as we see a reversal of a previously rapidly degenerative disease. As Pablo's body becomes stronger and the virus's grip on it begins to recede, he is able to leave the textual space within which he records most of his year, and he ventures out into his community, reconnecting with friends and family and forging new alliances as he strives to not only survive but also live with HIV.

Throughout the first three chapters of this study, I have primarily focused on individuals in interaction with a sexual partner, friend, or lover, or in solitude. In each case, there is an awareness of the position of these protagonists on society's margin because of their HIV status, but this status as other is seen through the eyes of individuals who have internalized society's proscription of HIV-positive individuals and whose actions result from the perceived negativity surrounding their conditions. All manifestations of agency on their part strive to overcome individual alterations in self-identity, and have less to do with constructing a space for themselves within the society at large or coming to terms with how to live in society as a subaltern being. Part of this failure to construct a space for their newly subaltern selves is due to the realities and perceptions of the epidemic as depicted in these works. Most works focus on the earlier years of the disease, when fatalities were the norm and promising medical advances were still in the distant future. In addition, social stigma was a force so strong that it shrouded any ability to rationally confront the disease as a simple biological reality, and it therefore often perpetuated mistruths and stereotypes that prevented people from accessing medical care.

The last chapter of my study differs significantly from these earlier depictions, both in the fact that it depicts a later moment in the history of the epidemic (1996, the year that AZT entered the scene), and in Lemebel's insistence on deconstructing the social meanings of the disease to show the possibility of subverting the notion of the subaltern to create a new space in society for those previously marginalized. Lemebel's crónica illustrates the plurality and cohesiveness that derive from the creation of a community of individuals previously cast out of society because of AIDS, homosexuality, and transvestism, all conditions relegating them to the periphery. His text illustrates an astute awareness of this seemingly compromised position on society's margins. Lemebel appropriates this ambivalent liminal state, celebrating the multiple hybridities of the individuals to assert their identities and create a social space for them through his writing. Using the *crónica*, Lemebel gives voice to these previously silent, subjugated individuals, allowing them to construct their own version of nation and self, one defined by multiplicity of gender, time, and space and united by difference, transvestitism, and AIDS. Instead of conforming to the version of nation imposed by the dominant culture, these protagonists forge their own collective space out of the precise differences that were cause for their persecution. In the end, Lemebel's writing affords these *locas* a textual space from which to exert their agency and construct a space for themselves and their companions in a society that would prefer to negate their existence. Perhaps more than any other text that I have examined, Lemebel's *crónicas* provide an example of how a strong sense of agency, combined with a carefully constructed textual space that "writes" this community of *locas* into the social landscape, affords these protagonists the tools to confront the oppression wrought by AIDS, as well as the social subjugation prevalent in the lives of many who face the disease.

When I began to conceptualize this project, I was struck by the apparent lack of literary and critical attention paid to this topic in the realm of Spanish America. The seeming contradiction between a pervasive social topic that appeared to have been ignored in the realm of fictional narrative was difficult to comprehend, particularly from my position in the U.S. academia where critical and literary discourse on AIDS is abundant. In fact, as I mentioned, the words of Ricardo Chávez-Castaneda resonated with my initial findings: "el tema, dicho de la manera más simple, brilla por su ausencia." However, as I began to delve into contemporary Spanish American literature in search of representations of AIDS, I discovered some trends. First, AIDS *does* appear in narrative, but often it has been shrouded in silence and secrecy. The notion of the taboo is still very strong, so that those who have addressed the topic often do so using some of the aforementioned techniques of silence and metaphor common to individuals accustomed to maneuvering around a social taboo. Second, representations of individuals with AIDS are still connected to the margins, with many of the protagonists conceptualized as subjugated societal outcasts. Furthermore, the texts themselves are marginalized to some degree; the majority of authors I studied do not belong to the traditional literary canon, but rather are emerging writers or figures like Ramos Otero and Lemebel, whose work is renowned, but who seem to prefer to exist outside of the traditional spaces of literature.

The central question for future research, in my view, relates to how this disease will be depicted in the future. Will HIV-positive individuals consistently be depicted as others, or will there be a day when a shift occurs and the disease loses its connection to the margin? Given that HIV and AIDS are constantly evolving and affecting societies in different ways, particularly in relation to the treatments that are developed to combat them, it is likely that literary depictions of them will also continue to evolve, mutate, and shift as writers respond to a global epidemic with very personal implications. It remains to be seen how these shifts will be reflected in literature and how the textual archive of this epidemic will be transformed. It is my personal hope, however, that as societies begin to develop more effective treatments (and possibly a cure) for AIDS, future studies will have the option to explore not only the current connection that AIDS has with physical decline and death, but also the triumphant association with survival and life as individuals and societies find ways to usurp the power that AIDS currently wields in contemporary society.

WORKS CITED

Albuquerque, Severino J. *Tentative Transgressions: Homosexuality, AIDS and the Theater in Brazil.* Madison: University of Wisconsin Press, 2004.
Anderson, Benedict R O'G. *Imagined Communities: Reflections on the Origin and Spread of Nationalism.* New York: Verso, 1991.
Apter, Emily. "Fantom Images: Hervé Guibert and the Writing of 'Sida' in France." *Writing Aids: Gay Literature, Language and Analysis.* Ed. Timothy F. Murphy and Suzanne Poirer. New York: Columbia University Press, 1993.
Arenas, Reinaldo. *Antes que anochezca: Autobiografía.* Barcelona: Tusquets Editores, 1992.
Armus, Diego, ed. *Disease in the History of Modern Latin America: From Malaria to AIDS.* Durham, NC: Duke University Press, 2003.
———. "Disease in the Historiography of Modern Latin America." *Disease in the History of Modern Latin America: From Malaria to AIDS.* Ed. Diego Armus. Durham, NC: Duke University Press, 2003.
———. "Tango, Gender, and Tuberculosis in Buenos Aires, 1900–1940." *Disease in the History of Modern Latin America: From Malaria to AIDS.* Ed. Diego Armus. Durham, NC: Duke University Press, 2003.
Atenas, Dino Plaza. "Lemebel o el salto de doble filo." *Revista Chilena de Literatura* 54 (1999): 123–35.
Avrahami, Einat. *The Invading Body: Reading Illness Autobiographies.* Charlottesville: University of Virginia Press, 2007.
Bacchilega, Cristina. *Postmodern Fairy Tales: Gender Narratives and Strategies.* Philadelphia: University of Pennsylvania Press, 1997.
Bataille, Georges. *Eroticism.* Trans. Mary Dalwood. New York: Penguin Books, 1962.
Bellatín, Mario. *Salón de Belleza/Efecto Invernadero.* Mexico: Consejo Nacional Para la Cultura y las Artes, Ediciones del Equilibrista, 1996.
Bhabha, Homi. *Locations of Culture.* New York: Routledge, 1994.
Biron, Rebecca E. *Murder and Masculinity: Violent Fictions of Twentieth Century Latin America.* Nashville, TN: Vanderbilt University Press, 2000.
Blanco, Fernando and Juan G. Gelpí. "El desliz que desafía otros recorridos. Entrevista con Pedro Lemebel." *Nómada* 3 (1997): 93–98.

Blanco, José Joaquín. "Zapata: El vampiro en los años del SIDA." *Las intensidades corrosivas*. Villahermosa, Tabasco: Instituto de Cultura de Tabasco, 1990.
Blanqué, Andrea. "Adiós, Ten-Ying." *Querida muerte*. Montevideo: Prisma Ltda., 1993.
———. "Personal Interview." Ed. Jodie Parys. Montevideo, 1997.
Bliss, Katherine Elaine. "Between Risk and Confession: State and Popular Perspectives of Syphilis Infection in Revolutionary Mexico." *Disease in the History of Modern Latin America: From Malaria to AIDS*. Ed. Diego Armus. Durham, NC: Duke University Press, 2003.
Bromberg, Sarah. "Existential Feminism." *Feminist Issues in Prostitution*. International Conference on Prostitution. California State University, Northridge, 1997. http://www.feministissues.com/index.html.
———. "Liberal Feminism." *Feminist Issues in Prostitution*. International Conference on Prostitution. California State University, Northridge, 1997. http://www.feministissues.com/index.html, 1997.
Brophy, Sarah. *Witnessing AIDS: Writing, Testimony, and the Work of Mourning*. Toronto, ON: University of Toronto Press, 2004.
Butler, Judith. *Bodies That Matter: On the Discursive Limits of Sex*. New York: Routledge, 1993.
———. *Gender Trouble: Feminism and the Subversion of Identity*. New York: Routledge, 1990.
Cady, Joseph. "Immersive and Counter-immersive Writing about AIDS: The Achievement of Paul Monette's Love Alone." *Writing AIDS: Gay Literature, Language and Analysis*. Ed. Timothy F. Murphy and Suzanne Poirer. New York: Columbia University Press, 1993.
Connell, R. W. *Masculinities*. Berkeley: University of California Press, 1995. 84.
Cranwell, Elizabeth Azcona. "Susan Sontag contra las metáforas del SIDA" *La Nación* July (1990): 1–2.
Crimp, Douglas, ed. *AIDS: Cultural Analysis, Cultural Activism*. Cambridge, MA: MIT Press, 1988.
Cruz-Malavé, Arnaldo. "Toward an Art of Transvestism: Colonialism and Homosexuality in Puerto Rican Literature." *¿Entiendes?: Queer Readings, Hispanic Writings*. Ed. Emilie L. Bergmann and Paul Julian Smith. Durham, NC: Duke University Press, 1995.
Cuarón, Carlos. "Sólo con tu pareja." Alfonso Cuarón. México, D.F.: IMCINE, 1991.
Cunningham, Lucia Guerra. "Ciudad neoliberal y los devenires de la homosexualidad en las crónicas urbanas de Pedro Lemebel." *Revista Chilena de Literatura* 56 (April 2000): 71–92.
Denneny, Michael. "AIDS Writing and the Creation of a Gay Culture." *Confronting AIDS through Literature*. Ed. Judith Laurence Pastore. Chicago: University of Illinois Press, 1993.
Dollimore, Jonathan. *Death, Desire, and Loss in Western Culture*. London: Penguin Press, 1998.
Edelman, Lee. "The Mirror and the Tank: AIDS, Subjectivity and the Rhetoric of Activism.'" *Writing AIDS: Gay Literature, Language and Analysis*. Ed. Timothy F. Murphy and Suzanne Poirer. New York: Columbia University Press, 1993.
Martínez, Tomás Eloy. *El vuelo de la reina*. Buenos Aires: Alfaguara, 2002.
Esslin, Martin. *An Anatomy of Drama*. New York: Hill and Wang, 1976.
Fernández, Juan Enrique. "Personal Interview." Ed. Jodie Parys. Montevideo, 1997.
Figueroa, Alvin Joaquín. "Feminismo y homosexualidad: Las voces de Luisa Valenzuela, Manuel Ramos Otero y Carmen Valle." *New Voices in Latin American Literature*. Ed. Ollantay Press. Vol. III. New York: Ollantay Press Literature/Conversation Series, 1993.
Foster, D. W., ed. *Chicano/Latino Homoerotic Identities*. Garland Reference Library of the Humanities, vol. 16, 1999.
Frank, Arthur W. *The Wounded Storyteller: Body, Illness, and Ethics*. Chicago, IL: The University of Chicago Press, 1995.
Galindo, Alberto S. *Atlas of AIDS: Culture, Circulation and AIDS in Latin America*. Doctoral Dissertation: Princeton University, 2006.

Garabano, Sandra. "Lemebel: Políticas de consenso, masculinidad y travestismo." *Chasqui* 32.1: 47–55.
Garasa, Delfín Leocadio. "SIDA y literatura." *La Nación-suplemento literario* (Feb. 3, 1991): 6.
Gilman, Sander L. "AIDS and Syphilis: The Iconography of Disease." *AIDS: Cultural Analysis, Cultural Activism*. Ed. Douglas Crimp. Cambridge, MA: MIT Press, 1988.
Gottlieb, Michael and Jerome E. Groopman, eds. *Acquired Immune Deficiency Syndrome: Proceedings of a Shering Corporation-UCLA Symposium* (held in Park City, Utah, February 5–10, 1984). New York: Liss, 1984.
Graziano, Frank. *Divine Violence: Spectacle, Psychosexuality, & Radical Christianity in the Argentine "Dirty War."* Boulder, CO: Westview Press, 1992.
Griffero, Ramón. "El secreto de Berlín." *Soy de la Plaza Italia*. Santiago de Chile: Neptuno Editores, 1992.
———. "Personal Correspondence." Ed. Jodie Parys, December 2003.
Grimm, Jacob and Wilhelm Grimm. "Rapunzel." *Grimm's Fairy Tales*. Ann Arbor, MI: Borders Classics.
Henderson, Mae, ed. *Borders, Boundaries, and Frames: Cultural Criticism and Cultural Studies*. New York: Routledge, 1995.
Hernández, Wilfredo. "Homosexualidad, rebelión sexual y tradición literaria en la poesía de Manuel Ramos Otero." *Sexualidad y nación*. Ed. Daniel Balderston. Pittsburgh, PA: Instituto Internacional de Literatura Iberoamericana, 2000. 225–41.
———. "Política homosexual y escritura poética en Manuel Ramos Otero." *Chasqui* 29.2 (2000): 73–95.
Hicks, Emily. *Border Writing: The Multidimensional Text*. Minneapolis: The University of Minnesota Press, 1991.
Ingenschay, Dieter. "Hemispheric Looks at Literary AIDS Discourses in Latin America." *Iberoamericana* 20 (2005): 141–56.
Jacoby, Roberto. "Introduction." *Un año sin amor*, by Pablo Pérez. Buenos Aires: Perfil Libros, 1998
Jacoby, Susan. *Wild Justice: The Evolution of Revenge*. New York: Harper and Row, 1983.
Jeftanovic, Andrea. "El cronista de los márgenes: Interview with Pedro Lemebel." *Lucero* 11 (Spring 2000): 74–83.
Jones, James W. "Refusing the Name: The Absence of AIDS in Recent American Gay Male Fiction." *Writing AIDS: Gay Literature, Language and Analysis*. Ed. Timothy F. Murphy and Suzanne Poirer. New York: Columbia University Press, 1993.
Kaminsky, Amy K. *After Exile: Writing the Latin American Diaspora*. Minneapolis: University of Minnesota Press, 1999.
Kleinman, Arthur, M.D. *The Illness Narratives: Suffering, Healing, and the Human Condition*. Basic Books, 1988.
Knapp, Bettina L. *Exile and the Writer: Exoteric and Esoteric Experiences; a Jungian Approach*. University Park: Pennsylvania State University Press, 1991.
Krueger, Steven F. *AIDS Narratives: Gender and Sexuality, Fiction and Science*. New York: Garland, 1996.
Kuhnheim, Jill S. "El mal del siglo veinte: Poesía y SIDA." *Revista de Crítica Literaria Latinoamericana* 29.58. (2003): 115–29.
Lacan, Jacques. "The Mirror Stage as Formative of the Function of the I as Revealed in Psychoanalytic Experience." Trans. Alan Sheridan. *Écrits: A Selection*. New York: W. W. Norton, 1977. 1–7.
Larvie, Patrick. "Nation, Science, and Sex: AIDS and the New Brazilian Sexuality." *Disease in the History of Modern Latin America: From Malaria to AIDS*. Ed. Diego Armus. Durham, NC: Duke University Press, 2003.
Lemebel, Pedro. *Loco afán: crónicas de sidario*. Santiago de Chile: LOM Ediciones, 1996.
Liguori, Ana Luisa. "El SIDA y sus metáforas." *Debate feminista*. 3 (1991): 279–89.

Llamas, Ricardo. "La reconstrucción del cuerpo homosexual en tiempos de SIDA." *Construyendo sidentidades: Estudios desde el corazón de una pandemia.* Ed. Ricardo Llamas. México: Siglo Veintiuno Editores, 1995.
MacCabe, Colin. "Introduction." *Eroticism*, by George Battaille. Trans. Mary Dalwood. New York: Penguin Books, 1962.
Maier, Linda S. "A Mirror Game: Diffraction of Identity in *La vida breve*." *Romance Quarterly* 34.2 (1987): 223–32.
Mallach, Nelson. "Elefante." *Historia de un deseo: El erotismo homosexual en 28 relatos argentinos contemporáneos.* Ed. Leopoldo Brizuela. Buenos Aires: Planeta, 2000.
McClennen, Sophia A. *The Dialectics of Exile: Nation, Time, Language, and Space in Hispanic Literatures.* West Lafayette, IN: Purdue University Press, 2004.
Merced, Jorge B. "Teatro y SIDA." *Ollantay* 2.2 (1994): 20–26.
Morris, David B. *Illness and Culture in the Postmodern Age.* Los Angeles: University of California Press, 1998.
———. "The Plot of Suffering." *Evil after Postmodernism.* Ed. Jennifer L. Geddes. New York: Routledge, 2001.
Murphy, Timothy F. and Suzanne Poirier, eds. *Writing Aids: Gay Literature, Language, and Analysis.* New York: Columbia University Press, 1993.
Musiak, Diego. "Fotos del alma." Ed. Diego Musiak. Buenos Aires: Adagio Films, 1995.
Navarro, Ray. "Eso, me está pasando." *Queer Looks: Perspectives on Lesbian and Gay Film and Video.* Ed. Martha Gever, Pratibha Parmar, and John Greyson. New York: Routledge, 1993.
Nelson, Emmanual S., ed. *AIDS: The Literary Response.* New York: Twayne, 1992.
Nodarse, Frank Padrón. "El "otro": Cine y SIDA." *La Gaceta de Cuba* 34.2 (1996).
Ortiz, Ricardo L. "Pleasure's Exile: Reinaldo Arenas's Last Writing." *Borders, Exiles, Diasporas.* Ed. Elazar Barkan and Marie-Denise Shelton. Stanford, CA: Stanford University Press, 1998.
Pastore, Judith Laurence, ed. *Confronting AIDS through Literature: The Responsibilities of Representation.* Urbana: University of Illinois Press, 1993.
Paternostro, Silvana. *In the Land of God and Man: Confronting Our Sexual Culture.* New York: Penguin Books, 1998.
Pérez, Pablo. *Un año sin amor.* Buenos Aires: Perfil Libros, 1998.
Pino, Ángeles Mateo del. "Chile, una loca geografía o las crónicas de Pedro Lemebel." *Hispamérica* 80/81 (1998): 17–29.
Posso, Karl. *Artful Seduction: Homosexuality and the Problematics of Exile.* Ed. European Humanities Research Centre. University of Oxford: Legenda, 2003.
Powell, David A. "Public vs. Private in the Diary Form: George Sand's *Journal D'un Voyageur Pendant La Guerre.*" *Autobiography, Historiography, Rhetoric: A Festschrift in Honor of Frank Paul Bowman.* Ed. Mary Donaldson-Evans, Lucienne Frappier-Mazur, and Gerald Prince. Atlanta: Rodopi, 1994.
Prieto, Ricardo. "Personal Interview." Ed. Jodie Parys. Montevideo, 1997.
———. "Pecados mínimos." *Teatro.* Montevideo: Proyección, 1993.
Otero, Manuel Ramos. *Invitación al polvo.* Río Piedras, Puerto Rico: Plaza Mayor, 1991.
Rodríguez Matos, Carlos, ed. *POESÍdA.* Jackson Heights, NY: Ollantay Press, 1995.
Romero-Cesareo, Ivette. "Moving Metaphors: The Representation of AIDS in Caribbean Literature and Visual Arts." *Displacements and Transformations in Caribbean Cultures* (2008): 100–126.
Rosati, Roxana Delbene. "Resisting a Stigmatized Identity: Patients' Strategies for the Management of the HIV/AIDS Stigma in a Public Hospital in Uruguay." *Sociolinguistic Studies* 1.2 (2007).
Rosenkrantz, Guillermina. *El cuerpo indómito: Espacios del exilio en la literatura de Manuel Puig.* Buenos Aires: Ediciones Simurg, 1999.
Said, Edward. *Borders, Boundaries, and Frames: Cultural Criticism and Cultural Studies.* Ed. Mae Henderson. New York: Routledge, 1995.

———. "Mind of Winter: Reflections on Life in Exile." *Harper's Magazine*. September (1984): 54.

Sánchez, Margarita. "Ser inmune desde adentro: SIDA, escritura y resistencia en las Américas." Doctoral Dissertation: Rutgers University, 2000.

Sandoval, Alberto. "Staging AIDS: What's Latinos Got to Do with It?" *Negotiating Performance: Gender, Sexuality and Theatricality in Latino America*. Ed. Diana Taylor and Juan Villegas. Durham, NC: Duke University Press, 1994.

Santiago, Héctor. "Testimonio sobre el SIDA." *Ollantay* 2.2 (1994): 27–33.

Sarduy, Severo. *Pájaros de la playa*. Barcelona: Tusquets, 1993.

Scarry, Elaine. *The Body in Pain: The Making and Unmaking of the World*. New York: Oxford University Press, 1985.

Schulz-Cruz, Bernard. "Antes que anochezca: El exorcismo de Arenas." *Ideología y subversión: Otra vez Arenas*. Ed. Reinaldo Sánchez and Humberto López Cruz. Salamanca: Centro de Estudios Ibéricos y Americanos de Salamanca, 1999. 51–61.

Sherry, Michael S. "The Language of War in AIDS Discourse." *Writing AIDS: Gay Literature, Language and Analysis*. Ed. Timothy F. Murphy and Suzanne Poirer. New York: Columbia University Press, 1993.

Sifuentes-Jáuregui, Ben. *Transvestism, Masculinity and Latin American Literature*. New York: Palgrave Macmillan, 2002.

Singer, Linda. *Erotic Welfare: Sexual Theory and Politics in the Age of Epidemic*. Ed. Judith Butler and Maureen MacGrogan. New York: Routledge, 1993.

Smallman, Shawn. *The AIDS Pandemic in Latin America*. Chapel Hill, NC: University of North Carolina Press, 2007.

Smith, Paul Julian. *Vision Machines: Cinema, Literature, and Sexuality in Spain and Cuba, 1983–1993*. New York: Verso, 1996.

Solari, Ana. "Luna negra de noviembre." *Mujeres de mucha monta*. Montevideo: Arca, 1992.

———. "Personal Interview." Montevideo, 1997.

Sontag, Susan. *Illness as Metaphor and AIDS and Its Metaphors*. New York: Picador USA, 1988.

Tomso, Gregory. "The Humanities and HIV/AIDS: Where Do We Go from Here?" *PMLA* 125.2 (2010): 443–53.

Torres, Daniel. "El 'Hombre de papel' en Invitación al polvo de Manuel Ramos Otero." *Chasqui* 29.1 (2000): 33–49.

Treichler, Paula A. "AIDS, Homophobia and Biomedical Discourse: An Epidemic of Signification." *AIDS: Cultural Analysis/Cultural Activism*. Ed. Douglas Crimp. Cambridge, MA: MIT Press, 1988.

Ulloa, Justo C. and Leonor Álvarez de Ulloa. "La función del fragmento en *Colibrí* de Sarduy." *MLN* 109.2 (1994): 268–82.

———. "*Pájaros de la playa* and Sarduy's Hidden Metaphor of Illness and Decay." *Between the Self and the Void: Essays in Honor of Severo Sarduy*. Ed. Alicia Rivero-Potter. Temple University: Society of Spanish and Spanish-American Studies, 1998. 121–35.

———. "*Pájaros de la playa* de Severo Sarduy: Final del juego." *Hispamérica* 78 (1997): 17–27.

Valenzuela, Luisa. "Escribir con el cuerpo." *Alba de América* 11, 20:1 (1993): 35–40.

Vega, José Luis. "La poesía de Manuel Ramos Otero." *Homenaje a Manuel Ramos Otero 1948–1990: Concierto para un recuerdo*. Ed. Universidad de Puerto Rico. Río Piedras, Recinto de Río Piedras, 1992.

Vilaseca, David. "Enjoy Your Symptoms! AIDS as a Source of 'Enjoyment' in Reinaldo Arenas's 'Antes que anochezca.'" *Identity and Discursive Practices: Spain and Latin America*. Ed. Francisco Dominguez. Bern, Switzerland: Peter Lang, 2000.

Watney, Simon. "The Spectacle of AIDS" *AIDS: Cultural Analysis/Cultural Activism*. Ed. Douglas Crimp. Cambridge, MA: MIT Press, 1988.

Wilson, Adela H. *La dificultad de ser gay en Chile . . . y en todo lugar*. Santiago de Chile: Editorial Sudamericana, 2000.

INDEX

abjection, and disavowal of patriarchal taboos against homosexuality, 59
Achugar, Hugo, 87n13
acquired immunodeficiency syndrome. See AIDS
action phase, 22, 25, 41, 48, 55
"Adiós, Ten-Ying" (Blanqué), 11–12, 58, 60–62, 82–92, 174–75; contrast between two bodies in, 83; death in, 83; direct treatment of HIV/AIDS in, 83, 88–89; fairy tales in, 61–62, 83–84, 86, 88, 91–92; narrative style of, 61–62, 82–84, 90–91; as opening a dialogue about sexuality and AIDS, 88; positive nature of, 82, 91–92; prostitution in, 60–61, 85, 88–89; romanticization of eroticism in, 83; sex as subject of, 89; sexuality and eroticism in, 82
agency, 10, 22, 26, 61, 173–78; authorial, 90–91; and control over others, 55–56; diminishing, 119; elimination of, 28; elusiveness of, 56; exertion of, 24, 25, 34–35, 43, 50, 53, 86; loss of, 14, 33; prostitution and, 85, 88; use of weapon to assert, 21
aggression, harnessing of, 25
AIDS (acquired immunodeficiency syndrome): absence of in Spanish American literature, 5–6; as advantage, 154–55; in Chile, 150, 151–56; as colonization, 152; and community-building, 139–40; as component of self, 95; conceptualization of women and, 47–48; as consequence vs. as punishment, 91; conservative hegemonic discourse of, 92; and creation of hybrid bodies, 142; cultural meaning of, 4; and death, 11–14, 46, 53, 58, 62–65, 71, 74, 76–79, 82, 83, 154, 165; as direct route to death, 110–11; direct treatment of, 68, 79–81, 83, 88–89, 153, 154; emergence of as literary topic in Spanish American literature, 1–2; emotional and mental struggles of, 98; eroticism and, 57–93; exploitation and commercialization of, 169; "fatal strategies" of inevitability and mortality, 45, 50; fear about, 19, 21, 53, 76, 95, 98, 132; as foreign disease, 31; as "gay" disease, 37, 115; gender dichotomy in, 116; global threat of, 112, 169; harsh cultural climate surrounding, 98; historical record of effects of, 148; hopelessness and, 53; impossibility of living with, 113; as incurable disease, 123; as indicator of individual and social vulnerabilities, 46; innocent victims vs. those deserving of, 23; as instrument of resistance,

185

155; interaction as accentuating meaning of, 95; international quilt, 169–70; and Lacanian symptom (*sinthome*), 6; and lepers, 13; and liminality, 153; local approach to, 170; and marginalization, 14, 31, 144, 147–48, 155, 170, 172; as marker of individual and social identity, 15; masculine signifier attached to, 116; mirror as site of articulation of, 51; misconceptions of, 4, 31–32, 37–38, 95; moral meaning of, 4; multiplicity of meaning of, 5; mythological connotations of, 3; negativity/pessimism about, 53; omnipotence of, 116; and otherness, 114; performative/celebratory aspect of, 155; personification of, 112, 116; as plague, 5, 7, 10, 19, 21, 30, 39, 45–47, 174; and poetry, 59; as principal marker of identity, 125; as protagonist, 3; reevaluation of preconceived notions of, 61, 83–84, 85; refusal to name, 5, 11, 30, 50–51, 53–54, 55; reuniting of community through, 153; reverence toward, 116; "secret" as reference to, 44–45; and sexuality, 89; and sexuality, desire, and death, 58; shame about, 4, 95, 97–98, 115; silence about, 5, 6–7, 55, 61, 62, 68, 80, 83, 84, 87–88, 92, 103, 147, 147n8, 178; sinister side of sexual relations and, 9; as social event, 46; social meanings of, 1, 4; stereotypes of, 3, 10–11, 24, 54, 114, 174, 177; stigmas of, 3, 4, 21, 22, 45, 55, 92, 167, 172; taboos about, 3–5, 24, 45, 54, 55, 62, 63, 68, 84, 87–89, 92, 147, 175, 178; as unnatural disease, 6; and writing, 3
AIDS and Its Metaphors (Sontag), 3, 19, 23. *See also* Sontag, Susan
AIDS literature, 30, 31, 178; Spanish American, 1–2, 5, 7, 8; in U.S., 2
AIDS narratives: confluence of gender, sexuality, fiction and science in, 23; in U.S., 2
The AIDS Pandemic in Latin America (Smallman), 38
Albuquerque, Severino: categorization of depiction of AIDS in Brazilian theater, 112n8; *Tentative Transgressions*, 111–12; "Neoexpressionist Paradigm," 112; "Neorealist Paradigm," 112
alienation, 99, 123, 155; radical, 97; through sexual orientation and gender, 97

Allende, Salvador, 15, 139, 150, 151; assassination of, 148
Álvarez de Ulloa, Leonor, 7
Anatomy of Drama, An (Esslin), 117
Anderson, Benedict: *Imagined Communities*, 142, 170
año sin amor, Un (Pérez), 13, 14, 95, 98–100, 122–37, 138–39, 175–76; AIDS as center stage, 124; AIDS and self-identification, 136; AIDS as uniting force, 135; alienation, 123; alternating beings, 125–26; anonymous homosexual sex, 125, 129, 131–32, 135; anxiety, 126, 132; AZT/DDI, 122, 132, 134, 137; corporeal signification, 124, 131; as corporeal text, 127, 131; depression, 123, 132–34; detachment, 124; diary form of, 15, 123, 129, 130, 136; erasure with body, 128; ever-presence of AIDS, 123; homeopathic regimens, 132, 134; identity and self, 124, 125, 135–36; inner exile, 123, 124, 126, 128, 137; interactions, 123; isolation, 123, 126, 128, 132, 134; loneliness, 123, 124, 126, 130, 132–33; narrative technique of, 124; overemphasis of body, 125; preoccupation with failing health, 129; premonition of death, 129; private and public spheres, 124, 136; as public discourse on AIDS, 136–37; rejection of literary community, 128; search for self, 127–28, 135; self-actualization, lack of, 126; shift in text, 135; solitary separation, 123, 128; soul, 127–28; temporality, 129–30; textual vs. physical body, 133; writing, 126–29, 131; writing to imaginary other, 131
Antes que anochezca [Before Night Falls] (Arenas), 6, 18n1; as love–hate relationship with Cuba, 6
antiretroviral drugs, 53, 111, 122–23, 131, 132, 137, 177
apocalyptic metaphor, 10, 19, 21, 45, 53–54, 111–12, 114, 118, 121, 174
Apter, Emily, 24
"Aquí estoy" (Miranda), 94
Arenas, Reinaldo, 6, 8, 59; *Antes que anochezca [Before Night Falls]*, 6, 18n1
Argentina: authoritarian regime in, 21, 33, 36–37, 96, 105, 158; writing about AIDS in, 8
Armus, Diego: *Disease in the History of Modern Latin America*, 3–5
Artful Seduction (Posso), 106

Index 187

artifice, 155–56
Atenas, Dino Plaza. *See* Plaza Atenas, Dino
authoritarian discourses, 10
authoritarian regimes, 21–22; in Argentina, 21, 33, 36–37, 96, 105, 158; in Chile, 21, 43, 96, 139, 142, 143, 148–50; metaphors of, 36–37; in Uruguay, 21, 22, 54, 96
authority: institutional, 25; masculine, 25, 35–37, 56; narrative, 91
avengers: as dominating bodies, 10; as mirroring bodies, 10; and metarevenge narratives, 19; and sexual justice, 32; solitariness/independence of, 18, 33; and victims' bodies, 20
Avrahami, Einhat, 172
AZT, 122, 132, 134, 137, 153

Bacchilega, Christina: *Postmodern Fairy Tales*, 12, 61, 84
Bataille, Georges, 12, 62–63, 67, 69, 83, 87; *Eroticism*, 62, 65; and violence, 62–63
Baudrillard, Jean, 45
Before Night Falls. See *Antes que anochezca*
behavior: dictatorial, 36; extreme/obsessive, 26; laws governing, 25; proscribed/socially unacceptable, 4, 86; risky, 44, 88, 115
Bellatín, Mario: *Salón de belleza*, 29n3, 139n1
Bhabha, Homi, 142–44, 150, 168, 170; *Locations of Culture*, 15, 141, 143–44
Bienvenido—Welcome, 8
Biron, Rebecca E., 25, 35
bisexuality, hidden among Latin men, 37
Blanqué, Andrea: "Adiós, Ten-Ying," 11–12, 58, 60–62, 82–92, 174–75; *Querida muerte*, 92
Bliss, Katherine, 4
blood, infection by tainted, 22, 23
bodily destruction, interplay of literary production and, 5
body/bodies: absent, poem as, 75; alteration of conceptualization of, 74–75, 96; altered nature of, 9, 22; appropriation of power over one's, 11; as central preoccupation of AIDS narratives, 22; communicative, 20; conversion of into pseudo-prisons, 138; as co-protagonists in narrative, 62; disciplined, 20; disintegrated, 63, 79, 131; dominant

and dominated, 22; dominating, 10, 20, 25, 27, 40, 51, 56; as element of self-identity, 1; erasure with, 128; erotic, 64–66, 70–77; extrasignification of, 124; Frank's typology of wounded, 10, 20; HIV-infected, as weapon, 21, 25, 37; homosexual, 125; hybrid, 15, 142; immortal, 89; literary, creation of, 74–75; mind, soul and, 127–28; mirroring, 10, 20, 40, 51, 56; mirror reflecting transformation of, 51; overemphasis of, 125; oversignified, 125; physical vs. figurative, 75; as portal to pleasure, 92; reduction by AIDS to, 126n9; reintegration of mind and, 25, 34; in sensuality vs. in disease, 62; separation of AIDS-infected from social, 12–14; sexualized, 58, 71, 75, 83, 125; as site of infection, 22; solitary, 94–137; textual, 133; of transvestite, 159; as weapon, 10, 17–56; wounded, 20, 40; writing about, 126, 128; writing with, 126–28. *See also* social body
Body in Pain, The (Scarry), 10, 20–21
bolero verses, 65
border crossings: literal and figurative, 96; transvestism and, 157
border metaphor, 144
border writing, 144–45, 146; Lemebel and, 145, 147
Border Writing (Hicks), 144
Brazil: HIV epidemic in, 4
Bromberg, Sarah, 85
"bugarrón," use of term, 65, 68
Butazzoni, Fernando, 87n13
Butler, Judith: *Gender Trouble*, 156–58

Cady, Joseph, 54
Camacho, Bernardo, 86
Campra, Rosalba, 169
cancer: metaphorical language and, 3; mythological connotations of, 3; stigmas of, 3
Caribbean: literary and visual representations of AIDS in, 7; unity, 65
Castillo, Ana, 57
catharsis, 117–18, 121
Catholic Church, mandates against contraception by, 38–39
censorship, authorial agency and, 90–91
Cernuda, Luis: influence on Ramos Otero, 63–64; *La realidad y el deseo*, 63
Céspedes, Juan Eduardo, 37

Chávez-Castaneda, Ricardo, 5–6, 178
Chicano/Latino Homoerotic Identities (Foster), 7n11
Chicano representations of AIDS, 7n11
Chile: alternate history of AIDS in, 152; authoritarian regime in, 21, 43, 96, 139, 142, 143, 148–50; cultural borders in, 144; cultural nationalism of, 141–44, 149, 169; diachronic vision of political and social climate in, 151; discussion of AIDS in, 147–48; emergence of AIDS in, 150, 151–56; erasure of homosexuals and transvestites in, 141, 149, 150; exile from, 149; gay community in, 149–50; and globalization, 160–61; homogenized citizenry in, 158; patriarchy in, 148–49, 158, 159–60; pre-dictatorship, 141, 149; rigid delineation of sexuality and gender in, 160; totalizing vision for society in, 158; transition to democracy in, 143, 149; transvestite (*loca*) community in, 139–71; Unidad Popular in, 149–50, 163
cholera, plague metaphor and, 19, 46
cinema: representations of AIDS in, 8
Ciudad Vieja (Montevideo, Uruguay), 60, 83, 86
civic equality, 151
Cixous, Hélène: "The Laugh of Medusa," 126n9
Colibrí (Sarduy), 7
collective space, negotiation of position in, 3
colonization, 144, 148; AIDS as, 152
colonized subjects, 144
communicative body, 20
community: building of through AIDS, 139–40; cohesion and, 164; creation of, 3, 14–15, 142, 150, 155, 162; diminished sense of, 150; forging of through hybridity, 138–71; of gays and transvestites, 151; local and global, 168–71; *locas* and, 138–71; and nation-building, 142; reuniting of through AIDS, 153; of sufferers, 139; and writing, 139
condom use, Latin men and, 37–38
Connell, R. W., 36
consciousness-raising, 24–25
contraception, mandates against, 38–39
control: creative and linguistic, by *locas*, 162; façade of, 55–56; fear of loss of, 33; by hegemony, 144; lack of over AIDS, 24–26; patriarchy and, 116; over personhood, 55; physical, loss of, 32–33
counter-narratives, construction of, 144
Cranwell, Elizabeth, 8n14
criminal justice system, eschewal of, 33
cristo de la Rue Jacob, El (Sarduy), 7
crónica genre, 15, 141, 151; fluidity of, 146–47; as historical record, 147, 148; historical uses of, 146; Lemebel's restructuring of, 146–47, 152; and liminality, 171; multidimensionality of, 147; textual hybridity and, 145–48, 152; traditional, 146
cross-dressing, terminology surrounding, 139n1, 158
Cruz-Malavé, Arnaldo, 76n6
Cuba: Arenas and, 6; writing about AIDS in, 8
cuerpo homosexual, reduction of gay male to, 125
cuerpo indómito, El (Rosenkrantz), 99
cultural borders, 144, 146, 160
"cultural disenfranchisement," 98
cultural hybrid, Latin American national essence as, 169
cultural identity, 15, 144
cultural margins, 145
cultural meaning, 4
cultural nationalism, 141–44, 149, 169
cultural taboos, 45, 55. *See also* taboos
culture: dominant, 164, 169, 171, 178; popular, 20, 40, 51, 161; as unfixed entity at periphery, 144; without boundaries of nation, 144

DDI, 134
death: AIDS and, 11–14, 46, 53, 58, 62–65, 71, 74, 76–79, 82, 83, 154, 165; confluence of with desire and writing, 57–93; connection between life and, 15, 62, 83, 142; and disease and desire, 12; and eroticism and narrative, 12, 57–93; escape from, 96; impending 60, 62, 64, 95, 104, 113, 129, 174, 175; metaphorical, 58; metaphor of, 65, 69–71, 79; orgasm as type of, 69; power of AIDS over, 11; re-semanticization of, 167; and sexuality, 57
Death, Desire, and Loss in Western Culture (Dollimore), 12, 57–58
Denneny, Michael, 46
De perlas y cicatrices (Lemebel), 140n1
desire: confluence of with death and writ-

ing, 57–93; and disease and death, 12; and eroticism, 57–93; impossibility of fully satiating, 58; mutability as inner dynamic of, 58; and sexuality, 57–58
deviant behaviors, 4
diachronic historical time, 15, 141, 148–50
diary genre: 15, 123, 129, 130; as intimate portrayal of existence, 129, 130; subversion of, 136
dictatorships. *See* authoritarian regimes
didactic function, 39
didacticism, 112
disciplined body, 20
"disco gay, el," 164
disease: convergence of with fiction, 5; and desire and death, 12; and foreignness, 32, 46; as invasion of alien organisms, 28; metaphorical representations of, 19, 36; physical manifestations of, 4; role of in society, 3; sexualization of, 4; stigmatization of as mysterious, 3
Disease in the History of Modern Latin America (Armus), 3–5
disenfranchisement, cultural: exile as, 98
dislocations, forced, 96
displacement, physical and emotional, 44
dissidence, political, 6
Dollimore, Jonathan: *Death, Desire, and Loss in Western Culture*, 12, 57–58
dominating body, 10, 20, 25, 27, 40, 51, 56
domination, harnessing of, 25, 26
Donoso, Claudia, 158n10
drag: and gender identity, 156, 158; and heterosexuals, 158; subversive potential of, 157; use of term, 139n1
drama, as collective experience, 117
drug users: HIV risk and, 39; marginalization of, 31. *See also* IV drug use

Echevarren, Roberto, 87n11
ecstasy, and lethal sexuality, 57
Edelman, Lee, 51
"Elefante" (Mallach), 13, 14, 95, 97–98, 100–110, 123, 175, 176; anonymity, 104, 107–8; Bolivia, 104–6; clandestine homosexuality, 103; Cohen CD, 103–4, 107; communication gaps, 104–5; confrontation with true identity, 103, 108–9; dislocation, 105; erasure of past, 101–2, 103; fleeing prejudice and persecution, 103; foreignness, 105; homecoming, 109–10; language barriers, 104–5; mirror stage, 100–101, 108;
Narcissus myth, 108; narrative style of, 101; notion of gaze, 100, 107–9; separation between "I" and "self," 108–9; space, home, and location, 100, 110; as radical isolation, 95, 97–98, 101, 106; reflected image of self, 108–9; self-imposed exile, 100, 103, 105–6, 109; silence about AIDS, 103
Eloy Martínez, Tomás: *El vuelo de la reina*, 9, 10, 19, 20, 21, 25, 26–39, 41, 47, 50, 51, 55–56, 173
eroticism: and AIDS, 57–93, 95; Bataille's theories on, 12, 87; cultural meanings attached to, 4; and death and narrative, 12, 57–93; eschewing of convention as fuel for, 67; power of, 75; as remedy for discontinuity of human experience, 63, 68–69, 76; rethinking of, 18; in "El secreto de Berlín," 43; taboo as limiting factor of, 62; theory of types of, 62
Eroticism (Bataille), 62, 65
erotic seduction, 26
"escribir con el cuerpo," 126
esquina es mi corazón, La (Lemebel), 140, 140n3
Esslin, Martin: *An Anatomy of Drama*, 117
euphemism, 11
exile, 6, 13, 23, 43–44, 73; as cultural disenfranchisement, 98; exoteric vs. esoteric, 99; homosexuality and, 97, 106; inner, 123, 124, 126, 128, 137; "internal," 99; isolated, 2–3; isolation and, 94–137; language as central dialectic in, 104; literary/critical history of, 96; metaphorical use of, 96–97; as philosophical existence, 96; physical and psychological, 98, 120; as physical uprooting, 99, 101; as removal in space and spirit, 99; self-imposed, 12, 95, 96, 100, 103, 105–6, 109, 118–20, 124, 138, 175
existential feminism, views of prostitution in, 85, 88

fairy tales: images of women in, 84; importance of to narrative projects, 84; postmodern rewriting of, 61, 83–84, 91; subversion of, 61, 91; use of in "Adiós, Ten-Ying," 12, 61–62, 83–84, 91–92
fatalism, 122
"fatal strategies," 45, 50
fear: about AIDS, 19, 21, 53, 76, 95, 98, 132; apocalyptic metaphor and, 19;

about HIV transmission, 46; plague metaphor and, 19; propagation of, 32
female gender, performance of, 156–58
feminist theory: exile and, 98; prostitution and, 85
femininity: importance of in gender construction, 158; Lemebel and, 159–62; as marginality, 162
femme fatale, 26, 54
Fernández Pagliano, Alvaro, 87n11
fiction: confluence of with gender, sexuality and science, 23; convergence of disease and, 5; in *crónicas,* 152; destructive dominant, 35–36
foreignness: disease and, 32, 46; plague metaphor and, 19, 30–32
Fotos del alma, 8
France: AIDS as American disease in, 31; writing about AIDS in, 8
Frank, Arthur W.: *The Wounded Storyteller,* 10, 20, 40
freedom, 83, 86, 92, 175; and civic equality, 151; personal, 11; prostitution and, 88; sexual, 11, 48, 86, 91

Garabano, Sandra, 158–59, 168–69
gay community, Chilean, 149; AIDS and, 152; community with transvestites, 151; marginalization of, 164; and resistance, 155
gay male, reduction of to "cuerpo homosexual," 125
gay rights, 67
gaze: aversion of from one's body, 100, 107–9; avoidance of, 101, 107; backward, 92, 175; Lacanian notion of, 14, 100; outward, 162, 174; textual, 151
gender: AIDS and dichotomy of, 116; alienation through, 97; confluence of with sexuality, fiction, and science, 23; extrasignification of bodies because of, 124; female, as performed, 139n1, 156–58; plurality of, 156–63; as sexual hybridity, 15, 141; Spanish term for, 141n6
gender conflation, 160
gender-crossing, 156
gender identity: cultural meanings attached to, 4; and performance, 156–58
gender performance, 139n1, 156–58
Gender Trouble (Butler), 156–58
genetic malfeasance, 44
Germany, writing about AIDS in, 8

Gilman, Sander L., 31, 55, 114–15
Giovanetti Viola, Hugo, 87n11
global awareness, 169; female-centered, 161
Gravina, María, 87n11
GRID (Gay Related Immune Deficiency), 18n1
Griffero, Ramón: "El secreto de Berlín," 9, 10, 19, 20, 21–22, 26, 37, 39–47, 50, 51, 55–56, 173
Grimm Brothers: "Rapunzel," 61, 83–84
Guerra Cunningham, Lucía, 146, 157
Guibert, Hervé, 24, 128
Guillain-Barré syndrome, 56
guilt, 26, 40, 42–44, 95, 116, 121
Guzetti, César A., 36

Haiti, HIV-positive community in, 80
Haitians, as most at risk from HIV, 31, 55, 114
Halladj, Husayn Mansur, 57
health: illness vs., 15, 142; rethinking of, 18
health prototypes, perpetuation of by popular culture, 51
hegemonic culture, prejudice by, 39
hegemonic discourse, 92, 159
hegemonic subjugation, combating, 14–15, 157
hegemony: challenges to, 157, 159–60; counteracting, 144; dynamics of margin and, 144; homosexuality and transvestism as counter-discourse to, 160; and nation, 168; political, 11; rejection by, 162; repression from, 164; space occupied by, 149
hemophiliacs, as most at risk from HIV, 31, 55, 114
Henderson, Mae, 96
Hernández, Wilfredo, 63, 67–68, 72, 81
heroin addicts, as most at risk from HIV, 31, 55, 114
heterosexuality: drag and, 158; façade of, 65, 68
heterosexual transmission: focus on, 18n1; myth of low risk of, 37, 39, 48, 55; in *Pecados mínimos,* 115
heterosexual women, myth of lack of danger of infection, 48
heterosexual writers, AIDS and, 88
Hicks, Emily: *Border Writing,* 144, 146, 152
Historia de un deseo (Mallach), 105

Index

historical time. *See* diachronic historical time
HIV (human immunodeficiency virus): 4-H's of, 31, 55, 114–14; altered body and, 9; deliberate transmission of, 17–56; demonization of individuals with, 11; direct treatment of, 68, 79–81, 88–89, 154; double stigmatization of marginalized social groups and, 31; emergence of as epidemiological shift, 151; external location of origin of, 32; fears and misconceptions of, 95; hopelessness and, 53; humanizing of, 151; hysteria surrounding, 23; and liminality, 153; marginalization and, 1; means of transmission, 22; medical discourse and, 28; mythological connotations of, 3; negativity/pessimism about, 53; potential effects of, 1; promiscuity and, 115; as revenge, 17–56; as sexually transmitted disease, 4; silent transmission of, 9–10, 24; stigmas of, 3, 22, 28, 31–32, 44; survival, possibility of, 122; as weapon, 9–10
hologram metaphor, 146, 152
hombre de papel, metaphor of in *Invitación al polvo*, 64, 73–76, 82, 89
homoeroticism, 59, 66
homosexual body, situation of, 125
homosexuality, 4, 6, 59; clandestine, 103; as counter-discourse to patriarchy and hegemony, 160; and exile, 97, 106; and femininity, 160; and illness, 18n1; as marginality, 162; patriarchal taboos against in Puerto Rico, 59, 65, 67–68; silence about in Chile, 147n8; societal views of, 66–68
homosexuals: HIV/AIDS affecting only, 18n1; marginalization of, 31, 168; as most at risk from HIV, 31, 39, 55, 114; negative language and imagery used against, 141; as peripheral citizens, 147; triply marginalized, 144
human immunodeficiency virus. *See* HIV
hybridity, 15; forging of (comm)unity through, 138–71; gender as sexual, 15, 141; in Lemebel, 145–48; and liminality, 144; multiple, 144, 169; national–transnational, 15, 141–42; textual, 145–48
hysteria, HIV and, 23

identity: affirmation of, 77; of AIDS-altered individual, 10; AIDS as marker of individual and social, 15; body as primary marker of, 129; community and social, confluence of, 15; construction of new, 24, 43, 46, 84, 89, 100, 108, 110, 135, 136, 160, 167, 174; crisis of, 74; cultural, 144, 169; erasure of, 162; erosion of, 123; female, 158, 168; fluidity of, 163; future markers of, 172–79; gaze and role in construction of, 100; gender and, 156–58; of HIV-positive individual, 24, 44, 101; homosexual, 65–68; national, 141, 143, 149; new markers of, 13, 96, 108, 125; personal and communal, 169; reconceptualized, 10, 176; reconstruction of through memory and narrative, 90; reduced sense of, 124; stigmas and conceptualizations of, 4; transvestite, 76n6; true, 103, 105; underlying conceptions of, 37; as unfixed entity at periphery, 144; writing and, 127; writing as true marker of, 64. *See also* self-identity
illness: homosexuality and, 18n1; language of, 104; postmodernism and, 31; special significance of, 3; vs. health, 142
Illness and Culture in the Postmodern Age (Morris), 31
Illness as Metaphor (Sontag), 3
illness narratives, 31–32
Imagined Communities (Anderson), 142
immigrants, as vectors of illness, 32
infection phase, 22–24, 48, 55
infidelity, 4, 32, 38
innocence, loss of, 151
interpersonal relationships, rethinking of, 18
intertextuality, 63, 65
In the Land of God and Man (Paternostro), 37–38
Invitación al polvo (Ramos Otero), 11–12, 58–60, 63–82, 89, 90, 174–75, 178; abandonment, 71–72; alternation between erotic and elegiac, 63; and *bolero* verses, 65; "bugarrón," 65, 68; "La caja china," 77; celebration of homosexual love, 68; confluence of identities and countries, 65; confluence of literary and erotic desires, 73–75; confluence of love, sexuality, and death, 64; death, preparation for, 77–79; direct treatment of HIV/AIDS, 68, 76, 79–81; dissociation from time, 70–71; "Entre paréntesis," 77; erotic body, celebration

of, 64, 65–66; erotic body, deconstruction of, 64, 71, 76–77, 82; eroticism as means of avoiding discontinuity of being, 68–69, 76; identity, 77; as intertextual dialogue with Quevedo, 63, 64; "Invitación al polvo," 79; loss, 70–71; "Metáfora contagiosa," 79; metaphor of death, 70–71; metaphor of hombre de papel, 64, 73–76, 82, 89; "La nada de nuestros nunca cuerpos," 81; "Nobleza de sangre," 68, 78–81; optimism belying tragedy, 70; Poem #1, 65; Poem #2, 66; Poem #3, 70–71; Poem #4, 75; Poem #9, 69; Poem #10, 66; Poem #11, 69; Poem #12, 72; Poem #14, 72; Poem #19, 73; Poem #23, 72; Poem #25, 67; Poem #29, 73–74; polvo, 63, 72, 74, 79; "De polvo enamorado," 64–74; preoccupation with present, 75–76; "Puerta de polva," 79; quest for infinity/eternity, 69; realization of HIV status, 64; religion, 69, 78, 80–81; renunciation of love, 77; "La rosa," 81–82; rose, image of, 72; sacrilegious level of, 81; and societal views of homosexuality, 66–68; solitariness, 60, 64, 68–70, 73, 76; taboo, transgression of, 65, 67–68; time as theme, 70–71, 74–75; traditional poetic forms, 66; transgression of cultural and religious conventions, 80; universalization of AIDS experience, 76, 78, 79; "La víspera del polvo," 74–82; writing, importance of, 64, 73–76, 77, 82
isolated exile, 2–3
isolation, 13–14, 23, 48; emotional, 123; and exile, 94–137; radical, 13–14, 95, 97–98, 101, 106, 110; self-imposed, 12, 95, 96, 100, 103, 105–6, 109, 118–20, 124, 138, 175
IV drug use, 4, 39. See also drug users

Jacoby, Susan, 18, 33, 127
judgment, apocalyptic metaphor and, 19
Jungian psychology, 99
justice, and revenge as mutually exclusive, 18

Kaminsky, Amy K., 13, 97, 98, 99, 143
Kaposi sarcoma, 30, 51
Kleinman, Arthur, 31–32
Knapp, Bettina L., 99

Krueger, Stephen F., 23, 29, 47
Kuhnheim, Jill, 59

Lacan, Jacques: gaze, 14, 100; mirror stage, 100; "other," 14
Lacanian symptom (*sinthome*), AIDS envisioned as literal and metaphorical elements of, 6
Landrón, Eric: "Otra ruleta rusa," 17
language: as central dialectic in exile experience, 104; of illness, 104–5; manipulation of by Lemebel, 140, 153. See also metaphor
"Language of War in AIDS Discourse, The" (Sherry), 28
Larre Borges, Ana Inez, 87n13
Latino representations of AIDS, 7n11
Lemebel, Pedro: and breaking of literary barriers, 146; construction of as writer, 140; critical attention, 140; *crónica* as genre of choice, 140, 141, 146–47, 148, 152; *De perlas y cicatrices*, 140n1; *La esquina es mi corazón*, 140, 140n3; and gynocentric linguistic history, 161–62; history of homosexuality in Chile, 141; hybridity of genres of, 141; and liminal space, 141; *Loco afán: crónicas de sidario*, 15, 138–71, 177, 178; "el mariconaje guerrero," 141, 142; margin–hegemony, dynamics of, 144; mother of, 161–62; and multiple hybridities, 144; plurality of voices in works of, 141, 146, 154; rejection of paternal moniker by, 161–62; renaming of, 161; technique of, 141; "Tengo miedo torero," 141n4; textual insertion of into national identity, 149
liberal feminism, views of prostitution in, 85, 88
libro de la muerte, El (Ramos Otero), 58, 59
Liguori, Ana Luisa, 8n14
liminality/liminal space, 15, 88, 141, 143–44, 147, 168, 171; celebration of, 162; and HIV/AIDS, 153; and loss of public space, 150; and mothers, 162
listlessness, 95
literary production, interplay of bodily destruction and, 5
Llamas, Ricardo, 124–25
locas, 139–71; and artifice and performance, 155; celebratory image of, 150, 155, 158; and community, 155;

community of with gays, 151, 155; companionship shared by, 154; created selves of, 155, 159; detailed portrait of, 140; elusiveness of, 159; heterosexuals and seduction of, 165; and hybridity, 159–60; marginal existence of, 144; as outcasts, 163; and plurality of gender, 156–63; recreation of sense of community or nation by, 145; and reinvention of self, 160–62; as textual border-crossers, 160; textual history and testimony of, 152; unity of, 170; use of term, 157–58

Locations of Culture (Bhabha), 15, 141, 143–44

Loco afán: crónicas de sidario (Lemebel), 15, 138–71, 177, 178; AIDS as advantage, 154–55; AIDS as instrument of resistance, 155; (un)baptism, 161; border and margin, 159; as border writing, 145; as challenge to hegemonic discourse, 159–60; and Chilean history, 148–50; community reuniting due to AIDS, 153, 155; and constructed gender, 156–63; as counternarrative to dominant images of Chile, 142; death vs. life, 154–55; decentered nationless subjects, 145; diachronic time, 148–50; direct reference to AIDS, 153; disruption of sense of self, 139; emergence of AIDS in Chile, 150–56; femininity, 159–62; fictional elements of, 152; funerals, 167–68; gay community, 149–50, 152, 155, 164; global awareness, 160–61; HIV/AIDS as central topic, 140; hologram metaphor, 146, 152; Hollywood icons, 160–62; homosexuality and transvestism as counter-discourse to patriarchy and hegemony, 160; hybridity, 145–48, 152; importance of female figures, 159–62; liminality, 147; manipulation of language, 140, 153; metaphors, 140, 153; mixing of textual strategies, 152; multiple borders, 145; multiplicity, acceptance, and celebration of, 160; navigation of textual and cultural borders, 146; "La noche de los visones," 150, 151; notion of community, 139–40; plurality, 145–46, 154; and plurality of gender, 156–63; puns, 153; "La Regine de aluminios el mono," 155–56; renaming, 160–62; textual hybridity, 145–48; as textual record and witness, 147, 148, 152; tone of, 153; treatment of AIDS, 153; "El ultimo beso de Loba Lamar," 165–66. See also *locas*

loneliness, 123, 124, 126, 130, 132–33. See also isolation; solitariness

love: celebration of to achieve transcendence, 63; death of, 65; homoerotic representation of, 66; metonymic portrayal of, 65–66; as superseding prejudice and persecution, 67

"Luna negra de noviembre" (Solari), 9, 19, 20, 21, 22, 26, 47–56, 173; action and retaliation, 50; agency, 50; apocalyptic metaphor, 53–54; corporeal and mental transformation, 48; *femme fatale*, 26, 54; isolation, 48; marginalization, 48; metaphor of hopelessness, 53; mirroring, 51; realization phase, 48; refusal to name HIV/AIDS, 50–51, 53–54; role of women, 47–48; self-awareness, 51; violation of grammatical rules, 49

machismo, 38
Madonna, 161
Madres de la Plaza de mayo, Las, 158
Maier, Linda S., 100
"mal del siglo veinte: POESídA y SIDA, El" (Kuhnheim), 29n3
Mallach, Nelson: "Elefante," 13, 14, 95, 97–98, 100–110, 123, 175, 176; *Historia de un deseo*, 105
Maraudo, Laura, 87n13
Mardones, Pedro, 140, 161. See also Lemebel, Pedro
marianismo, 38
"mariconaje guerrero, el," 141, 142
marginalities, 162
marginalization: of AIDS, 14, 31, 144, 147–48, 155, 170, 172; of AIDS-infected individuals, 15, 31, 48, 144, 155; of deviant individuals, 22; and exile, 96; of HIV-positive individuals, 1; of homosexuals, 15, 31, 144, 150, 155, 168; multiple, 31, 144–45, 158; physical and psychological, 13; of practitioners of "unsafe" sex, 11–12; of prostitutes, 31, 155; of subordinates, 144; of transvestites, 15, 150, 155
margins: border and, 144, 159; cultural, 145; existence in, 142, 177; interstitial, 144; of public discourse, 62; relegation to, 114, 148–50, 163; of society, physical and psychological, 13, 96

Martínez, Tomás Eloy. *See* Eloy Martínez, Tomás
Marxist feminism, views of prostitution in, 85
masculine authority, 25, 35–37, 56
masculinity, 25, 157; authoritarianism and, 36; duality of, 25; grammatical, 116; murder and, 25, 35; violence and, 36
Mateo del Pino, Ángeles, 140
McCabe, Colin, 65, 69
McClennen, Sophia A., 13, 98, 104, 142–44, 169
men, societal expectations of, 38
metaphor/metaphorical language: apocalyptic, 10, 19, 21, 45, 53–54, 111–12, 114, 118, 121, 174; of border, 144; burden of, 23; of creative force, 75; of death, 65, 69–71, 79; elimination of, 80, 89, 153; of exile, 96–98; of hologram, 146, 152; of hombre de papel, 64, 73–76, 82, 89; and illness, 3–5; indirectness and, 44, 50, 59; and Lacanian symptom, 6; Lemebel's use of, 140, 153; military, 19–20, 21, 28–29, 32, 45, 118; of plague, 7, 10, 19, 21, 30, 36–37, 39, 45–47; and stereotypes of AIDS, 10–11, 23, 24, 55, 92, 153, 178
metarevenge narratives, 19, 41
Mexico, writing about AIDS in, 8
military/militaristic metaphor, 10, 19–20, 21, 28–29, 32, 45, 118
Miranda, Miguel: "Aquí estoy," 94
mirror: imagery of, 100–101; as site of articulation of AIDS, 51
mirroring body, 10, 20, 40, 51, 56
"mirror stage," 14, 100–101, 108
misogyny, 115
Molloy, Sylvia: *En breve cárcel*, 97
monogamous relationships, 18
Monsiváis, Carlos
moral condemnation, 3
morality, 42, 48, 55, 67, 85, 148, 173
Moreira, Jilia, 87n13
Morris, David B.: *Illness and Culture in the Postmodern Age*, 31
mortality, act of writing as means of facing, 5
mother, importance of in gender construction, 158, 161–62. *See also Pecados mínimos*
Mujeres de mucha monta, 47
Mundo, El, 68, 79–80
Muñoz, Carlos Basilio, 87n13

murder: in Argentinean authoritarian regime, 33; manifestation of domination through, 25; and masculinity, 25, 35; in *El vuelo de la reina*, 33–35; of women, 25
mutability, 58

narcissistic libido, 100
Narcissus, myth of, 108
narrative: collective, 84; confluence of with eroticism and death, 12; effect of AIDS on, 3; eroticism and, 82; illness, 31–32; metarevenge, 19, 41; revenge, 9–10, 18–20, 95
national identity: construction and production of, 143; pedagogical and performative aspects of, 15, 141; reductionism based on, 125
nationalism: authoritarian, 143; cultural, 141–44, 149, 169
national subject, construction and production of, 143
national–transnational hybridity, 15, 141–42
nation-building, 142–43
Negotiating Performance (Taylor and Villegas), 7n11
New York, HIV-positive community in, 80
"Nobleza de sangre" (Ramos Otero), 68, 78–81; appearance of in *El Mundo*, 68, 79–80
Nuyorican community, 8n14

objectification, 33, 42
old age, vs. youth, 15, 142
Ollantay Theater Magazine, 7n11, 8n14
Onetti, Juan Carlos: *La vida breve*, 100
Ortiz, Ricardo L., 6
ostracism, 23
Otero, Manuel Ramos. *See* Ramos Otero, Manuel
"other"/otherness, 14, 19, 30–32; extrasignification of bodies because of, 124; PWAs and, 114; as reflection of self, 94. *See also* foreignness
"Otra ruleta rusa" (Landrón), 17

Pájaros de la playa (Sarduy), 7, 18n1
Paternostro, Silvana: *In the Land of God and Man*, 37–38
patriarchy, 116; in Chile, 148–49, 158–59,

162, 168; homosexuality and transvestism as counter-discourse to, 160; taboos rooted in, 59
Pecados mínimos (Prieto), 2, 13–14, 53n11, 95, 97–98, 110–22, 123, 175; apocalyptic metaphor, 111–12, 114, 118, 121; audience identification, 117–18; catharsis, lack of, 117–18, 121; coffin as symbol, 120; dark picture of AIDS, 113, 121; deviation from dramatic convention, 118; didacticism, 112; father, 116; gender dichotomy, 116; Julia (mother), 113–14, 117, 119–21; larger-than-life position of AIDS, 111; meaning of home, 119; misogyny, 115; performance of, 110n4; physical space as self-imposed exile, 118–20; physical vs. psychological exile, 120; radical isolation, 110; sadism, 111, 113–14, 121; shocking and scandalous effect of, 118; study of medicine, 114, 120; temporal organization of, 111; women, 115–16
people with AIDS (PWAs): need to identify and categorize, 95; as risk to society, 95; social attitudes surrounding, 95–96; stereotypical representation of, 114–15. See also AIDS
Pérez, Pablo: *Un año sin amor*, 13, 14, 95, 98–100, 122–37, 138–39, 175–76
performance: of gender, 139n1, 156–58; *locas* and, 155, 160, 162
performativity, 157
Peri-Rossi, Cristina, 59
Perlongher, Néstor, 59
persecution: on basis of sexuality, 67; escape from, 31, 43–44, 96, 103; fear of, 106
phallic privilege, 36
phallocentric symbolic order, 126n9
physical space, as self-imposed exile, 118–20
Pinochet, Augusto, 15, 43, 139, 140, 150, 158, 160, 163; coup by, 148; and disappearance and elimination of citizens, 149; as self-proclaimed "Father of the Nation," 148
plague conditions, positive aspects of, 46
plague metaphor, 7, 10, 19, 21, 30, 36–37, 39, 45–47
Plaza Atenas, Dino, 145, 146, 168
plurality, 145; of gender, 156–63; textual, 146
POESídA, 59
poetry: as absent body, 75; heterosexual love, 63; Latin American, 59; as marginalized genre, 59; power of to outlast sexuality, love and life, 75, 78; as "puerta de polvo," 79; relationship of with death, 59; traditional, 59, 66
popular culture, mirroring body and, 20, 40, 51, 161
Porzecanski, Teresa, 87n13
Posso, Karl: *Artful Seduction*, 106
postdictatorial texts, 10, 21, 25
Postmodern Fairy Tales (Bacchilega), 12, 61
postmodernism, 61; illness and, 31; and nation-building, 142–43; rewritings of fairy tales, 61, 83–84, 91
Powell, David A., 130
power: façade of, 33, 35, 55–56; of fairy tales, 61; interchange of, 10; lack of, 25, 56; over one's body, 11; patriarchy and, 159–60; to wreak destruction, 25
prejudice: on basis of sexuality, 67; escape from, 103–5; by hegemonic culture, 39; against homosexuality, 68
Prieto, Ricardo, 87n11; *Pecados mínimos*, 2, 13–14, 53n11, 95, 97–98, 110–22, 123, 175
private discourse, 130, 136
private space, and public space, 163–68
private sphere, vs. public sphere, 124, 157
promiscuity, 4, 48, 70, 87, 115
prophylactic use, avoidance of, 41–42, 70, 132
prostitution, 140; in "Adiós, Ten-Ying," 60–61, 85, 88–89; and agency, 85, 88; emancipation and, 84–85; HIV risk and, 39, 47; marginalization of, 31; reevaluation of preconceived notions of, 61
public discourse, 130, 136
public space: loss of, 150, 164; and private space, 163–68
public sphere: shrinking, 163; vs. private sphere, 157
Puerto Rico, 8n14; HIV-positive community in, 80; Ramos Otero as pioneer in, 68; taboos against homosexuality in, 59, 65, 67–68; writing about AIDS in, 8
Puig, Manuel, 97, 99
PWAs. See people with AIDS

Querida muerte (Blanqué), 92
Quevedo, Francisco de, 63, 64
Quintans, Juan José, 87n13

race, reductionism based on, 125
"radical alienation," 97
radical feminism, views of prostitution in, 85
"radical isolation," 13–14, 95, 97–98, 101, 106, 110; as distinct from traditional exile, 97
rage, 20, 25–26, 40, 42, 48–49, 55–56, 113, 116, 122, 173
Ramos Otero, Manuel: centrality of homosexual experience in work of, 67; influence of Cernuda on, 63–64; *Invitación al polvo*, 11–12, 58–60, 63–82, 174–75, 178; *El libro de la muerte*, 58, 59; as pioneer in Puerto Rico, 68; as spokesperson for homosexual community, 79; and transvestism, 73, 76n6
rape: manifestation of domination through, 25; minimization and dismissal of, 34; rhetoric of, 28; transmission of HIV through, 19–20, 21, 23; and victim blaming, 44; in *El vuelo de la reina*, 28–29, 32
"Rapunzel," use of in "Adiós, Ten-Ying," 61, 83–84, 86, 91–92
realidad y el deseo, La (Cernuda), 63
realization phase, 22, 24, 48, 55
remembrance, theme of, 170
renaming, 160–62
repression, 7, 13; of cultural taboos, 55; from hegemony, 164; as phase of homosexual experience, 59; social and biological, 168
re-semanticization: of death, 167; of life and self, 98
research questions, lists of, 2, 5, 7
retribution, 9, 20; desire for, 18, 33; as overriding theme, 54
revenge: evolution of, 18; HIV as, 17–56; and justice as mutually exclusive, 18; as overriding theme, 54; phallocentric vs. gynocentric, 26
revenge narratives, 9–10, 18–20, 95; the body as weapon in, 20–56
risky behaviors, participation in, 44, 88, 115
Rodríguez de Tió, Lola, 65
Rodríguez Julia, Edgardo, 146
Rosenkrantz, Guillermina, 96–97, 99, 101; *El cuerpo indómito*, 99
Rossiello, Leonardo, 87n11

sadism, 42, 111, 113–14, 121
Said, Edward: "Mind of Winter," 96

Salón de belleza (Bellatín), 29n3, 139n1
Sánchez, Margarita, 155, 163
San Francisco, HIV-positive community in, 80
Sarduy, Severo, 6, 7, 8, 59; *Colibrí*, 7; death of, 7; *El cristo de la Rue Jacob*, 7; *Pájaros de la playa*, 7, 18n1
Scarry, Elaine: *The Body in Pain*, 10, 20–21, 33
science, confluence of with gender, sexuality, and fiction, 23
"secret," use of term, 26, 44–46
"secreto de Berlín, El" (Griffero), 9, 10, 19, 20, 21–22, 26, 37, 39–47, 50, 51, 55–56, 173; confluence of HIV-positive person and serial killer, 43; displacement, 44; eroticism, 43; exile, 43; genetic malfeasance, 44; plague metaphor, 39, 45–47; protagonist as simulacrum of HIV, 43; sadism, 42; "el secreto," 44–45; violence, 39–40
self: AIDS as component of, 95; appropriation of female images for reinvention of, 161–62; constructed, 156, 159; deconstruction of, 76; erasure of from social body, 95, 138; fragmentation of, 28; invention of through corporeal or linguistic means, 160–62; other as reflection of, 94; poet as true self, 76; re-semanticizing of, 98; rethinking of conceptualization of, 1, 24, 138; sense of, 23; separation between "I" and "self," 108–9; separation between individual and reflected, 100, 108–9; vulnerability of, 24
self-actualization, 126
self-awareness, 51, 136
self-censorship, 99, 123
self-determinacy, 84
self-discovery, 129
self-flagellation and condemnation, 138
selfhood: stigmas and concept of, 4; writing and, 126
self-identity: AIDS as part of, 136; body as element of, 1; as female, 156; responses to alteration in, 95, 177
self-imposed exile/isolation, 12, 95, 96, 100, 103, 105–6, 109, 118–20, 124, 138, 175
self-reflection, 56, 108, 174
serial killers, HIV-positive individuals as, 43
Serra, Margarita, 87n13
sex, 10, 18; anonymous/casual, 52, 99, 120, 125, 126, 129, 135, 164; enjoyment of, 70; heterosexual, 115; safe, 48; as

Index

suicide, 118; unprotected, 39, 46, 89, 115, 132; violent acts during and after, 39
sexual activity: risk associated with, 11, 39; safe vs. unsafe, 11, 48; silence and denial about, 39
sexual attitudes, in Latin America, 37–39
sexual exploration, 11–12; men and, 38
sexual expression, power of AIDS over, 11
sexual fluidity, 160
sexual freedom, limitations on, 48
sexuality, 7; celebration of, 87; as celebration of life, 62; confluence of with gender, fiction and science, 23; cultural meanings attached to, 4; and death, 57; disavowal of punitive images of, 93; and love as fountain of possibility and inspiration, 60; and pleasure, 70; reevaluation of preconceived notions of, 61, 85, 92; as remedy for discontinuity of human experience, 63; resistance of to strict rules, 160; rethinking of, 18; rigid delineation of, 160; as route to freedom, independence, pleasure and adventure, 86–87; secrecy and, 45, 67, 87; taboos and, 63, 67, 87; transgression of boundaries of, 12
sexual landscape, drastically altered, 57
sexual liberation, 67
sexual liberties, 151
sexually transmitted diseases, 4
sexual orientation: alienation through, 97, 106; extrasignification of bodies because of, 124
shame: about AIDS, 4, 95, 97–98, 115; secrecy, sexuality and, 45
Sherry, Michael S.: "The Language of War in AIDS Discourse," 28
"SIDA y literatura" (Garasa), 8n14
Sifuentes-Jáuregui, Ben: *Transvestism, Masculinity, and Latin American Literature*, 157–58
silence: about AIDS, 5, 6–7, 55, 61, 62, 68, 80, 83, 84, 87–88, 92, 103, 147, 147n8, 178; cult of, 5; repressive, 22; about unprotected sex, 39
Smallman, Shawn, 22–23; *The AIDS Pandemic in Latin America*, 38
Smith, Paul Julian, 44–45; *Vision Machines*, 50
social body: cleansing of, 13; self-erasure from, 95, 138; separation of AIDS-infected body from, 12–14, 96, 173; wounded, 36
social cleansing, 36

social dynamism, 160
socialist feminism, views of prostitution in, 85
social liberties, 151
socially unacceptable behaviors, 4
social withdrawal, 96
Solari, Ana, 87n11; "Luna negra de noviembre," 9, 19, 20, 21, 22, 26, 47–56, 173
solitariness, 60. See also isolation; loneliness
solitary body, AIDS and, 94–137
"solitary separation," 13–14, 95, 98–100, 123, 128
Solo con tu pareja, 8
Sontag, Susan, 8n14, 10, 28, 32, 45, 46, 53, 79, 89, 112, 118; *AIDS and Its Metaphors*, 3, 19, 23; *Illness as Metaphor*, 3
Soviet Union, AIDS as American disease in, 31
Spanish America: AIDS literature in, 1–2, 5, 7, 8; dearth of literary criticism on AIDS in, 5–6, 8; dearth of theory on AIDS literature in, 8–9
stereotypes: of AIDS, 3, 10–11, 24, 54, 114, 174, 177; of deviance, 22
stigmas: of AIDS, 3, 4, 21, 22, 45, 55, 92, 167, 172; of disease, 3–4, 23, 28, 31–32, 44; of HIV, 3, 22, 28, 31–32, 44
stigmatization, double, 31
Stonewall, 67–68
stylistics, 10, 11
subjugated persons, ability of to appropriate position, 144
subjugation, 31, 144, 173, 178
suicide, sex as, 118
syphilis, 4; plague metaphor and, 19, 46

taboos: about AIDS 3–5, 24, 45, 54, 55, 62, 63, 68, 84, 87–89, 92, 147, 175, 178; and eroticism, 62–63; against homosexuality, 59; repression of, 55; and sexuality, 63, 67, 84, 87; transgression of, 63, 65, 67–68, 84, 87, 92
Taylor, Elizabeth, 153, 161
"Tengo miedo torero" (Lemebel), 141n4
Tentative Transgressions (Albuquerque), 111–12
theater: catharsis in, 117–18, 121; as instrument of social innovation, 117; role of audience in, 117; as subversive, 117
Tomso, Gregory, 8n14
Torres, Daniel, 65, 68, 72
torture: "cure" through, 36; escape from, 96; manifestation of domination through,

25; physical, 20–21; psychological, 20, 22, 114; remorse or conscience over, 155; rhetoric of, 21; use of, 10; in *El vuelo de la reina*, 33
totalitarianism, 37
transnationalism, 169
transvestism, 59, 76n6; in Chile, 139–71; as counter-discourse to patriarchy and hegemony, 160; and female gender performance, 157–58; fetishism of, 73; as marginality, 162; and segregation in Chile, 141; use of term, 139. *See also locas*
Transvestism, Masculinity, and Latin American Literature (Sifuentes-Jáuregui), 157–58
transvestites: bodies of, 159; as peripheral citizens, 147; power of, 165; utopic snapshot of, 150. *See also locas*
Treichler, Paula A., 31
tuberculosis: as disease of passion, 3–4; metaphorical language and, 3; mythological connotations of, 3; stigmas of, 3; as "white plague," 4

Ulloa, Justo C., 7
United Kingdom, positive messages about AIDS in, 45
United States: AIDS as African or Haitian disease in, 31; cinematic representations of AIDS in, 8; literary response to AIDS in, 7–8; positive messages about AIDS in, 45; work of Latinos in, 7, 7n11
unity, forging of through hybridity, 138–71
"unmaking," 33
urban spaces, 15, 141
Uruguay: authoritarian regime in, 21, 22, 54, 96; first case of AIDS in, 2; lack of overt discussion of sexuality and AIDS in literature of, 87–88; prevalence of HIV/AIDS in, 87n12; silence about HIV/AIDS in, 62, 92, 112

Valenzuela, Luisa, 126n9; "Escribir con el cuerpo," 126, 127
vampiro de la colonia Roma, El (Zapata), 7
Vega, José Luis, 63
venereal disease, irreverence toward, 70
vengeance. *See* revenge
victim blaming, 23, 44

victimization, 20; and manipulative desire, 20
victimizers: as dominating bodies, 25
victims: innocent, 23; lack of agency of, 28, 34; of rape, 44
victim–victimizer relationship, 10
vida breve, La (Onetti), 100; anguish and rapture in, 100
Vilaseca, David, 6–7
violence: Bataille and, 62–63; escape from, 31; as expression of power, 20–21; glorification of, 62; and masculine identities, 36; transmission of HIV through, 20, 23
Vision Machines (Smith), 50
volition, 23–24, 98
vuelo de la reina, El (Eloy Martínez), 9, 10, 19, 20, 21, 25, 26–39, 41, 47, 50, 51, 55–56, 173; connections to Argentinean authoritarianism, 36–37; "la enfermedad," 30; façade of power, 33, 35; fiction of absolute masculine authority, 35–36; foreignness/otherness, 30–32; "el mal," 29–30; marginalization, 31, 32; metaphorical impotence, 28, 35; military metaphor, 28–29, 32; murder, 33–35; plague metaphor, 30; as postdictatorial work, 25; significance of Momir, 30; "unmaking," 33; use of rape, 28–29, 32, 34; torture, 33; xenophobia, 30

war, metaphor of. *See* military/militaristic metaphor
"war on AIDS," 28
weapon, AIDS-infected body as, 10, 17–56, 95, 155–56, 173
whorehouse, 164–65
Wilson, Adela H., 147; as pseudonym, 147n8
women: conceptualization of in cultural narrative of AIDS, 47–48; emancipation of through prostitution, 84–85; images of in fairy tales, 84; murder of, 25; portrayal of as evil, 115; as scapegoats, 115–16; societal expectations of, 38–39, 84–86; subversion of traditional roles of, 85–86; vulnerability of to HIV infection, 39; and writing, 126n9
"wounded bodies," 10, 20, 40
Wounded Storyteller, The (Frank), 10, 20

writing: act of as means of facing mortality, 5, 15; about body, 127–28; with body, 126–28; confluence of with desire and death, 57–93; counter-immersive, 54; and identity, 127; negative outcomes of, 126; personal effect of, 126; role of, 3; role of in *Un año sin amor*, 126–29; role of in *Invitación al polvo*, 64, 73–76, 77, 82; as stripping of body, 129; and women, 126n9

Writing AIDS: Gay Literature, Language and Analysis, 54

Xaubet, Horacio, 87n13
xenophobia: plague metaphor and, 19, 30; propagation of, 32

"Yeguas del Apocalipsis, Las," 140
youth, vs. old age, 15, 142

Zapata, Luis: *El vampiro de la colonia Roma*, 7

TRANSOCEANIC STUDIES
Ileana Rodriguez, Series Editor

The Transoceanic Studies series rests on the assumption of a one-world system. This system—simultaneously modern and colonial and now postmodern and postcolonial (global)—profoundly restructured the world, displaced the Mediterranean *mare nostrum* as a center of power and knowledge, and constructed dis-centered, transoceanic, waterways that reached across the world. The vast imaginary undergirding this system was Eurocentric in nature and intent. Europe was viewed as the sole culture-producing center. But Eurocentrism, theorized as the "coloniality of power" and "of knowledge," was contested from its inception, generating a rich, enormous, alternate corpus. In disputing Eurocentrism, books in this series will acknowledge above all the contributions coming from other areas of the world, colonial and postcolonial, without which neither the aspirations to universalism put forth by the Enlightenment nor those of globalization promoted by postmodernism will be fulfilled.

Learning to Unlearn: Decolonial Reflections from Eurasia and the Americas
  Madina V. Tlostanova and Walter D. Mignolo

Oriental Shadows: The Presence of the East in Early American Literature
  Jim Egan

www.ingramcontent.com/pod-product-compliance
Lightning Source LLC
Chambersburg PA
CBHW030138240426

43672CB00005B/171